Envisioning

Saint Germain's

Golden Age

Spiritualizing the World, vol 5

Envisioning Saint Germain's Golden Age

KIM MICHAELS

Copyright © 2017 Kim Michaels. All rights reserved. No part of this book may be used, reproduced, translated, electronically stored or transmitted by any means except by written permission from the publisher. A reviewer may quote brief passages in a review.

MORE TO LIFE PUBLISHING

www.morepublish.com

For foreign and translation rights,

contact info@ morepublish.com

ISBN: 978-87-93297-36-4

The information and insights in this book should not be considered as a form of therapy, advice, direction, diagnosis, and/or treatment of any kind. This information is not a substitute for medical, psychological, or other professional advice, counseling and care. All matters pertaining to your individual health should be supervised by a physician or appropriate health-care practitioner. No guarantee is made by the author or the publisher that the practices described in this book will yield successful results for anyone at any time. They are presented for informational purposes only, as the practice and proof rests with the individual.

For more information: *www.ascendedmasterlight.com* and *www.transcendencetoolbox.com*

CONTENTS

Introduction 7
1 | Awakening those who can bring in the Golden Age 11
2 | Invoking the awakening of the forerunners 23
3 | An all-encompassing shift in consciousness 43
4 | Invoking a realistic view of nature 65
5 | Invoking an all-encompassing shift in consciousness 85
6 | The secret about the rise and fall of Golden Ages 101
7 | Invoking the dynamics of the Golden Age 115
8 | The grand illusion of the scarcity of resources 141
9 | Invoking the abundance consciousness 155
10 | Be MORE than normal! 181
11 | Invoking the will to be MORE than normal! 193
12 | Politics and education in the Golden Age 217
13 | Invoking the politics and education of the Golden Age 231
14 | I challenge you to rethink the concept of ownership 261
15 | Invoking a new view of ownership 273
16 | Invoking a new view of corporations 297
17 | Is it consequential for bringing in the Golden Age? 313
18 | Invoking the awakening of Saint Germain's own 323
19 | Saint Germain is the Buddha for the Aquarian age 343
20 | Diversity is the master key to the Golden Age 347
21 | The Alpha and the Omega of the Golden Age 365
22 | Elitism is the key to understanding history 383
23 | The questions most people cannot even ask 395
24 | Invoking an end to suppression by the power elite 413
25 | Invoking the exposure of the power elite 439
26 | Invoking a new awareness of history 465

INTRODUCTION

This book belongs to the series *Spiritualizing the World*. The books in this series are given by the ascended masters as workbooks that provide the knowledge and practical tools we need in order to make a contribution to solving concrete world problems. This book contains the knowledge and the tools we need in order to change our mindset and thereby set the stage for the manifestation of the Golden Age planned by Saint Germain. These books do not contain foundational knowledge about ascended masters and their teachings. In order to make the most efficient use of this book, you need to have a general knowledge of the following topics:

- You need to know who the ascended masters are, how they give their teachings and how you can make the best use of them on a personal and planetary level. You can find extensive teachings on this in the books: *How You Can Help Change the World* and *The Power of Self*.

- You need to know how the earth functions as a cosmic schoolroom. You need to know your own role and the authority you have as a spiritual being in embodiment. You need to know the role of the ascended masters and how only we who are in embodiment can give them the authority to use their unlimited power to affect change on earth. You can find more on these topics in the first book in this series: *How You Can Help Change the World*.

- You need to know how to use the practical tools given by the ascended masters. You can find more on this topic in: *How You Can Help Change the World* and on the website: *www.transcendencetoolbox.com*.

- You need to know about the existence and methods of the dark forces who are ultimately responsible for creating war on earth. You can find foundational teachings on this in: *Cosmology of Evil*.

How to use this book

There is no one way of using the teachings and tools in this book. However, if you want to make a significant contribution to bringing society forward, it is suggested that you start by following this program:

- You read one of the chapters in the book completely in order to increase your understanding of the topic.

- You give the invocation associated with that chapter once a day for nine days while studying the same chapter again.

The reasoning behind this program is that the chapters in the book form a progression. As you give an invocation for one chapter, you are also clearing your own consciousness from certain energies and illusions. This makes it easier for you to absorb and apply the teachings from the next chapter.

You can, of course, also read the book all the way through and then select one or more invocation(s) that you give several times. It is always more powerful to give an invocation once a day for nine or 33 days.

Please note that even though the dictations in this book were given at a conference in the United States (and therefore talk about America), the teachings apply to many parts of the world. You can therefore use this book to help people anywhere move towards the Golden Age.

If you feel burdened

The purpose of this book is not to merely give you intellectual knowledge. The real purpose is that you give the invocations, whereby you give the ascended masters the authority to remove the dark forces and energies that cause people to be stuck in repeating old patterns. These forces will not be happy that you contribute to the process of removing them from the earth. They may therefore seek to direct psychic energy at you that can make you feel burdened in various ways. Their purpose is to make you stop (or prevent you from starting) your efforts.

If you feel burdened, you can use some of the decrees and invocations for spiritual protection found on *www.transcendencetoolbox.com*. Most people can quickly come to a point where they are no longer vulnerable to the attacks from dark forces.

The dark forces will always seek to inflate any condition in our personal lives that makes us vulnerable. If you have particular issues, it may be helpful to use other tools that address those issues in a more direct manner. The ascended masters have given many invocations and decrees that can help you deal with specific topics, and you can find most of them on *www.transcendencetoolbox.com*. Some tools are found in the other books by Kim Michaels, and you can find them on *www.morepublish.com*.

NOTE: The first dictations in this book where given at a conference in Los Angeles in July of 2007. The dictations from Chapter 20: *Diversity is the master key to the Golden Age* were given at a conference in Kazakhstan in July of 2013.

1 | AWAKENING THOSE WHO CAN BRING IN THE GOLDEN AGE

My beloved hearts, I Mary come to you with great joy—with a great, bubbling, overflowing sense of joy for your presence here at this particular place in the City of Angels on the West Coast of the United States. We have much that we would like to see accomplished for this city and for this state of California.

I must tell you that if there is going to be a major shift in the United States – from the old Piscean-age consciousness to the consciousness of the Aquarian age – well, then, my beloved, that shift can only start in one place and that is here in the state of California. There is no other place in the United States where there is such a concentration of people who at inner levels have reached the spiritual maturity where they are ready to fully embrace the Aquarian-age consciousness, the age of spiritual freedom, the consciousness of spiritual freedom. This new consciousness must sweep through this nation, if it is to free itself from the shackles, not only of the old consciousness of the Piscean age, but of the consciousness of those lifestreams who for eons have formed a power elite. They have weighted down this planet and have kept the majority of the people in a state of virtual or physical slavery to the elite and to their state of consciousness.

What I would like to impart to you is that we have the potential to create an astonishing and unique breakthrough in the consciousness of the people in this city and even in the entire state. Thereby, many of these people who have volunteered to come into embodiment in this state at this particular time will suddenly be awakened to the reality that they came here for a greater purpose. They did not simply come here to enjoy the sunshine or the surfing or the good material lifestyle that has almost become a religion in itself, not only in this state but throughout these United States.

Do not accept the old ways of thinking

What is needed is simply that these people are awakened to the purpose that they themselves chose before they came into embodiment. Do you see that I am not talking here about forcing anyone to do something that they do not want to do? I am, in fact, talking about reawakening people to the reality of what they chose before they came into embodiment. This is reawakening people to the greatest joy, the greatest love that they have—the love that propelled them to make a not inconsiderable sacrifice to come into embodiment at a time when this planet is at a crucial point. The weight of negative energy is at the highest it has been for a very long time, simply because those forces who would like to see this planet stay in the old consciousness are doing everything they can to prevent people

1 | Awakening those who can bring in the Golden Age

from breaking through and throwing off the shackles of the old ways, the old ways of thinking.

You have watched this movie [*October Sky*] of one person who in a small mining town broke through the old consciousness, broke through the consciousness that you can only go down into the ground to dig out a living in the dirt and the dust that will eventually kill you—but there is no other way so you just have to do it. This person broke through and said: "No, there is another way. I will not accept that this is my lot in life, just because I was born in this particular place at this particular time." There are thousands – tens of thousands – of people, who volunteered to come into embodiment in California right now to have that same breakthrough of consciousness of saying: "No, I will not accept that this is the limit for what I can do and how I can live my life. I know there is more, I know there is a higher way of life and I am willing to be the forerunner, I am willing to be the example, I am willing to speak out. I am willing to demonstrate in my own life that there is more, there is a higher lifestyle than materialism, than depression, than atheism, than the old form of religion that is so rigid and stifled in doctrines and dogma that it might as well be atheism, for they are not worshiping the Living God but a dead god of their own making."

When you think about this movie and you think about the qualities of the main character – and you realize that you have had some of these qualities – well, I want to ask you: How many of you during that movie saw yourselves as that person? If you think back at your life, you will realize that you have been unique individuals. You have dared to stand out from the crowd. You have dared to think beyond what your parents, your peers and your society have conditioned you to think. You have been willing to think outside the box.

You might look at your life and say you have not accomplished anything significant in the outer. Nevertheless, what I want you to realize is that you have been willing to think outside the box. Why can I say this? Because of the fact that you are sitting here listening to a person who thinks that he is letting a spiritual being speak through him. My beloved, how many in the world would be willing to do this? Therefore, you know that you are willing to think outside the box, do you not?

What I want you to realize is that even if you think that you have not done much in your life, well your life is not over, is it? You still have a potential. I want you to lock in to the fact that the very reality that you are open to a higher teaching, to a higher way of thinking, means that you have the potential to come up much higher than you have come up so far. I am not asking you to feel guilty. I am not asking you to feel inadequate. I am not asking you to look at your life as a failure. I am simply asking you to recognize that the very fact that you are here and listening to this, means that you have the potential to be among those who are the forerunners for a breakthrough into a new awareness, a new state of consciousness. No matter how old you are, no matter how short or long of a life-span you have left, you can fulfill that potential and make a significant contribution.

I am not talking necessarily about shooting rockets into the sky or inventing this or that invention. I am talking about being who you are, daring to *be* who you are and radiating that consciousness, radiating that being. I must assure you that when you do that, you are radiating such a powerful matrix of light that it can reawaken those who have not yet dared to think outside the box because they have – as you saw in the movie with many of the people who had grown up in that little town – become overwhelmed by the mass consciousness of the environment where they have grown up.

They have accepted the limitations that were defined by that mass consciousness, and therefore they have not dared to think outside that box. They have not dared to lock in to their potential. They have not dared to even remember the purpose for which they came into embodiment. They are feeling so inadequate, so weighted down that they cannot even dare to conceive that they could be part of a new movement, a new movement in consciousness that is more significant than any awakening you have seen in recorded history.

Dare to lock in to that potential. Dare to look at your life and realize that you have much to offer, that God in you has much to offer this world. Even if the world does not seem to want it, even if the people around you in your own family, among your friends and co-workers, do not seem to want it. It is not a matter of evaluating whether other people want your gift. It is only a matter of radiating that light, of giving that gift. The victory is not in other people's response or lack of response. The victory is in radiating the light.

Victory is in giving

The sun does not evaluate its own success based on what people on earth do with the sun's rays. The sun only evaluates success based on the amount of light that it is radiating and the quality of that light. The sun is not here to be concerned about people, for they have their free will. The sun (or rather the spiritual beings who serve as the hierarchs for the physical sun) is here to radiate light. You are here to radiate the light that you are – the light of your God Flame – by being who you are—even right here in the physical universe where there are so many forces that are arrayed against being. Do you not see, even in this movie, how an entire town has been so locked down by a certain consciousness that they can only work in these dirty, dangerous jobs underground in order to make a living? Yet, who owns the mine? Who makes the profit off the sweat and the risk that these people are taking? Is there not somewhere someone who forms an elite who is reaping the profit off the people's labor? Is that elite not dependent upon keeping the people in a state of consciousness where they will keep walking that treadmill of thinking that this is the only way to make a living.

Look around you here in California. Surely, you have a much better economy than they have in that little mining town in West Virginia. Surely, you have many job opportunities, you can have even better pay and a better lifestyle. Is there still not someone who is reaping the profit off what you are doing? Whether you are working for yourself or whether you are working in a job, there is someone somewhere who is reaping a greater profit than you are because they have somehow managed to get an entire state, an entire population, locked in a mental box, in a mindset, that allows them to reap a profit off other people's labor without giving anything in return.

This, my beloved, is a completely ungodly principle that you will see throughout the history of this planet where there have always been those who want to receive without giving in return. The principle of God is what was described in Jesus' parable about the servants who received ten, five and two talents. Two of the servants multiplied them and one buried them in the ground. You see, the principle of God is simple: If you multiply what you are given, you will receive much more in return. When you are willing to multiply in your own life, you are multiplying the abundance that is available for everyone on earth. Those who bury the talents in the ground – and not only bury them in the ground but seek to receive from others rather

1 | Awakening those who can bring in the Golden Age

than multiplying their own – they are the ones who form an elite, who are seeking to take advantage of others.

This is precisely the consciousness that must be overthrown for the Aquarian age to manifest. People need to realize that they do not need any overlords in the physical octave, in the material realm. They do not need a priesthood who tells them they can only be saved by following the priesthood's every command—or they will burn forever in hell. Neither do they need a political priesthood who tells them that unless they vote for them (or allow them to do whatever they want once they are elected), calamity will happen, the economy will fail, the stock market crash, or this or that. Nor do the people need an economic elite behind the scenes who are pulling the strings of the politicians – the political marionettes – who are simply dancing to the tune of the hidden power elite.

The people have the power to thrive without an elite

I can assure you that if you removed the power elite from the state of California tomorrow, the economy would not collapse. Surely, there would be an adjustment—there would be a *major* adjustment. But the economy would not stop to function, the economy would not collapse. The political system would not collapse. People would step up to the plate and fill the roles that are now being filled by the elite or those who are controlled by the elite. The elite can survive only by beating down the people, by making them believe that they are as nothing, that they cannot govern themselves, that they cannot run their societies or their communities. This is the lie that has been perpetrated upon humankind for a very, very long time, as described in Maitreya's book.

It is as big of a lie as when it was first released in this world. There is absolutely no amount of argumentation – no matter how subtle, no matter how seemingly sophisticated – that can make it any less of a lie. It is a lie for the simple reason that God is in everyone. As Jesus said: "With men this is impossible, but with God all things are possible." When the people are not beaten down by an elite, God in them will step up to the plate and they will be able to govern themselves and to run the economy and their families. This is an absolute truth that I am telling you. The people have power, and the power elite can survive only by preventing the people from unleashing the power that is found where? Well, the power is found in the Kingdom of God that is within you, within every human being.

If you will take another look at the teachings of Jesus, you will see that he was anti-establishment, anti-elite, from the very beginning. He came to set the people free from the elite who had managed to make the people believe that they needed the elite in order to be saved, in order to run their society, in order to keep law and order, in order to keep the government going, in order to keep the economy going—whatever you have. This is the lie that is daily being perpetrated upon the people through the mainstream media who are also subject to the lie. They think that they cannot survive without the elite and therefore they must promote the mindset and the belief system of the elite. Even though many of them know that it is a lie that they are writing in their newspapers or broadcasting on their television stations.

Overcoming a spiritual crisis

What I desire to have you focus on is victory in being. Part of that victory in being is to help people overcome the sense of

1 | Awakening those who can bring in the Golden Age

being in crisis mode, the sense of being overwhelmed to the point where many are so burdened by their everyday problems, their problems in their families, their jobs, their problems with health or mental health. Look at how many people – even in this state where there is such great material affluence – are in a spiritual or emotional crisis, having various mental problems, having no sense of purpose in their lives, being so focused on themselves and their immediate situation that they cannot step back and realize that: "I did not come here for the purpose of being burdened by these problems. I came here for a greater goal. I came here out of a greater love. When I reconnect to that, I can solve all these problems and get on with my mission in life."

They cannot even consider that they have a mission in life because they are so burdened by the spiritual crisis. That is why we have prepared the *Spiritual Crisis Toolkit*. We ask you to make calls for the awakening of the people in Los Angeles and California. Make calls that they will wake up and realize their own personal potential, their own personal Divine plans, but also realize the potential and the Divine plan for this state and what it can do for the American nation.

I trust most of you are not considering yourself in an immediate spiritual crisis. That is why I ask you to look beyond and use the *Spiritual Crisis Toolkit* for those many, many people who are burdened by various conditions that prevent them from locking in to their Divine plans and their purpose for coming into embodiment. I ask you to visualize the collective consciousness of this state of California and this city of Los Angeles in a polarity with the city of San Francisco and how your calls and the invocations you give, even your consciousness itself, are releasing your own Flame of Being. This flame will break through the cloud, the dark cloud, that is hanging over this state and dispel the doom and gloom, the limited mindset, even the fear of calamities, various prophecies, such as earthquakes or whatever you have that could hit this state.

So many people are so afraid of what might happen that they dare not express their Christhood today, even though it is precisely the expression of Christhood today that can prevent the calamities of tomorrow from ever manifesting. I ask you to visualize how you break up this cloud and how the light of your combined higher selves, your I AM Presences, forms a mighty sun over this state and this city that will break through and dispel the clouds until the people feel a new awakening, a new lightness of being, a new awareness of a new day, a new state of consciousness.

This is my message for tonight, as I can assure you that we have much more to say about the state of California, its potential for making a contribution to bringing the United States out of the Piscean mental box and into—not the Aquarian mental box, for there is no mental box that can hold the consciousness of Aquarius. Is it not based on the Freedom flame of Saint Germain himself who cannot be put in any mental box conceived of by human beings?

Thus, you will indeed hear from Saint Germain in these coming days, for he is the master who will bring into the physical the matrix of what we desire to release right now of the Golden Age consciousness. We desire to pull back the veil, so that there can be a physical anchoring of at least some part of the vision that Saint Germain holds for the Golden Age in California, America and beyond.

I ask you to consider vibration, energy. I am not speaking softly for I do not come as the gentle Mother. I come as the fiery Mother to awaken you. Tune in to the energies that we are releasing, and allow yourself to feel the acceleration in your forcefield, in your mind. Allow yourself to come up with that acceleration and to just let go of the old consciousness that you cannot rise—for you *can* rise if you are willing. You can rise up with us. I can assure you that we are willing to rise and we are willing to see you rise. Thus, my beloved, be sealed in the fiery love of Mother Mary.

2 | INVOKING THE AWAKENING OF THE FORERUNNERS

In the name I AM THAT I AM, Jesus Christ, I call to all ascended masters working on manifesting the Golden Age, especially Mother Mary and Saint Germain, to radiate into the collective consciousness an impulse that will awaken those who came into embodiment in order to be the forerunners for Saint Germain's Golden Age. Help people see that we can build a new future by working with the ascended masters and letting go of the old way of looking at life, including…

[Make personal calls.]

Part 1

1. Mother Mary, radiate into the collective consciousness the awareness that the spiritually mature people need to fully embrace the Aquarian-age consciousness and free ourselves from the shackles, not only of the consciousness of the Piscean age, but of the consciousness of those lifestreams who for eons have formed a power elite.

> O blessed Mary, Mother mine,
> there is no greater love than thine,
> as we are one in heart and mind,
> my place in hierarchy I find.
>
> **O Mother Mary, generate,**
> **the song that does accelerate,**
> **the earth into a higher state,**
> **all matter does now scintillate.**

2. Mother Mary, radiate into the collective consciousness the awareness that will awaken people to the reality that we have volunteered to come into embodiment at this particular time for a greater purpose.

> I came to earth from heaven sent,
> as I am in embodiment,
> I use Divine authority,
> commanding you to set earth free.

> O Mother Mary, generate,
> the song that does accelerate,
> the earth into a higher state,
> all matter does now scintillate.

3. Mother Mary, radiate into the collective consciousness the awareness that will awaken people to the purpose that we ourselves chose before we came into embodiment.

> I call now in God's sacred name,
> for you to use your Mother Flame,
> to burn all fear-based energy,
> restoring sacred harmony.

> O Mother Mary, generate,
> the song that does accelerate,
> the earth into a higher state,
> all matter does now scintillate.

4. Mother Mary, radiate into the collective consciousness the awareness that will reawaken people to the greatest joy, the greatest love that we have—the love that propelled us to come into embodiment at a time when this planet is at a crucial point.

> Your sacred name I hereby praise,
> collective consciousness you raise,
> no more of fear and doubt and shame,
> consume it with your Mother Flame.

> O Mother Mary, generate,
> the song that does accelerate,
> the earth into a higher state,
> all matter does now scintillate.

5. Mother Mary, radiate into the collective consciousness the awareness that the weight of negative energy is at the highest it has been for a very long time, because the dark forces are doing everything they can to prevent people from breaking through and throwing off the shackles of the old ways of thinking.

> All darkness from the earth you purge,
> your light moves as a mighty surge,
> no force of darkness can now stop,
> the spiral that goes only up.

> **O Mother Mary, generate,**
> **the song that does accelerate,**
> **the earth into a higher state,**
> **all matter does now scintillate.**

6. Mother Mary, radiate into the collective consciousness the awareness that will help people break through and say: "No, I will not accept that this is the limit for what I can do and how I can live my life. I know there is more, I know there is a higher way of life and I am willing to be the forerunner, I am willing to be the example, I am willing to speak out.

> All elemental life you bless,
> removing from them man-made stress,
> the nature spirits are now free,
> outpicturing Divine decree.

> **O Mother Mary, generate,**
> **the song that does accelerate,**
> **the earth into a higher state,**
> **all matter does now scintillate.**

7. Mother Mary, radiate into the collective consciousness the awareness that will help people say: "I am willing to demonstrate in my own life that there is more, there is a higher lifestyle than materialism, than depression, than atheism, than the old form of religion that is so rigid and stifled in doctrines and dogma that it might as well be atheism, for they are not worshiping the Living God but a dead god of their own making."

> I raise my voice and take my stand,
> a stop to war I do command,
> no more shall warring scar the earth,
> a golden age is given birth.
>
> **O Mother Mary, generate,**
> **the song that does accelerate,**
> **the earth into a higher state,**
> **all matter does now scintillate.**

8. Mother Mary, radiate into the collective consciousness the awareness that will help the spiritual people realize that we have been unique individuals. We have dared to stand out from the crowd. We have dared to think beyond what our parents, our peers and our society have conditioned us to think. We have been willing to think outside the box.

> As Mother Earth is free at last,
> disasters belong to the past,
> your Mother Light is so intense,
> that matter is now far less dense.

**O Mother Mary, generate,
the song that does accelerate,
the earth into a higher state,
all matter does now scintillate.**

9. Mother Mary, radiate into the collective consciousness the awareness that will open people to a higher teaching, to a higher way of thinking, and to the potential to come up much higher than we have come up so far.

In Mother Light the earth is pure,
the upward spiral will endure,
prosperity is now the norm,
God's vision manifest as form.

**O Mother Mary, generate,
the song that does accelerate,
the earth into a higher state,
all matter does now scintillate.**

Part 2

1. Mother Mary, radiate into the collective consciousness the awareness that will awaken those who have the potential to be among the forerunners for a breakthrough into a new awareness, a new state of consciousness.

O Saint Germain, you do inspire,
my vision raised forever higher,
with you I form a figure-eight,
your Golden Age I co-create.

**O Saint Germain, what love you bring,
it truly makes all matter sing,
your violet flame does all restore,
with you we are becoming more.**

2. Mother Mary, radiate into the collective consciousness the awareness that by daring to be who we are and radiating that consciousness, we are radiating such a powerful matrix of light that it can reawaken those who have not yet dared to think outside the box.

O Saint Germain, what Freedom Flame,
released when we recite your name,
acceleration is your gift,
our planet it will surely lift.

**O Saint Germain, what love you bring,
it truly makes all matter sing,
your violet flame does all restore,
with you we are becoming more.**

3. Mother Mary, radiate into the collective consciousness the awareness that will help people lock in to our potential and remember the purpose for which we came into embodiment, so we can be part of a new movement in consciousness that is more significant than any awakening we have seen in recorded history.

O Saint Germain, in love we claim,
our right to bring your violet flame,
from you Above, to us below,
it is an all-transforming flow.

> **O Saint Germain, what love you bring,**
> **it truly makes all matter sing,**
> **your violet flame does all restore,**
> **with you we are becoming more.**

4. Mother Mary, radiate into the collective consciousness the awareness that will help us dare to look at our lives and realize that we have much to offer, that God in us has much to offer this world.

> O Saint Germain, I love you so,
> my aura filled with violet glow,
> my chakras filled with violet fire,
> I am your cosmic amplifier.

> **O Saint Germain, what love you bring,**
> **it truly makes all matter sing,**
> **your violet flame does all restore,**
> **with you we are becoming more.**

5. Mother Mary, radiate into the collective consciousness the awareness that it is not a matter of evaluating whether other people want our gift. It is only a matter of radiating the light, of giving the gift. The victory is not in other people's response, the victory is in radiating the Light.

> O Saint Germain, I am now free,
> your violet flame is therapy,
> transform all hang-ups in my mind,
> as inner peace I surely find.

**O Saint Germain, what love you bring,
it truly makes all matter sing,
your violet flame does all restore,
with you we are becoming more.**

6. Mother Mary, radiate into the collective consciousness the awareness that we are here to radiate the light that we are, the light of our God Flames, by being who we are in the physical universe.

O Saint Germain, my body pure,
your violet flame for all is cure,
consume the cause of all disease,
and therefore I am all at ease.

**O Saint Germain, what love you bring,
it truly makes all matter sing,
your violet flame does all restore,
with you we are becoming more.**

7. Mother Mary, radiate into the collective consciousness the awareness that the power elite have locked the entire population in a mental box, in a mindset that allows them to reap a profit off other people's labor without giving anything in return.

O Saint Germain, I'm karma-free,
the past no longer burdens me,
a brand new opportunity,
I am in Christic unity.

**O Saint Germain, what love you bring,
it truly makes all matter sing,
your violet flame does all restore,
with you we are becoming more.**

8. Mother Mary, radiate into the collective consciousness the awareness that this is an ungodly principle that is seen throughout the history of this planet where there have always been those who want to receive without giving in return.

O Saint Germain, we are now one,
I am for you a violet sun,
as we transform this planet earth,
your Golden Age is given birth.

**O Saint Germain, what love you bring,
it truly makes all matter sing,
your violet flame does all restore,
with you we are becoming more.**

9. Mother Mary, radiate into the collective consciousness the awareness that the principle of God is that if we multiply what we are given, we will receive more in return. Those who bury the talents in the ground form an elite who are seeking to take advantage of others.

O Saint Germain, the earth is free,
from burden of duality,
in oneness we bring what is best,
your Golden Age is manifest.

> O Saint Germain, what love you bring,
> it truly makes all matter sing,
> your violet flame does all restore,
> with you we are becoming more.

Part 3

1. Mother Mary, radiate into the collective consciousness the awareness that this consciousness must be overthrown for the Aquarian age to manifest. People need to realize that they do not need any overlords in the material realm.

> O blessed Mary, Mother mine,
> there is no greater love than thine,
> as we are one in heart and mind,
> my place in hierarchy I find.

> O Mother Mary, generate,
> the song that does accelerate,
> the earth into a higher state,
> all matter does now scintillate.

2. Mother Mary, radiate into the collective consciousness the awareness that we do not need a priesthood who tells us we can only be saved by following their every command.

> I came to earth from heaven sent,
> as I am in embodiment,
> I use Divine authority,
> commanding you to set earth free.

> **O Mother Mary, generate,**
> **the song that does accelerate,**
> **the earth into a higher state,**
> **all matter does now scintillate.**

3. Mother Mary, radiate into the collective consciousness the awareness that we do not need a political priesthood who tells us that unless we vote for them, or allow them to do whatever they want once they are elected, calamity will happen.

> I call now in God's sacred name,
> for you to use your Mother Flame,
> to burn all fear-based energy,
> restoring sacred harmony.

> **O Mother Mary, generate,**
> **the song that does accelerate,**
> **the earth into a higher state,**
> **all matter does now scintillate.**

4. Mother Mary, radiate into the collective consciousness the awareness that we do not need an economic elite behind the scenes who are pulling the strings of the politicians, the political marionettes who are simply dancing to the tune of the hidden power elite.

> Your sacred name I hereby praise,
> collective consciousness you raise,
> no more of fear and doubt and shame,
> consume it with your Mother Flame.

**O Mother Mary, generate,
the song that does accelerate,
the earth into a higher state,
all matter does now scintillate.**

5. Mother Mary, radiate into the collective consciousness the awareness that if we removed the power elite tomorrow, the economy or the political system would not collapse. People would step up to the plate and fill the roles that are now being filled by the elite.

All darkness from the earth you purge,
your light moves as a mighty surge,
no force of darkness can now stop,
the spiral that goes only up.

**O Mother Mary, generate,
the song that does accelerate,
the earth into a higher state,
all matter does now scintillate.**

6. Mother Mary, radiate into the collective consciousness the awareness that the elite can survive only by beating down the people, by making us believe that we are as nothing, that we cannot govern ourselves, that we cannot run our societies or communities.

All elemental life you bless,
removing from them man-made stress,
the nature spirits are now free,
outpicturing Divine decree.

**O Mother Mary, generate,
the song that does accelerate,
the earth into a higher state,
all matter does now scintillate.**

7. Mother Mary, radiate into the collective consciousness the awareness that this is a lie. It is a big lie, and no amount of argumentation can make it any less of a lie. It is a lie for the simple reason that God is in everyone.

I raise my voice and take my stand,
a stop to war I do command,
no more shall warring scar the earth,
a golden age is given birth.

**O Mother Mary, generate,
the song that does accelerate,
the earth into a higher state,
all matter does now scintillate.**

8. Mother Mary, radiate into the collective consciousness the awareness that when the people are not beaten down by an elite, God in us will step up to the plate and we will be able to govern ourselves and to run the economy and our families.

As Mother Earth is free at last,
disasters belong to the past,
your Mother Light is so intense,
that matter is now far less dense.

> **O Mother Mary, generate,**
> **the song that does accelerate,**
> **the earth into a higher state,**
> **all matter does now scintillate.**

9. Mother Mary, radiate into the collective consciousness the awareness that the people have power, and the power elite can survive only by preventing the people from unleashing the power that is found in the Kingdom of God that is within every human being.

> In Mother Light the earth is pure,
> the upward spiral will endure,
> prosperity is now the norm,
> God's vision manifest as form.

> **O Mother Mary, generate,**
> **the song that does accelerate,**
> **the earth into a higher state,**
> **all matter does now scintillate.**

Part 4

1. Mother Mary, radiate into the collective consciousness the awareness that Jesus was anti-establishment, anti-elite, from the very beginning. He came to set the people free from the elite who had managed to make the people believe that they needed the elite in order to be saved and in order to run society.

O Saint Germain, you do inspire,
my vision raised forever higher,
with you I form a figure-eight,
your Golden Age I co-create.

**O Saint Germain, what love you bring,
it truly makes all matter sing,
your violet flame does all restore,
with you we are becoming more.**

2. Mother Mary, radiate into the collective consciousness the awareness that this lie is daily being perpetrated upon the people through the mainstream media who are also subject to the lie.

O Saint Germain, what Freedom Flame,
released when we recite your name,
acceleration is your gift,
our planet it will surely lift.

**O Saint Germain, what love you bring,
it truly makes all matter sing,
your violet flame does all restore,
with you we are becoming more.**

3. Mother Mary, radiate into the collective consciousness the awareness that people in the media think they cannot survive without the elite and therefore they must promote the mindset and the belief system of the elite.

O Saint Germain, in love we claim,
our right to bring your violet flame,
from you Above, to us below,
it is an all-transforming flow.

**O Saint Germain, what love you bring,
it truly makes all matter sing,
your violet flame does all restore,
with you we are becoming more.**

4. Mother Mary, radiate into the collective consciousness the awareness that will help people overcome the sense of being in crisis mode, the sense of being overwhelmed by their everyday problems.

O Saint Germain, I love you so,
my aura filled with violet glow,
my chakras filled with violet fire,
I am your cosmic amplifier.

**O Saint Germain, what love you bring,
it truly makes all matter sing,
your violet flame does all restore,
with you we are becoming more.**

5. Mother Mary, radiate into the collective consciousness the awareness that will help people step back and realize: "I did not come here for the purpose of being burdened by these problems. I came here for a greater goal. I came here out of a greater love. When I reconnect to that, I can solve all these problems and get on with my mission in life."

O Saint Germain, I am now free,
your violet flame is therapy,
transform all hang-ups in my mind,
as inner peace I surely find.

**O Saint Germain, what love you bring,
it truly makes all matter sing,
your violet flame does all restore,
with you we are becoming more.**

6. Mother Mary, radiate into the collective consciousness the awareness that will help people wake up and realize their own personal potential, their own personal Divine plans, but also realize the potential and the Divine plan for what we can do for the world.

O Saint Germain, my body pure,
your violet flame for all is cure,
consume the cause of all disease,
and therefore I am all at ease.

**O Saint Germain, what love you bring,
it truly makes all matter sing,
your violet flame does all restore,
with you we are becoming more.**

7. Mother Mary, radiate into the collective consciousness the awareness that will help people break through the dark cloud of doom and gloom and the fear of calamities.

O Saint Germain, I'm karma-free,
the past no longer burdens me,
a brand new opportunity,
I am in Christic unity.

**O Saint Germain, what love you bring,
it truly makes all matter sing,
your violet flame does all restore,
with you we are becoming more.**

8. Mother Mary, radiate into the collective consciousness the awareness that we cannot be so afraid of what might happen that we dare not express our Christhood today, for it is the expression of Christhood today that can prevent the calamities of tomorrow from manifesting.

O Saint Germain, we are now one,
I am for you a violet sun,
as we transform this planet earth,
your Golden Age is given birth.

**O Saint Germain, what love you bring,
it truly makes all matter sing,
your violet flame does all restore,
with you we are becoming more.**

9. Mother Mary, radiate into the collective consciousness a mighty spiritual sun that will break through and dispel the clouds until the people feel a new awakening, a new lightness of being, a new awareness of a new day, a new state of consciousness.

O Saint Germain, the earth is free,
from burden of duality,
in oneness we bring what is best,
your Golden Age is manifest.

**O Saint Germain, what love you bring,
it truly makes all matter sing,
your violet flame does all restore,
with you we are becoming more.**

Sealing

In the name of the Divine Mother, I call to all ascended masters for the sealing of myself and all people in my circle of influence in the creative flow of the Divine Mother, the River of Life. I call for the multiplication of my calls by all ascended masters so that we form the perfect figure-eight flow of "As Above, so below." Thus, I accept that this is fully manifest, because the mouth of the Lord, the Divine Mother that I AM, has spoken it. Amen.

3 | AN ALL-ENCOMPASSING SHIFT IN CONSCIOUSNESS

Saint Germain I AM, and I come to give you a discourse to prepare your consciousness for the shift that must take place, if we are to bring in the Golden Age and shift the consciousness of the people of the world, the people of this nation of America, the people of this state of California from the Piscean age consciousness to the Aquarian age consciousness.

As Mother Mary did indeed speak about yesterday, it is true that there is an immense potential for this shift to begin here in the state of California and to spread throughout America, and from here beyond. Certainly, as we have said recently, there is an equally great potential for a shift to begin in Europe and spread from there as well and there is a potential for a shift to begin in South America and spread from there. You see, we of the ascended masters do not put all of our eggs in one basket. Right now, I am given a platform here in California, so I am talking about the specific egg that I have laid here in the nest of this beautiful state.

Life is influenced by the consciousness of duality

My beloved, it says in Genesis that God created man in his own image and after his likeness. While this is true, it must be recognized by all sincere spiritual seekers that we are not in the original state of innocence at which man and the earth were created. The earth right now has fallen very far below that state of innocence. In fact, I will prepare your consciousness to begin to accept just how far this planet has fallen below.

First, you need to recognize that as a result of the planet falling below its original state of innocence, human beings have departed from their original matrix, the original image of God in which they were created. They have violated the first two commandments, the commandment to not have any other gods before me, and to not take onto thyself any graven image.

They have created images based on the duality consciousness. They have then used those images to create false gods after the image and likeness of the dualistic consciousness—in many cases even after the image and likeness of those fallen beings that Maitreya has exposed in his book. These are the beings who want to set themselves up as gods on earth. They want to be worshiped as gods on earth because they are not willing to come into oneness with the God in heaven whereby they could be Gods in the spiritual realm.

They have been given the earth as a temporary playground where they could outplay that consciousness until they either have had enough of it or have spent their opportunity and thus face the second death. I need you to understand that almost everything on this planet is influenced by the consciousness of duality, the consciousness of the fallen beings that is anti-God, that is based on a denial of God. This is a denial that God is here on this planet, even a denial that God created this planet, even a denial that God exists.

3 | An all-encompassing shift in consciousness

Why is there such cruelty in nature?

I want you to think back to the movie you watched before the invocation was given [A movie about nature]. You see the beautiful images of nature, you see the cute polar bear cubs that climb out of their nest for the first time. Certainly, you feel love and compassion for these beautiful animals. Do you realize that the mother of those cute bear cubs – in order to feed and raise those cubs – has to go out and kill a seal, who also has young that will then starve to death if they are not eaten by the bear? You see the wonderful caribou that migrate over the Alaskan tundra, and then you see the wolves stalking them. You feel compassion for the young caribou and wish it could escape the wolf, and you feel a sense of terror and regret over seeing it be eaten.

You see, this is how nature currently functions on this planet. What has been done on this planet is that humankind has been sold a pack of lies—worse than a pack of wolves. One of these lies is that nature is something that is inevitable, that is beyond human comprehension, beyond human power to change. The way things are, are simply the way things are and there ain't nothing you can do about it. Well, this is a lie, perpetrated by those forces and beings in other realms, in the mental and emotional realms, who have sought to control humankind.

Yes, there are certain groups of people on this planet who are spreading these lies and serving as instruments. As I recently said in Ireland, I want you to think beyond, because if you only focus on physical conspiracies, you will not grasp the full picture, and thus you will not be able to make and facilitate the shift in consciousness that needs to occur.

What they want you to believe is that you, the people, have no power to change the big things on earth including nature and what they have come to call the balance of nature or the ecosystem. How many of you were brought up to believe that nature was beyond the influence of human beings—except through technology? Certainly, you were brought up to believe that your consciousness could not change certain basic, fundamental things in nature. You could not change the fact that there are birds or animals of prey on this planet who must kill in order to survive. This is something that either God created that way or it just evolved by chance and thus, either way, it is beyond the power of human beings.

The truth about the balance of nature

On the one hand, you have been brought up to believe in the very subtle lie that human beings have no ultimate power over nature. At the same time, you have been brought up to believe that human beings can destroy nature and can *only* destroy nature. After all, there is nature and then there is human beings, and somehow there is a disconnect between the two. You have been brought up with the naive belief that the planet was once an idyllic place where all the animals lived and there was no humans to destroy and pollute.

Therefore, you should feel bad about being a human being on this planet. You should voluntarily submit yourself to the lie that there are too many people on this planet. You will notice even this movie, how it is part of the greater propaganda without any deliberate intent of the people who made it. Think back to the very opening words that 200 years ago there were only two billion people on this planet, today there are six billion people crowding the planet.

Well, does this not show you how they want you to believe that on the one hand you have no ability to influence the big

3 | An all-encompassing shift in consciousness

picture and the balance and order of nature, but on the other hand you are an alien creature in nature who can only destroy? Do you see that now they are trying to sell you on the next lie of global warming. Well, if humankind has the ability to influence the planetary weather through global warming, then does this not disprove the claim that humankind has no power to change the order of nature?

When you start realizing that humankind does have a destructive capability that has reached global proportions, is it that difficult to take the next step and realize that perhaps humankind has an even greater power—that is greater than the power of technology? This is the power of consciousness whereby humankind has both the ability to destroy and the ability to uplift and to purify this planet, bringing it back to the original purity but even going beyond and co-creating the kingdom of God on earth.

Look at nature and look at the animal species. Consider why the balance of nature, as they call it, requires that an animal population must be kept at a certain level by animals of prey in order to avoid growing so large that it depletes its own food supply? You see, my beloved, what is called the balance of nature – where certain animal species must be held in check by others – is really not a state of balance, is it? If you think logically, you realize that if there was truly balance in nature, then there would be no risk that a population could grow too large for the food supply in the area where it lived. If there was truly balance on this planet, there would be a higher regulatory mechanism that would keep animal populations at the ideal level so that there was no need for disease, famine, starvation or animals of prey.

What you have been brought up to see as the balance of nature is the *unbalance* of nature. Where did that unbalance come from? Well, it came from man. It came through the minds of those in the fallen consciousness. Do you not see that the state of certain animals being hunted and killed by others is a dualistic state where some must be killed so that others can survive? This is clearly duality for those who are aware of what duality means.

You have only two options. Either this imbalance evolved spontaneously or it was created by God. Certainly, there are many religious people who are deeply confused, thinking that God must have created lions and wolves. Yet, does it really make sense that in paradise there were lions and wolves? Does it really make sense – as you have seen from early childhood the pictures of Noah's ark – that Noah brought lions and wolves onto the ark? My beloved, just imagine for a moment being stuffed in a small boat along with wolves and lions and trying to keep order. This is simply not a realistic scenario. Even on a humorous note, if you believe the Bible literally, then Noah brought two of each animal onto the ark. Well, which species was he going to sacrifice so the lion could get its next meal? There were only two goats so he couldn't feed them some of the leftovers, he had to feed them the only two. You see, my beloved, this simply makes no sense whatsoever.

Did God create the imbalance in nature?

You need to step away from the literal interpretation and realize there is a deeper reality here. The deeper reality is that God did not create the current animal species that are found on this planet, nor did he create the state of imbalance that you see. This was created as an outpicturing of the state of consciousness of humankind. Surely, Maitreya has explained in his book that the presence of intelligent human-like beings on this planet goes very far back, much further back than

3 | An all-encompassing shift in consciousness

acknowledged by any mainstream religion and even by science itself. The fact of the matter is that almost every aspect of nature on this planet is an outpicturing of the duality, the imbalance, the inharmony in the collective consciousness of humankind. This goes for earthquakes and natural disasters, as Mother Mary has explained, it goes for diseases in your physical bodies, diseases in animal populations, it goes for the entire idea of overpopulation that necessitates diseases or starvation, it goes for poisonous animals of any kind, all kinds of parasites that prey upon humans and animals. All of this is an outpicturing of the dualistic state of consciousness.

I want you to consider this from different perspectives. Consider what you saw on this clip: On the farthest-most northern tip, it is so extremely cold that an animal species has had to adapt to this by growing very long fur and by developing a life cycle where the mother hibernates for several months during the winter, then gives birth to her cubs. She brings them out in the spring because the summer is so short that they have no opportunity to grow big before the next winter unless they start as soon as they can leave the nest or the den. You see the extreme that nature has gone through to adapt to these conditions. What I want you to realize from this is the extreme conditions that are found in the collective human consciousness. What you realize when you see how these extreme patterns are embedded even in nature herself, is how deeply certain thoughtforms, certain ideas, certain beliefs, certain attachments are embedded in the collective psyche.

For each animal species you see on this planet, there is a group of people – you cannot identify them by outer characteristics but only by their consciousness – who have in their consciousness the very thoughtforms that have precipitated that animal species in its extreme form of adaptability to some state of imbalance on the earth. These people are very attached to these thoughtforms. They are not about to give up those thoughtforms, at least not until we have a dramatic shift in consciousness.

A profound shift in consciousness is needed

I am not giving you these ideas to make you feel overwhelmed or burdened. I am giving you these ideas because you who are the aware people need to recognize just how deep of a shift in consciousness I am talking about. When you begin to realize this, you will acknowledge a very important principle. In order to free yourself from the collective consciousness on this planet, you have to be willing to literally rethink everything you were brought up to believe. You must question even the most subtle beliefs that are not what we might say political ideologies or religious ideologies. They are the subtle beliefs that nobody questions because they have been part of the collective consciousness for so long that everybody takes them for granted.

I want you to realize, that part of walking the path to Christhood is that you are willing to question what everybody else takes for granted so that you can free yourself from these collective illusions. Therefore, you become a forerunner for adopting and accepting a higher state of consciousness that is free of these age-old illusions. When you become one of those forerunners, my beloved, you can then fill your place, holding the balance for millions of others as the shift in consciousness spreads like rings in the water.

It is a reality that we of the ascended masters walk a tightrope. We are inevitably releasing the energies from Above that will bring forth a shift in consciousness, but we have to do this in a very delicate manner. If we were to release these energies too quickly, then people would be awakened so quickly that they could not adapt, they could not accept the changes. They would go through a state of withdrawal, of an identity crisis, of not knowing who they are.

Holding the spiritual balance for others

You all know this because most if not all of you have at some point on your spiritual path, maybe several times, gone through a certain identity crisis where you had to be willing to question everything that you believed. You had to be willing to let go of everything that you believed and give all your beliefs to God and let him give back what is real. You must realize that not everybody on the planet is ready to do that – is willing and capable of doing that – and therefore there needs to be someone who can hold the balance as the shift in consciousness occurs.

When you are willing to question these deep beliefs, these illusions, and you overcome those illusions and you accept the truth of Christ that will make you free, then you can hold the balance for many other people, potentially for millions of other people. As they accept the new consciousness, they will not be overwhelmed. They will not lose their sense of continuity and identity but will be able to make a much quicker transition into the higher state of consciousness.

This is crucial because, as Mother Mary has said, if we do not have a certain shift in consciousness, the physical planet will not be able to withstand the energy without massive earth changes. If enough people can make the shift in consciousness, then the broader number of people that are necessary can awaken. Therefore, we can avoid the earth changes that otherwise will come to pass.

There is a high potential that the transition into the Aquarian age consciousness can happen smoothly, gradually. Or there is the low potential that humankind will continue business as usual until the planet simply can no longer bear the weight of their karma on the one side and the weight of the new light that is being released on the other. It is therefore torn apart by the difference between the two.

Humankind *will* be awakened, but it will be an extremely rude awakening compared to the high potential of them gradually shifting into the higher consciousness without even fully realizing what is happening. People simply wake up and say: "Hey, I no longer believe in these old beliefs. I no longer believe this is impossible. I no longer believe that we the people have no power to govern ourselves."

The elite as the "saviors" of the people

I ask you to consider what has happened over this last year or so. What you have seen over this last year is a steady decline in the American people's support for the war in Iraq and support for the president. What that really signifies is that the people have stopped supporting the agenda behind the war in Iraq. That agenda was not the war on terror, was not to fight the terrorists on foreign soil instead of fighting them at home, as Bush has said over and over again. The real agenda was the agenda of the power elite, which has many facets that I will not here go into.

What I want you to realize is that because of the clearing of consciousness, the clearing of the heart, the American people have begun to realize that they will not support their president when their president is not *their* president but is the president of the elite. The people are beginning to realize that they can

3 | An all-encompassing shift in consciousness

no longer allow their leaders to follow the agenda of the elite instead of following the agenda of the ascended masters—who are really behind the people. Our agenda is what is best for the people of this nation.

To return to my concepts that everything in nature, even the balance of nature, is affected by the consciousness of humankind, one of the subtle beliefs behind this idea is that there are certain aspects of life on this planet that are beyond the power of the people and thus you need someone outside yourself to do something for you. This is the lie that Jesus has exposed in such detail, such richness and with such eloquence on his website [*www.askrealjesus.com*]. The fallen beings elevated his example to an idol that he is the *only* Son of God and everybody needs him in order to be saved. In reality, his true mission was to show everyone that they can find the kingdom of God within them and thus do not need an external savior.

The fallen beings who came to this planet (and who are attempting to set themselves up as gods on earth) are getting the people to worship them as gods on earth. What they have attempted to do from the very beginning is a very simple strategy. Through their fallen consciousness, through their dualistic consciousness, they create a state of imbalance on the planet, and then they set themselves up as those who can save the people from that imbalance. You see it today. They are the ones who have misused science and technology in their greed to create multinational corporations that have no respect for the environment, no respect for the people they employ. These are the ones who have created the pollution that is threatening the ecosystem on this planet.

If anyone is responsible for global warming, they are the ones who are responsible for it. Of course, we have given teachings already on the reality of global warming, but what I want you to realize is that pollution is first and foremost created by the elite. Now that the problem is there and has been recognized by the people, well, then the power elite comes in with the second part of their strategy, which is to set themselves up as the saviors who can tell the people how to overcome this problem.

For nigh a century, they were trying to hide the fact that pollution could have an influence on the environment so that they could continue to have the biggest possible short-term profits by polluting. Now that the consciousness of the people has shifted – where they could no longer get away with this – they are trying to use the new environmental awareness to their advantage by setting themselves up as the saviors of the people. This is what they have done over and over again. Every single problem on this planet is created through the consciousness of duality. Although many of the people have fallen into duality, it is first and foremost the elite – of the most rigid and closed-minded fallen beings – who are upholding that consciousness as the dominant state of consciousness on earth.

Through that consciousness, a problem is created and then the elite comes in and says: "Ah, but we have the only solution—and it is that you, the people, give us more control over you and then we will solve the problem and take you to heaven on earth." This is, of course, a complete fallacy. Obviously, you cannot solve a problem with the same state of consciousness that has created that problem. How can those who are the most blinded by the duality consciousness solve the problems created through the duality consciousness? Obviously, the elite will never save the people.

For a time, a particular elite will be able to use the problem to control the people until the people start seeing through the illusion. Then what happens? Well, what happens is that now an aspiring power elite begins to form and they say: "No, the established power elite is wrong, but we are the real saviors.

We have the real solution. So follow us instead of following the old elite." Is it not time for a critical mass of people to awaken to the reality that you have come into embodiment to rise above this dualistic game, to totally leave it behind, to expose it for what it is and to stand up and say: "The emperors of duality have nothing on!"

Saint Germain's strategy for the Golden Age

If there was one concept I would like you to accept, it is the very fact that even though humankind has created a false god in their own image and likeness, the very fact that some people are stupid does not mean that God is stupid. We of the ascended masters are not stupid, we are not unintelligent. I have been an ascended being for over 400 years. I have known that I would be the hierarch for the Age of Aquarius. I have known full well from my last embodiments – where I was up against these fallen beings – what they planned to do with this planet.

I have had a long time to plan a strategy. Part of that strategy is that I have gathered – over the centuries – lifestreams of light who are loyal to me, who are loyal to the Flame of Freedom, who see the Flame of Freedom. These lifestreams have been trained over many lifetimes. They have volunteered to come into embodiment at this specific time because they wanted to support the cause of Saint Germain, which is to bring the Aquarian age consciousness and the Golden Age of Aquarius into physical manifestation as quickly as possible in this 21st century.

You are all among them. If you think I am not stupid, then realize you are not stupid either. You know within what is the reality of your Divine plan. If you made a Divine plan, it was because you and I both knew that you had a very realistic potential of fulfilling that plan—because you have what it takes. You have the experience from past lives, you have the knowledge and the understanding, you have the momentum.

What you need to do is let go of this entire outer consciousness that has been put upon you from day one that you crawled out of your mother's womb and gave your first cry—even while you were in the womb. It says that you are nothing, that you are no good, that you cannot make a difference, that the problems on this planet are too big for you to have any impact. What difference can one person make?

My beloved, look at it as the unreality it is and realize that you are in embodiment because, in the deeper parts of your being, you know that this is all lies. You know that with men this is impossible but with God in you all things that are part of your Divine plan are indeed possible.

Let go of the dream of one true religion

We are not here talking about everybody on this planet coming to accept even the existence of the ascended masters, coming to accept a particular teaching or a particular organization. It was the Piscean age where one organization was supposedly the only one. This is the Aquarian age where we are about awakening everyone to their Divine plan. There are many different people who are part of my bands. They have many different talents – many different Divine plans – for many different things must happen. Many shifts must occur for this planet to go through the transition into a higher state of consciousness.

It is not realistic to create a new Aquarian age religion and spend all of your efforts and attention on converting everybody to that religion. This is a dream of the Piscean age. I ask all spiritual people to fully and finally let go of this dream and realize that it had its place in the Piscean, but it no longer has any place in the Aquarian age. We are talking about an age of freedom, of spiritual freedom, where every person is under his own vine and fig tree of his I AM Presence and Holy Christ Self. You do not need one centralized organization in the Aquarian age. You need a universal awakening. You need a universal awareness that is not focused on any particular individual, institution, doctrine or philosophy. It is about people everywhere waking up and realizing that they have a mission to raise the consciousness in some way—and then *they do it!*

If many people come together under a certain teaching and find inspiration in that teaching, then that is good. Do not let the outer organization, the outer guru or the outer teaching become a hindrance to the expression of your Christhood. Do not feel that you have to force the expression of your Christhood into a certain mold or a certain matrix, for, my beloved, this is not being.

Learn from every situation

Again, you have the eternal question: "To Be or not to Be." I am asking you to *be* here below all that you already are Above by locking in to that Divine plan, by letting go of any expectations you have – any attachments you have – to what your Divine plan should or should not be. There are no shoulds in being. There are no do's or don'ts in Christhood. There is only the spontaneous act of being the Christ in action in this particular situation. There is not the evaluation: "Oh I should do this, I should not do that." Everything becomes spontaneous.

Look at the life of Jesus. You can look back and say: Was it wise for Jesus to overturn the tables of the money changers in the temple? Was it not the very incident that alerted the power elite of the Jewish religion to how dangerous Jesus was and made them decide to kill him? If Jesus had sat there and considered before he went to the temple what he should do and what he should not do, he might indeed with his outer mind have reasoned himself out of doing anything drastic. You see, it was not a mistake for him to overturn those tables, no matter the fact that he could have done it with a little less fervor and a little less anger. This was something that needed to happen for his plan to be fulfilled.

Do not look at your life with the analytical mind and say: "Oh back then I made this or that mistake. I should never have done it." My beloved, it is wise to look back at your life and say: "If I did something, I did it because I had to do it, if nothing else because I needed to learn a certain lesson. By doing that particular thing, I had the opportunity to learn that lesson faster. Even if I did not take that opportunity back then, I can take the opportunity today." It may be too late to undo the past, but it is never too late to learn the lesson from the past. If you learn that lesson, nothing is wasted, for you have indeed used even a mistake to come up higher on the path.

Tune in to the etheric blueprint for the Golden Age

I realize that I have given you as much as you can handle in one installment, for your cups are beginning to overflow and there is no longer room for my words and my light and you need time to digest. I will give you one last thought that I desire you to ponder. Consider how we of the ascended masters look at planet earth and what is happening on earth. Be willing to consider that we look at it in a very different way than the way you look at it and the way most people look at it. We have a broader perspective, a broader view. We have a more long-term view. We are non-attached. I am not fault-finding you, for you are in embodiment and you naturally look at the earth from the inside. I am telling you that there is value in once in a while stepping outside by considering how we in the ascended realm look at earth.

There may be many prophecies, there may be many portents about what could happen on the earth. I tell you that we of the ascended masters do not look at the earth and look at history as some period of growth, then a calamity, then a backward step, then a little climb, then another calamity. We do not look at life on earth as a stop-and-go as a backwards-and-forwards process. We see that behind everything that has happened on earth (even some of the big calamities that you are aware of: the sinking of Atlantis, the sinking of Lemuria, the sinking of past civilizations that Maitreya mentions in his book), there has been a progression in consciousness. Even though there have been great calamities on this planet, behind all of them has been an upward movement.

Everything that happens on this planet, good or bad, serves as a lesson that at some level in the etheric realm is anchored in the collective consciousness. This means that even though there has been great turbulence in the physical octave, great turbulence in the emotional octave, great turbulence in the mental realm, even in some of the lower levels of the identity realm, there are higher levels of the identity realm where there has been a steady progression in awareness.

That awareness is anchored in the etheric realm right now. It is literally humankind's treasure laid up in heaven. It is there for people to draw upon and you who are the more spiritually aware, I encourage you to consider that you can tune in to your own identity body and to the collective etheric body, and you can then draw down those lessons that have been learned over eons of time on this planet. Thereby, you can tune in to the new age of Aquarius, you can tune in to the Golden Age. You do not think that I sat down and created the matrix for the Golden Age without looking back, learning and drawing upon the lessons of history? I did not design a Golden Age without considering what has gone before on this planet. Naturally, I want the Golden Age of Aquarius to build upon everything that has been learned on this planet.

In the etheric realm of planet earth is what you might call a vast database or library where all the positive lessons that have been learned – individually and collectively – on this planet are stored and cannot be destroyed by anything that takes place in the lower realms. At any point in time, no matter how dark it might seem for those in embodiment, there is a potential that a critical mass of people can raise their consciousness, tune in to the matrix for a Golden Age in the etheric realm and bring that to their outer awareness. Gradually, they can awaken other people so that a momentum builds and a shift occurs that will bring that Golden Age matrix from the etheric into the mental where even more people can grasp it and another shift occurs. Then, it is brought into the emotional to the point where more and more people overcome the sense of doom and gloom, the sense of limitation, the sense of what is impossible. They begin to truly accept in the feeling world that there can be a Golden Age, that there can be a better future no matter how gloomy it might look.

This will bring forth the point where more and more people start acting on the highest potential instead of acting on the lowest potential. We need a critical mass of people who will begin to live their lives as if the Golden Age is already inevitable and is already beginning to manifest in the material realm. Do you see that this is the highest state of consciousness you can reach?

3 | An all-encompassing shift in consciousness

It is not a matter of *believing* that perhaps, maybe, sometime in the future there can be a Golden Age. No, my beloved, we need those here in embodiment who will accept that the Golden Age is not a matter of *if,* and it is not a matter of *when*—it is a matter of NOW. *Now and here!* Because you accept that only the Golden Age consciousness is ultimately real. Thus, reality will inevitably be projected onto the Mother Light and the Mother Light will outpicture that reality. You live your life as if the Golden Age is already manifest. If you will live your life as if the Golden Age is manifest, then it *will* be manifest in your life—when you have no doubt and fear, no room for any lower emotions or any lower beliefs or doubts.

Dare to tune in to your Divine plan individually. Dare to tune in to the fact that in the etheric realm, the Golden Age is already a manifest reality. It is simply a matter of you accepting it with all levels of your consciousness, and it will manifest in your individual life. As a critical mass of people do the same – because perhaps they see your example, or they are simply pulled up by your consciousness even though they have never met you – then, when that critical mass is reached, you will see a widespread manifestation of the Golden Age.

No limits to growth

You already see aspects of this here in the state of California. Do you not see how this state has been the seat of much innovation? Take a look at the computer industry, of how that industry has brought incredible wealth that was simply not there 30 years ago. Do you see why there is no limit to growth, as they said back in the 70's and 80's, when they had an entire movement funded by the power elite to make people believe that there were limits to economic growth, limits to the growth of the size of the human population. Surely, there are limits—if you accept that there are limits. If you do *not* accept that there are limits, there *are* no limits. As I started out saying, everything on this planet is affected by the consciousness of humankind. The limitations that are here in the physical are the outpicturings of the limitations in the mind, the collective mind. Change your mind, get rid of the limitations in the mind and you will change the physical. This is an inevitable reality, and it is the most important thing that needs to happen right now—that people awaken to this reality and this potential.

Once again, your cups are full and more than full. I thank you from the bottom of my heart for providing a platform whereby you can hold the balance for my releasing this teaching. I hope you recognize that as you individually raise your consciousness, and as you raise your collective consciousness and come into greater oneness, then you make it possible for us to release more advanced teachings.

Do you not see that more advanced teachings are being brought forth now than two or three years ago? Do you not see that when Jesus brought out the book *The Mystical Teachings of Jesus*, he could only bring it out for a certain level of consciousness? Now it has been possible to expand that book and so to take it to a much higher level where the teachings, the true teachings of Christ, are given in a more direct form. You are all part of this. Truly, as we have said many times, we of the ascended masters can give a certain teaching, but unless there are people who are willing to internalize that teaching and multiply the talents, well, then we cannot give any more.

I want you to credit yourselves for the fact that the very reality that you have accepted this teaching has allowed me to bring forth the teaching I have brought forth today, has allowed Maitreya to bring forth his book, which could not have been brought forth even two years ago. I trust that you will return on the morrow with a willingness to once again step up to a higher level of consciousness so that I might speak again tomorrow and bring forth an even higher teaching that will be even more direct in addressing what needs to happen for the shift in consciousness and what the Golden Age might actually look like when it is physically manifest. Thus, I seal you in the love of my heart, in the Freedom Flame. I look forward to seeing you again tomorrow.

4 | INVOKING A REALISTIC VIEW OF NATURE

In the name I AM THAT I AM, Jesus Christ, I call to all ascended masters working on manifesting the Golden Age, especially Archangel Michael, Elohim Hercules, Master MORE and Saint Germain, to radiate into the collective consciousness a realistic view of our relationship to nature. Help people see that we can build a new future by working with the ascended masters and letting go of the old way of looking at life, including...

[Make personal calls.]

Part 1

1. Saint Germain, radiate into the collective consciousness the awareness that although God created humans in his own image and likeness, we are not in the original state of innocence at which we and the earth were created.

> Michael Archangel, in your flame so blue,
> there is no more night, there is only you.
> In oneness with you, we're filled with your light,
> what glorious wonder, revealed to our sight.
>
> **Michael Archangel, your Knowing so strong,**
> **Michael Archangel, oh sweep us along.**
> **Michael Archangel, we're singing your song,**
> **Michael Archangel, with you we belong.**

2. Saint Germain, radiate into the collective consciousness the awareness that the earth has fallen very far below its original state of innocence.

> Michael Archangel, protection you give,
> within your blue shield, we ever shall live.
> Sealed from all creatures, roaming the night,
> we remain in your sphere, of electric blue light.
>
> **Michael Archangel, your Knowing so strong,**
> **Michael Archangel, oh sweep us along.**
> **Michael Archangel, we're singing your song,**
> **Michael Archangel, with you we belong.**

3. Saint Germain, radiate into the collective consciousness the awareness that as a result of the planet falling below its original state of innocence, human beings have departed from their original matrix, the original image of God.

> Michael Archangel, what power you bring,
> as millions of angels, praises will sing.
> Consuming the demons, of doubt and of fear,
> we know that your Presence, will always be near.
>
> **Michael Archangel, your Knowing so strong,**
> **Michael Archangel, oh sweep us along.**
> **Michael Archangel, we're singing your song,**
> **Michael Archangel, with you we belong.**

4. Saint Germain, radiate into the collective consciousness the awareness that we have created images based on duality. We have used those images to create false gods after the image and likeness of the dualistic consciousness.

> Michael Archangel, God's will is your love,
> you bring to us all, God's light from Above.
> God's will is to see, all life taking flight,
> transcendence of self, our most sacred right.
>
> **Michael Archangel, your Knowing so strong,**
> **Michael Archangel, oh sweep us along.**
> **Michael Archangel, we're singing your song,**
> **Michael Archangel, with you we belong.**

5. Saint Germain, radiate into the collective consciousness the awareness that there are fallen beings who want to set themselves up as gods on earth, because they are not willing to come into oneness with the God in heaven whereby they could be Gods in the spiritual realm.

> Michael Archangel, you are the best friend,
> from all worldly dangers you do us defend,
> the devil no match for your power of light,
> and therefore our souls can freely take flight.

> **Michael Archangel, your Knowing so strong,**
> **Michael Archangel, oh sweep us along.**
> **Michael Archangel, we're singing your song,**
> **Michael Archangel, with you we belong.**

6. Saint Germain, radiate into the collective consciousness the awareness that almost everything on this planet is influenced by the consciousness of duality.

> Michael Archangel, as children we play,
> we're bringing the earth into a new day,
> we raise it from all of the patterns so old,
> our planet's life story is by us retold.

> **Michael Archangel, your Knowing so strong,**
> **Michael Archangel, oh sweep us along.**
> **Michael Archangel, we're singing your song,**
> **Michael Archangel, with you we belong.**

4 | Invoking a realistic view of nature

7. Saint Germain, radiate into the collective consciousness the awareness that the consciousness of the fallen beings is anti-God, is based on a denial of God. This is a denial that God is here on this planet, that God created this planet, that God exists.

> Michael Archangel, God's power you show,
> that you are invincible, this we do know,
> you are undivided and thus can withstand,
> anything coming from serpentine band.
>
> **Michael Archangel, your Knowing so strong,**
> **Michael Archangel, oh sweep us along.**
> **Michael Archangel, we're singing your song,**
> **Michael Archangel, with you we belong.**

8. Saint Germain, radiate into the collective consciousness the awareness that it is a complete lie that nature is something that is inevitable, is beyond human comprehension, beyond human power to change.

> Michael Archangel, come raise now the earth,
> giving her thus a complete rebirth,
> collective the mind that we do now raise,
> for this we do give our infinite praise.
>
> **Michael Archangel, your Knowing so strong,**
> **Michael Archangel, oh sweep us along.**
> **Michael Archangel, we're singing your song,**
> **Michael Archangel, with you we belong.**

9. Saint Germain, radiate into the collective consciousness the awareness that the idea that there is nothing we can do about nature is a lie, perpetrated by the dark forces who seek to control humankind.

> Michael Archangel, the earth is now new,
> covered in Blue-flame as the morning dew,
> our planet now sparkles throughout all of space,
> as we are receiving your infinite Grace.
>
> **Michael Archangel, your Knowing so strong,**
> **Michael Archangel, oh sweep us along.**
> **Michael Archangel, we're singing your song,**
> **Michael Archangel, with you we belong.**

Part 2

1. Saint Germain, radiate into the collective consciousness the awareness that if we only focus on physical conspiracies, we will not grasp the full picture, and thus we will not be able to make and facilitate the shift in consciousness that needs to occur.

> O Hercules Blue, we're one with your will,
> all space in our beings with Blue Flame you fill,
> a beacon that radiates light to the earth,
> bringing about our planet's rebirth.

**O Hercules Blue, all life you defend,
giving us power to always transcend,
in you the expansion of self has no end,
as we in God's infinite spirals ascend.**

2. Saint Germain, radiate into the collective consciousness the awareness that it is a lie that we have no power to change the big things on earth including nature, the balance of nature or the ecosystem.

O Hercules Blue, your wisdom so great,
within us a sense of knowing create,
a new frame of reference we suddenly gain,
for going beyond duality's pain.

**O Hercules Blue, all life you defend,
giving us power to always transcend,
in you the expansion of self has no end,
as we in God's infinite spirals ascend.**

3. Saint Germain, radiate into the collective consciousness the awareness that it is also a lie that we can only destroy nature. It is a lie that there is nature and then there is human beings, and there is a disconnect between the two.

O Hercules Blue, we lovingly raise,
our voices in giving God infinite praise,
in feeling your flame, so clearly we see,
transcending the self is the true alchemy.

> O Hercules Blue, all life you defend,
> giving us power to always transcend,
> in you the expansion of self has no end,
> as we in God's infinite spirals ascend.

4. Saint Germain, radiate into the collective consciousness the awareness that it is a lie that the planet was once an idyllic place where all the animals lived and there were no humans to destroy and pollute.

> O Hercules Blue, all life now you heal,
> enveloping all in your Blue-flame Seal,
> we're grateful for playing a personal part,
> In God's infinitely intricate work of art.

> O Hercules Blue, all life you defend,
> giving us power to always transcend,
> in you the expansion of self has no end,
> as we in God's infinite spirals ascend.

5. Saint Germain, radiate into the collective consciousness the awareness that we do not need to feel bad about being humans or believe the lie that there are too many people on this planet.

> O Hercules Blue, your Temple of Light,
> revealed to us all through our inner sight,
> your power allows us to forge on until,
> we pierce every veil and climb every hill.

> O Hercules Blue, all life you defend,
> giving us power to always transcend,
> in you the expansion of self has no end,
> as we in God's infinite spirals ascend.

4 | Invoking a realistic view of nature

6. Saint Germain, radiate into the collective consciousness the awareness that the fallen beings want us to believe that on the one hand we have no ability to influence the big picture and the balance of nature, but on the other hand we are alien creatures in nature who can only destroy.

> O Hercules Blue, I pledge now my life,
> in helping this planet transcend human strife,
> duality's lies are pierced by your light,
> restoring the fullness of our inner sight.
>
> **O Hercules Blue, all life you defend,**
> **giving us power to always transcend,**
> **in you the expansion of self has no end,**
> **as we in God's infinite spirals ascend.**

7. Saint Germain, radiate into the collective consciousness the awareness that if humankind has the ability to influence the planetary weather through global warming, it disproves the claim that we have no power to change the order of nature.

> O Hercules Blue, we set all life free,
> from the subtlest lies of duality,
> the prince of this world no more has a bond,
> for with you we go completely beyond.
>
> **O Hercules Blue, all life you defend,**
> **giving us power to always transcend,**
> **in you the expansion of self has no end,**
> **as we in God's infinite spirals ascend.**

8. Saint Germain, radiate into the collective consciousness the awareness that humankind has a power that is greater than the power of technology. It is the power of consciousness whereby we have both the ability to destroy and the ability to uplift this planet.

> O Hercules Blue, in oneness with thee,
> we open our hearts to your reality,
> your electric-blue fire within us reveal,
> our innermost longing for all that is real.

> **O Hercules Blue, all life you defend,**
> **giving us power to always transcend,**
> **in you the expansion of self has no end,**
> **as we in God's infinite spirals ascend.**

9. Saint Germain, radiate into the collective consciousness the awareness that the balance of nature is the unbalance of nature. It came from the fallen consciousness.

> O Hercules Blue, you fill every space,
> with infinite Power and infinite Grace,
> you embody the key to creativity,
> the will to transcend into Infinity.

> **O Hercules Blue, all life you defend,**
> **giving us power to always transcend,**
> **in you the expansion of self has no end,**
> **as we in God's infinite spirals ascend.**

Part 3

1. Saint Germain, radiate into the collective consciousness the awareness that God did not create the animal species on this planet, nor did he create the state of imbalance. Both were created as an outpicturing of the state of consciousness of humankind.

> Master MORE, come to the fore,
> we will absorb your flame of MORE.
> Master MORE, our will so strong,
> our power centers cleared by song.
>
> **Master MORE, your Sacred Heart,**
> **from this we will no more depart,**
> **we are forever in your flow,**
> **of Diamond Will that you bestow.**

2. Saint Germain, radiate into the collective consciousness the awareness that the presence of intelligent human-like beings on this planet goes much further back than acknowledged by any mainstream religion and science.

> Master MORE, your wisdom flows,
> as our attunement ever grows.
> Master MORE, we have a tie,
> that helps us see through Serpent's lie.
>
> **Master MORE, your Sacred Heart,**
> **from this we will no more depart,**
> **we are forever in your flow,**
> **of Diamond Will that you bestow.**

3. Saint Germain, radiate into the collective consciousness the awareness that almost every aspect of nature on this planet is an outpicturing of the imbalance in our consciousness, causing earthquakes, natural disasters, diseases in our physical bodies and in animal populations.

> Master MORE, your love so pink,
> there is no purer love, we think.
> Master MORE, you set us free,
> from all conditionality.

> **Master MORE, your Sacred Heart,**
> **from this we will no more depart,**
> **we are forever in your flow,**
> **of Diamond Will that you bestow.**

4. Saint Germain, radiate into the collective consciousness the awareness that the extreme conditions found in the collective human consciousness are embedded in nature, and this shows how deeply certain thoughtforms and ideas are embedded in the collective psyche.

> Master MORE, we will endure,
> your discipline that makes us pure.
> Master MORE, intentions true,
> as we are always one with you.

> **Master MORE, your Sacred Heart,**
> **from this we will no more depart,**
> **we are forever in your flow,**
> **of Diamond Will that you bestow.**

5. Saint Germain, radiate into the collective consciousness the awareness that for each animal species on this planet, there is a group of people who have in their consciousness the very thoughtforms that have precipitated that animal species in its extreme form of adaptability to some state of imbalance.

> Master MORE, our vision raised,
> the will of God is always praised.
> Master MORE, creative will,
> raising all life higher still.

> **Master MORE, your Sacred Heart,**
> **from this we will no more depart,**
> **we are forever in your flow,**
> **of Diamond Will that you bestow.**

6. Saint Germain, radiate into the collective consciousness the awareness that in order to free ourselves from the collective consciousness on this planet, we have to be willing to rethink everything we were brought up to believe.

> Master MORE, your peace is power,
> the demons of war it will devour.
> Master MORE, we serve all life,
> our flames consuming war and strife.

> **Master MORE, your Sacred Heart,**
> **from this we will no more depart,**
> **we are forever in your flow,**
> **of Diamond Will that you bestow.**

7. Saint Germain, radiate into the collective consciousness the awareness that we need to question even the most subtle beliefs that nobody questions because they have been part of the collective consciousness for so long that everybody takes them for granted.

> Master MORE, we are so free,
> eternal bond from you we see.
> Master MORE, we find rebirth,
> in flow of your eternal mirth.

> **Master MORE, your Sacred Heart,**
> **from this we will no more depart,**
> **we are forever in your flow,**
> **of Diamond Will that you bestow.**

8. Saint Germain, radiate into the collective consciousness the awareness that walking the path to Christhood means that we are willing to question what everybody else takes for granted so that we can free ourselves from these collective illusions.

> Master MORE, you balance all,
> the seven rays upon our call.
> Master MORE, forever MORE,
> we are the Spirit's open door.

> **Master MORE, your Sacred Heart,**
> **from this we will no more depart,**
> **we are forever in your flow,**
> **of Diamond Will that you bestow.**

9. Saint Germain, radiate into the collective consciousness the awareness that it is a lie that there are certain aspects of life on this planet that are beyond the power of the people and thus we need someone outside ourselves to do something for us.

> Master MORE, your Presence here,
> filling up the inner sphere.
> Life is now a sacred flow,
> God Power we on all bestow.
>
> **Master MORE, your Sacred Heart,**
> **from this we will no more depart,**
> **we are forever in your flow,**
> **of Diamond Will that you bestow.**

Part 4

1. Saint Germain, radiate into the collective consciousness the awareness that the fallen beings create a state of imbalance on the planet, and then they set themselves up as those who can save the people from that imbalance.

> O Saint Germain, you do inspire,
> my vision raised forever higher,
> with you I form a figure-eight,
> your Golden Age I co-create.
>
> **O Saint Germain, what love you bring,**
> **it truly makes all matter sing,**
> **your violet flame does all restore,**
> **with you we are becoming more.**

2. Saint Germain, radiate into the collective consciousness the awareness that the fallen beings are the ones who in their greed have misused science and technology to create multinational corporations that have no respect for the environment or people.

> O Saint Germain, what Freedom Flame,
> released when we recite your name,
> acceleration is your gift,
> our planet it will surely lift.

> **O Saint Germain, what love you bring,**
> **it truly makes all matter sing,**
> **your violet flame does all restore,**
> **with you we are becoming more.**

3. Saint Germain, radiate into the collective consciousness the awareness that the fallen beings have created the pollution that is threatening the ecosystem. Pollution is first and foremost created by the elite.

> O Saint Germain, in love we claim,
> our right to bring your violet flame,
> from you Above, to us below,
> it is an all-transforming flow.

> **O Saint Germain, what love you bring,**
> **it truly makes all matter sing,**
> **your violet flame does all restore,**
> **with you we are becoming more.**

4. Saint Germain, radiate into the collective consciousness the awareness that the power elite now comes in with the second part of their strategy, which is to set themselves as the saviors who can tell the people how to overcome this problem.

> O Saint Germain, I love you so,
> my aura filled with violet glow,
> my chakras filled with violet fire,
> I am your cosmic amplifier.

> **O Saint Germain, what love you bring,**
> **it truly makes all matter sing,**
> **your violet flame does all restore,**
> **with you we are becoming more.**

5. Saint Germain, radiate into the collective consciousness the awareness that the fallen beings are trying to use the new environmental awareness to their advantage by setting themselves up as the saviors of the people.

> O Saint Germain, I am now free,
> your violet flame is therapy,
> transform all hang-ups in my mind,
> as inner peace I surely find.

> **O Saint Germain, what love you bring,**
> **it truly makes all matter sing,**
> **your violet flame does all restore,**
> **with you we are becoming more.**

6. Saint Germain, radiate into the collective consciousness the awareness that it is first and foremost the elite who are upholding that consciousness of duality as the dominant state of consciousness on earth.

> O Saint Germain, my body pure,
> your violet flame for all is cure,
> consume the cause of all disease,
> and therefore I am all at ease.
>
> **O Saint Germain, what love you bring,**
> **it truly makes all matter sing,**
> **your violet flame does all restore,**
> **with you we are becoming more.**

7. Saint Germain, radiate into the collective consciousness the awareness that when a problem is created by the elite, then the elite says: "The only solution is that you, the people, give us more control over you and then we will solve the problem and take you to heaven on earth."

> O Saint Germain, I'm karma-free,
> the past no longer burdens me,
> a brand new opportunity,
> I am in Christic unity.
>
> **O Saint Germain, what love you bring,**
> **it truly makes all matter sing,**
> **your violet flame does all restore,**
> **with you we are becoming more.**

8. Saint Germain, radiate into the collective consciousness the awareness that this is a complete fallacy because we cannot solve a problem with the same state of consciousness that has created that problem.

> O Saint Germain, we are now one,
> I am for you a violet sun,
> as we transform this planet earth,
> your Golden Age is given birth.

> **O Saint Germain, what love you bring,**
> **it truly makes all matter sing,**
> **your violet flame does all restore,**
> **with you we are becoming more.**

9. Saint Germain, radiate into the collective consciousness the awareness that those who are the most blinded by the duality consciousness cannot solve the problems created through the duality consciousness. The elite will never save the people.

> O Saint Germain, the earth is free,
> from burden of duality,
> in oneness we bring what is best,
> your Golden Age is manifest.

> **O Saint Germain, what love you bring,**
> **it truly makes all matter sing,**
> **your violet flame does all restore,**
> **with you we are becoming more.**

Sealing

In the name of the Divine Mother, I call to all ascended masters for the sealing of myself and all people in my circle of influence in the creative flow of the Divine Mother, the River of Life. I call for the multiplication of my calls by all ascended masters so that we form the perfect figure-eight flow of "As Above, so below." Thus, I accept that this is fully manifest, because the mouth of the Lord, the Divine Mother that I AM, has spoken it. Amen.

5 | INVOKING AN ALL-ENCOMPASSING SHIFT IN CONSCIOUSNESS

In the name I AM THAT I AM, Jesus Christ, I call to all ascended masters working on manifesting the Golden Age, especially Saint Germain and Master MORE, to radiate into the collective consciousness the need for an all-encompassing shift in consciousness. Help people see that we can build a new future by working with the ascended masters and letting go of the old way of looking at life, including…

[Make personal calls.]

Part 1

1. Saint Germain, radiate into the collective consciousness the awareness that an established elite will use a problem to control the people until the people start seeing through the illusion. Then, an aspiring elite will claim that they can save the people from the old elite.

> O Saint Germain, you do inspire,
> my vision raised forever higher,
> with you I form a figure-eight,
> your Golden Age I co-create.

> **O Saint Germain, what love you bring,**
> **it truly makes all matter sing,**
> **your violet flame does all restore,**
> **with you we are becoming more.**

2. Saint Germain, radiate into the collective consciousness the awareness that it is time for people to awaken to the reality that we have come into embodiment to rise above this dualistic game, to totally leave it behind, to expose it for what it is and to stand up and say: "The emperors of duality have nothing on!"

> O Saint Germain, what Freedom Flame,
> released when we recite your name,
> acceleration is your gift,
> our planet it will surely lift.

**O Saint Germain, what love you bring,
it truly makes all matter sing,
your violet flame does all restore,
with you we are becoming more.**

3. Saint Germain, radiate into the collective consciousness the awareness that even though people have created a false god in their own image and likeness, the fact that some people are stupid does not mean that God is stupid.

O Saint Germain, in love we claim,
our right to bring your violet flame,
from you Above, to us below,
it is an all-transforming flow.

**O Saint Germain, what love you bring,
it truly makes all matter sing,
your violet flame does all restore,
with you we are becoming more.**

4. Saint Germain, radiate into the collective consciousness the awareness that it is time for all people who love Saint Germain to awaken to our Divine plans and our knowledge that with God in us, it is possible to change the earth.

O Saint Germain, I love you so,
my aura filled with violet glow,
my chakras filled with violet fire,
I am your cosmic amplifier.

**O Saint Germain, what love you bring,
it truly makes all matter sing,
your violet flame does all restore,
with you we are becoming more.**

5. Saint Germain, radiate into the collective consciousness the awareness that all spiritual people need to fully and finally let go of the dream that there is only one true religion or spiritual philosophy.

O Saint Germain, I am now free,
your violet flame is therapy,
transform all hang-ups in my mind,
as inner peace I surely find.

**O Saint Germain, what love you bring,
it truly makes all matter sing,
your violet flame does all restore,
with you we are becoming more.**

6. Saint Germain, radiate into the collective consciousness the awareness that we need a universal awareness that is not focused on any particular individual, institution, doctrine or philosophy. It is about people everywhere waking up and realizing that we have a mission to raise consciousness.

O Saint Germain, my body pure,
your violet flame for all is cure,
consume the cause of all disease,
and therefore I am all at ease.

**O Saint Germain, what love you bring,
it truly makes all matter sing,
your violet flame does all restore,
with you we are becoming more.**

7. Saint Germain, radiate into the collective consciousness the awareness that we cannot let an outer guru or teaching become a hindrance to the expression of our Christhood.

O Saint Germain, I'm karma-free,
the past no longer burdens me,
a brand new opportunity,
I am in Christic unity.

**O Saint Germain, what love you bring,
it truly makes all matter sing,
your violet flame does all restore,
with you we are becoming more.**

8. Saint Germain, radiate into the collective consciousness the awareness that the ascended masters look at planet earth in a very different way than the way most people look at it.

O Saint Germain, we are now one,
I am for you a violet sun,
as we transform this planet earth,
your Golden Age is given birth.

**O Saint Germain, what love you bring,
it truly makes all matter sing,
your violet flame does all restore,
with you we are becoming more.**

9. Saint Germain, radiate into the collective consciousness the awareness that the masters do not look at life on earth as a backwards-and-forwards process. They see that behind everything that has happened on earth, there has been a progression in consciousness.

> O Saint Germain, the earth is free,
> from burden of duality,
> in oneness we bring what is best,
> your Golden Age is manifest.
>
> **O Saint Germain, what love you bring,**
> **it truly makes all matter sing,**
> **your violet flame does all restore,**
> **with you we are becoming more.**

Part 2

1. Saint Germain, radiate into the collective consciousness the awareness that even though there have been great calamities on this planet, behind all of them has been an upward movement.

> Master MORE, come to the fore,
> we will absorb your flame of MORE.
> Master MORE, our will so strong,
> our power centers cleared by song.

**Master MORE, your Sacred Heart,
from this we will no more depart,
we are forever in your flow,
of Diamond Will that you bestow.**

2. Saint Germain, radiate into the collective consciousness the awareness that everything that happens on this planet, good or bad, serves as a lesson that at some level in the etheric realm is anchored in the collective consciousness.

Master MORE, your wisdom flows,
as our attunement ever grows.
Master MORE, we have a tie,
that helps us see through Serpent's lie.

**Master MORE, your Sacred Heart,
from this we will no more depart,
we are forever in your flow,
of Diamond Will that you bestow.**

3. Saint Germain, radiate into the collective consciousness the awareness that even though there has been great turbulence in the physical, emotional, mental and identity realms, there has been a steady progression in awareness.

Master MORE, your love so pink,
there is no purer love, we think.
Master MORE, you set us free,
from all conditionality.

> **Master MORE, your Sacred Heart,**
> **from this we will no more depart,**
> **we are forever in your flow,**
> **of Diamond Will that you bestow.**

4. Saint Germain, radiate into the collective consciousness the awareness that this higher consciousness is anchored in the etheric realm and we can draw upon it.

> Master MORE, we will endure,
> your discipline that makes us pure.
> Master MORE, intentions true,
> as we are always one with you.

> **Master MORE, your Sacred Heart,**
> **from this we will no more depart,**
> **we are forever in your flow,**
> **of Diamond Will that you bestow.**

5. Saint Germain, radiate into the collective consciousness the awareness that we can tune in to our own identity bodies and to the collective etheric body, and we can then draw down the lessons that have been learned over eons of time on this planet.

> Master MORE, our vision raised,
> the will of God is always praised.
> Master MORE, creative will,
> raising all life higher still.

> **Master MORE, your Sacred Heart,**
> **from this we will no more depart,**
> **we are forever in your flow,**
> **of Diamond Will that you bestow.**

5 | Invoking an all-encompassing shift in consciousness

6. Saint Germain, radiate into the collective consciousness the awareness that we can tune in to the new age of Aquarius, we can tune in to the Golden Age.

> Master MORE, your peace is power,
> the demons of war it will devour.
> Master MORE, we serve all life,
> our flames consuming war and strife.
>
> **Master MORE, your Sacred Heart,**
> **from this we will no more depart,**
> **we are forever in your flow,**
> **of Diamond Will that you bestow.**

7. Saint Germain, radiate into the collective consciousness the awareness that you created the matrix for the Golden Age by looking back, learning and drawing upon the lessons of history.

> Master MORE, we are so free,
> eternal bond from you we see.
> Master MORE, we find rebirth,
> in flow of your eternal mirth.
>
> **Master MORE, your Sacred Heart,**
> **from this we will no more depart,**
> **we are forever in your flow,**
> **of Diamond Will that you bestow.**

8. Saint Germain, radiate into the collective consciousness the awareness that you want the Golden Age of Aquarius to build upon everything that has been learned on this planet.

Master MORE, you balance all,
the seven rays upon our call.
Master MORE, forever MORE,
we are the Spirit's open door.

Master MORE, your Sacred Heart,
from this we will no more depart,
we are forever in your flow,
of Diamond Will that you bestow.

9. Saint Germain, radiate into the collective consciousness the awareness that in the etheric realm of planet earth is a vast database storing all the positive lessons that have been learned on this planet.

Master MORE, your Presence here,
filling up the inner sphere.
Life is now a sacred flow,
God Power we on all bestow.

Master MORE, your Sacred Heart,
from this we will no more depart,
we are forever in your flow,
of Diamond Will that you bestow.

Part 3

1. Saint Germain, radiate into the collective consciousness the awareness that there is a potential that a critical mass of people can raise their consciousness, tune in to the matrix for a Golden Age in the etheric realm and bring it to their outer awareness.

> O Saint Germain, you do inspire,
> my vision raised forever higher,
> with you I form a figure-eight,
> your Golden Age I co-create.
>
> **O Saint Germain, what love you bring,**
> **it truly makes all matter sing,**
> **your violet flame does all restore,**
> **with you we are becoming more.**

2. Saint Germain, radiate into the collective consciousness the awareness that we can awaken other people so that a momentum builds and a shift occurs that will bring the Golden Age matrix from the etheric into the mental where even more people can grasp it and another shift occurs.

> O Saint Germain, what Freedom Flame,
> released when we recite your name,
> acceleration is your gift,
> our planet it will surely lift.

**O Saint Germain, what love you bring,
it truly makes all matter sing,
your violet flame does all restore,
with you we are becoming more.**

3. Saint Germain, radiate into the collective consciousness the awareness that when the Golden Age matrix is brought into the emotional, more and more people overcome the sense of doom and gloom, the sense of limitation, the sense of what is impossible.

O Saint Germain, in love we claim,
our right to bring your violet flame,
from you Above, to us below,
it is an all-transforming flow.

**O Saint Germain, what love you bring,
it truly makes all matter sing,
your violet flame does all restore,
with you we are becoming more.**

4. Saint Germain, radiate into the collective consciousness the awareness that will help people accept in the feeling world that there can be a Golden Age, inspiring more and more people to start acting on the highest potential instead of acting on the lowest potential.

O Saint Germain, I love you so,
my aura filled with violet glow,
my chakras filled with violet fire,
I am your cosmic amplifier.

5 | Invoking an all-encompassing shift in consciousness

> **O Saint Germain, what love you bring,**
> **it truly makes all matter sing,**
> **your violet flame does all restore,**
> **with you we are becoming more.**

5. Saint Germain, radiate into the collective consciousness the awareness that we need a critical mass of people who will begin to live their lives as if the Golden Age is already inevitable and is already beginning to manifest in the material realm.

> O Saint Germain, I am now free,
> your violet flame is therapy,
> transform all hang-ups in my mind,
> as inner peace I surely find.

> **O Saint Germain, what love you bring,**
> **it truly makes all matter sing,**
> **your violet flame does all restore,**
> **with you we are becoming more.**

6. Saint Germain, radiate into the collective consciousness the awareness that the masters need those in embodiment who will accept that the Golden Age is not a matter of *if,* and it is not a matter of *when*—it is a matter of NOW. *Now and here!*

> O Saint Germain, my body pure,
> your violet flame for all is cure,
> consume the cause of all disease,
> and therefore I am all at ease.

**O Saint Germain, what love you bring,
it truly makes all matter sing,
your violet flame does all restore,
with you we are becoming more.**

7. Saint Germain, radiate into the collective consciousness the awareness that we need to accept that only the Golden Age consciousness is ultimately real. Thus, reality will inevitably be projected onto the Mother Light and the Mother Light will outpicture that reality.

O Saint Germain, I'm karma-free,
the past no longer burdens me,
a brand new opportunity,
I am in Christic unity.

**O Saint Germain, what love you bring,
it truly makes all matter sing,
your violet flame does all restore,
with you we are becoming more.**

8. Saint Germain, radiate into the collective consciousness the awareness that there are limits to growth only if we accept that there are limits. If we do not accept that there are limits, there are no limits.

O Saint Germain, we are now one,
I am for you a violet sun,
as we transform this planet earth,
your Golden Age is given birth.

**O Saint Germain, what love you bring,
it truly makes all matter sing,
your violet flame does all restore,
with you we are becoming more.**

9. Saint Germain, radiate into the collective consciousness the awareness that the limitations that are here in the physical are the outpicturings of the limitations in the collective mind. When we get rid of the limitations in the mind, we will change the physical. This is an inevitable reality, and the most important thing that needs to happen is that people awaken to this reality and potential.

O Saint Germain, the earth is free,
from burden of duality,
in oneness we bring what is best,
your Golden Age is manifest.

**O Saint Germain, what love you bring,
it truly makes all matter sing,
your violet flame does all restore,
with you we are becoming more.**

Sealing

In the name of the Divine Mother, I call to all ascended masters for the sealing of myself and all people in my circle of influence in the creative flow of the Divine Mother, the River of Life. I call for the multiplication of my calls by all ascended masters so that we form the perfect figure-eight flow of "As Above, so below." Thus, I accept that this is fully manifest, because the mouth of the Lord, the Divine Mother that I AM, has spoken it. Amen.

6 | THE SECRET ABOUT THE RISE AND FALL OF GOLDEN AGES

My beloved, I want to make sure that you understand the point I was making last night when I talked about what human beings call the balance of nature. This is really not a state of balance but a state that is created by humankind's collective consciousness, engaging in duality.

When you engage in the dualistic consciousness, it is inevitable that you create a problem. Then, in order to deal with that problem – to somehow cope with it instead of solving the problem – you use the duality consciousness to create a further complication—something that is even more complex. One problem leads to another, and the problems build upon each other until you have this complexity that seems so overwhelming that most people give up and say: "How could we possibly change these conditions?"

What is the alternative? Well, the alternative is to reach beyond duality, to reach for the Christ consciousness and thereby allow the Holy Spirit to flow into every aspect of life on earth. As I said last night, the imbalance of the human consciousness has created certain animal species, that will tend to grow in population until they deplete their food supply and thereby either die out or are drastically reduced in numbers. Therefore, the human consciousness has created animals that prey upon these other animal populations to keep some state of balance. The human consciousness has even precipitated diseases that keep animal populations in check.

The Holy Spirit is the perfect regulatory mechanism

If humankind, or at least a critical mass among them, would reach for the Christ consciousness and allow the Holy Spirit to flow through them, then the Holy Spirit would become the perfect regulating mechanism that could regulate every aspect of the environment. This would include overcoming all earthquakes, volcanic eruptions, all disruptive weather patterns. Indeed, the Holy Spirit can create the perfect climate that allows the growth of the maximum amount of crops that will then feed the maximum amount of people.

The Holy Spirit would make it unnecessary to have diseases, parasites, famines or any of the so-called regulatory mechanisms that you see in nature. The Holy Spirit is the one perfect regulatory mechanism that has no side effects but only causes everything to grow and become more.

The same holds true for human society. If a critical mass of people are the conduits for the regulatory mechanism of the Holy Spirit, then there will be no competition for jobs.

The Holy Spirit will make sure that only the number of people apply for a specific education that are needed to fill the jobs that are out there. The Holy Spirit will also make sure that the economy is in a constant state of growth that will give jobs to every human being, or at least everyone who is willing to work.

You see, once again, the pattern that the economy and all aspects of human society have become unbalanced because of the dualistic state of consciousness. This happens especially because of those who are the most trapped in that state of consciousness, namely those who form a power elite. They have become so trapped in duality and separation that they believe that they – in their separate sense of identity – know better than God how things should be done on planet earth, or even in the entire universe. They have set themselves up as those who know best.

In their duality, they inevitably create imbalances that lead to problems. Then, as I said last night, we have the ongoing pattern of an established power elite creating a problem and an aspiring power elite coming up, claiming that they can solve the problem created by the old power elite even though they are still in the consciousness of duality. Therefore, they must inevitably create another imbalance that leads to another problem, and so on ad infinitum. What can be done to break this cycle, to break this spiral? Well, the only thing that can be done is, as I said last night, that those who are my own, those who are loyal to the cause of freedom, awaken to who they are, awaken to their potential and decide to hold the spiritual balance for the awakening of humankind. This has an Alpha aspect where you raise your consciousness and hold the balance for many. It has an Omega aspect where you speak the truth that you know and demand change in society.

How can the power elite be allowed to reincarnate?

One of the questions that many of you have is why certain lifestreams – who are completely stuck in duality – are allowed to incarnate again and again on earth. Why are these same lifestreams allowed to ascend to leadership positions time and time again? Lifetime after lifetime they repeat the same old patterns of creating problems and they seem to be the only ones who cannot see it. They cannot see how disastrous it is to keep doing the same thing over and over again and expecting that one day paradise is going to descend on Iraq or on the Third Reich, or whatever ideal society they claim can be manifest on this planet, based on their dualistic ideologies.

Why do we allow such lifestreams to continue to reincarnate and to continue to become leaders of the people? Well, the reality is that we of the ascended masters are not allowing these lifestreams to reincarnate—*you are!* Humankind is allowing this and here is precisely why. As Maitreya explains in great detail in his book, there are two ways you can learn. The highest way of learning is that you learn from the ascended masters because you recognize that there is something beyond your own consciousness – something beyond duality, something beyond the ego – and thus you are willing to listen to a true teacher who has no selfish motives whatsoever.

If you are not willing (anymore) to listen to that true teacher, then what happens? Well, you lose contact with the true teacher, and then the false teachers become your teacher. You see, if the people had been willing to listen to the ascended masters, we could long ago have raised up a critical mass of people, who could then take leadership positions and lead from the level of the Christ mind—rather than from the mind of anti-christ. They would have replaced the power elite

6 | The secret about the rise and fall of Golden Ages

people who are trapped in duality. However, for this to happen, it would require that the people had reached a certain level of consciousness where they were actually able to recognize the difference between those who lead from the consciousness of Christ and those who lead from the consciousness of anti-christ. The people of the world have not yet reached that level, even though they are very close to breaking through to a realization that there is a higher reality and that not everything is a matter of argument and counter-argument.

When the people are not willing to reach for something beyond the consciousness of duality, then the fallen beings – those who are trapped in duality – become the teachers of the people by default. We allow this to happen because we have respect for free will. Also because we see that there is still a potential that the people can be awakened. After all, we see very clearly that these lifestreams who are stuck in duality are not likely to change their ways. When they ascend to positions of power, they will inevitably misuse that power. We see that when that abuse of power becomes severe enough, there is the potential that the people will finally wake up.

Obviously this is an awakening that happens the hard way, and we would prefer to see it the higher way. Again, we bow to the free will of the people who are in embodiment and therefore are the ones who determine what is allowed to occur and continue to occur on earth. The people are the ones who must wake up and say: "Enough is enough!" As Jesus has explained and as Maitreya explains, there is a top 10 percent and a bottom 10 percent. What really determines the fate of the planet is whether the 80 percent of the general population will blindly follow the blind leaders in the bottom 10 percent or whether they will wake up and open their eyes to follow the leaders in the top 10 percent.

Understanding the dynamics of a Golden Age

I desire to give you an understanding of the Golden Age, an understanding that has not been available on this planet since the times of Atlantis, for no one has been able to grasp it. You see, when we talk about past Golden Ages, we are indeed talking about a society that had a higher state of consciousness than the one you see on the planet today. Yet, I am not talking about a society in which all people had reached a certain state of Christhood.

Certainly, there have been Golden Ages in the past where everyone had a higher state of consciousness than the average person on earth today. This still did not mean that the entire population had reached a high level of Christhood. In a Golden Age the difference is that there is a critical mass of people among the top 10 percent who have reached that level of Christhood where they can consciously and knowingly lead by reaching up for a higher truth, coming from their higher selves and the ascended masters. Thereby, we have enough people in embodiment who are willing to be here below all that they are Above, being willing to be the mouthpieces and the instruments for the ascended masters.

Let me give you an essential truth that most do not understand. When you are in embodiment, even if you have reached a very high level of consciousness, you are still seeing everything through the physical body and the mind. You are inside the earth, the energy system of earth, looking at the earth from the inside. This cannot give you the same perspective that you have when you are an ascended being, residing in a higher realm, looking at the big picture—not only of the earth but of the entire universe.

Do you see what I am saying here? There is nothing wrong with being in embodiment. It is indeed necessary to have people in embodiment that have reached a high level of consciousness. These people will not fulfill their maximum potential unless they come into oneness with their own higher beings. Then, we of the ascended masters can work with them and impart to them the higher vision that we see. You in embodiment can receive this vision from us, but you cannot come up with it on your own. It simply is impossible to see the greater vision while you are inside the energy system of earth.

Do you see the mechanism here? This is indeed something that is designed specifically by the Creator. If you were completely able to see everything while you are in embodiment, would there really be the same drive to ascend? Again, as Maitreya explains in his book in greater detail, the Creator has designed the world of form in order to ensure maximum growth. It is simply a law that those who are in embodiment cannot see beyond a certain level—unless they connect to their higher beings and those who have already ascended.

Therefore, we have the figure-eight flow between heaven and earth, between the spiritual realm and the material world, which is the only way that the material world can be raised up to become the kingdom of God. You see, again, the River of Life is the only thing that can maintain maximum progress, maximum growth. This River of Life is the Holy Spirit, flowing into every aspect of life here below, causing it to transcend the patterns that have caused it to be frozen in a certain state.

Understanding ongoing growth

The law of God is continual, ongoing growth. This is expressed in the physical equivalent, namely the second law of thermodynamics, which basically says that if a system is not growing, it will collapse, it will self-destruct. The deeper understanding is that a system cannot grow unless it is connected to a higher reality outside itself and thus receives input from that higher reality. This causes it to transcend itself and come closer to manifesting – in the material universe – the thoughtforms that exist in a higher reality, namely the etheric realm, as I explained yesterday.

The need in human society is for the spreading of a new awareness that it is indeed possible, desirable and necessary that there are some among the leaders of humankind who are willing to rise up and say: "I can of my own self do nothing, it is the Father (meaning the I AM Presence) within me who is doing the work." What you see in the world today are leaders who are not willing to say this, for they truly believe that they are smart enough and powerful enough to do all things on their own. They believe they have the solution to every problem. They believe they can bring forth paradise on earth, even if it requires them to exterminate millions of people that seem to stand in the way of that paradise.

A critical mass of people need to come to the point where they are willing to stand up and say: "There is an alternative to the kind of leaders we have had in recorded history—those who are ego-centered, those who are stuck in duality. There is something beyond the duality consciousness, and we demand leadership that is beyond duality and we are willing to play our roles in taking up that leadership."

As those in the top 10 percent dare to come out and express that aspect, that level of Christhood, there are those among the people who will be awakened and say: "Oh but this is true, this is self-evident. Suddenly we see that this is self-evident whereas we could not see it yesterday, but now we see it and we want those kind of leaders in all aspects of society. For there *is* a higher truth. Everything is not relative and we cannot allow the duality consciousness to manipulate everything and turn it into a relativistic truth where those who are somehow in a privileged position can define a 'truth' that allows them to maintain or expand their power and privilege, at the cost of the general population living as virtual slaves of the elite."

The secret about the fall of Golden Ages

What you saw in past Golden Ages, and the very key to the establishment of a Golden Age, was that you had those people who were willing to reach beyond the material world, to reach beyond duality and demonstrate an entirely new form of leadership. Now, I want to give you another secret about Golden Ages that likewise has not been understood. Why have past Golden Ages come to a halt? Why have they started a decline that eventually lead, in many cases, to a cataclysmic collapse?

It was because, as I said yesterday, there are no free lunches. It is not possible for anything in the material realm to attain a state of permanency. This means that those among the top 10 percent who are capable of a certain degree of Christ leadership cannot allow themselves to begin to believe that they have reached some ultimate state and now they no longer need to look for the beam in their own eye, or they no longer need to look for a higher understanding—they no longer need to transcend themselves.

What happened in past Golden Ages was that there were people among the top 10 percent who had reached a certain degree of Christhood – but not the full Christhood – who somehow started believing that they belonged to an elite who was above and beyond the people. You see, my beloved, the trickiness? I am talking about the top 10 percent. These are people who have wisdom, vision and insight, even power beyond the average population. These are people who need to lead in order to bring society forward. The question is: Can they overcome all self-centeredness – all selfishness, all focus upon themselves – and attain a state that has been called servant leadership, which is really completely selfless leadership? In this state they realize that they are not separated from the people, they are not above the people—they are one with the people. As Christ said: "Inasmuch as you have done it unto the least of these my brethren, you have done it unto me." This is, my beloved, a very delicate challenge.

In past ages we have seen those who attained some degree of Christhood that allowed them to take up leadership positions, in some cases even religious leadership positions, and become prophets or seers that brought a higher vision for that society. After some time, the people started idolizing them and they started buying into the idolatry. They started – in very subtle ways – believing that they were special, that they were an elite above and beyond the people. Many of them were aware that there were people in a lower state of consciousness who were trying to form a power elite. They thought they were better than that power elite because, after all, they were open to a spiritual outlook on life.

Anything can be corrupted by the subtlety of the serpentine consciousness. It is possible for a person who has attained some degree of Christhood to stagnate, perhaps by becoming focused on doing an outer activity. The certainty creeps in that in order to serve my society, I do not have time to look at my own psychology and transcend myself—I need to focus on the outer service. This causes a lifestream to believe that it has reached some kind of plateau where it is now beyond reproach, beyond self-transcendence. Therefore, in very subtle ways, it shifts to the mechanism where it wants to defend its position, rather than continuing the process of life, of transcending its position to a higher and higher position. Or even being willing

6 | The secret about the rise and fall of Golden Ages

to step back from a certain position in society in order to allow someone else to learn by having that position.

As long as you are in the material universe, it is always possible to develop an attachment to something. Once you have developed an attachment, you can – in very subtle ways – begin to stagnate and then go backwards. This is precisely what happened in past Golden Ages where those who were not the power elite, but the spiritual elite, still developed, or never overcame, certain attachments that caused them to start seeing themselves as an elite that were better, more special, more privileged, more wise than the people.

As soon as this happens, what is the underlying mechanism? Well, the underlying mechanism is that you begin to deny the most fundamental reality of the world of form. This is expressed in a quote in the Gospel of John: "Without him was not anything made that was made." It means that the Christ and the Christ potential is in every human being, no matter how lowly they might seem in their present state of consciousness.

The higher you rise in Christhood – which is true leadership – the more you see the Christ in everyone and the more you work to free that Christ, to help people recognize their Christhood. It becomes a goal for you to raise up other people instead of raising yourself up in comparison to them. You want to raise up all life, rather than raising up an elite.

The eternal challenge of leadership

There can only be elitism when there is someone who is not part of the elite. This causes the elite to actually want to hold back those who are not in the elite. Then, again, you have a dualistic system of the haves and the have-nots where the population is divided into groups and there is a belief that these groups are fixed and it is impossible to ascend from the lowest to the highest.

Even the teaching that there is the top 10 percent, the bottom 10 percent and the people in the middle is in a sense a challenge that we hurl at you. On the one hand, we need you to recognize that you are part of the top 10 percent because you have a potential to manifest Christhood and bring society forward. At the same time, by giving you this realization, we do present you with a challenge: Can you keep your humility? Can you avoid falling into the trap of beginning to think that you are special?

Or will you recognize the fundamental truth that Christ expressed when he said: "I can of my own self do nothing, it is the Father within me." In other words, it is not this outer self that is higher than anyone else on earth. It is only through my connection to a higher reality (that is beyond this world) that I have any ability to do anything of value.

You now understand – as I dare say no one in the physical octave has understood for at least 10,000 years – the fundamental dynamic of what creates a Golden Age and what causes it to collapse—if it will not continue to transcend. A Golden Age is not a state of perfection that, once reached, will be maintained for a thousand years, as many Christians believe that when Christ comes again, he will establish a permanent kingdom that will last for a thousand years, or forever or whatever they believe. The Golden Age can only continue if society continues to transcend itself, which means that both the top 10 percent and a critical mass of the middle 80 must transcend themselves. If the bottom 10 percent will not transcend, well they will lose their opportunity to embody on this planet and will go elsewhere.

My beloved, with this understanding I leave you to ponder this until I shall speak to you again and give you further teachings, not only about the Golden Age in general but also about the potential to start a breakthrough in the Golden Age consciousness here in this state of California. Thus, I thank you for your attention, and I seal you in the love of my heart, in the Freedom Flame that I AM.

7 | INVOKING THE DYNAMICS OF THE GOLDEN AGE

In the name I AM THAT I AM, Jesus Christ, I call to all ascended masters working on manifesting the Golden Age, especially Archangel Jophiel, Elohim Apollo, Master Lanto, Saint Germain and Gautama Buddha to radiate into the collective consciousness an understanding of the dynamics of the Golden Age. Help people see that we can build a new future by working with the ascended masters and letting go of the old way of looking at life, including…

[Make personal calls.]

Part 1

1. Saint Germain, radiate into the collective consciousness the awareness that when we engage in the dualistic consciousness, it is inevitable that we create a problem. Then, in order to deal with that problem, we use the duality consciousness to create something that is even more complex.

> Jophiel Archangel, in wisdom's great light,
> all serpentine lies exposed to our sight.
> So subtle the lies that creep through the mind,
> yet you are the greatest teacher we find.
>
> **Jophiel Archangel, exposing all lies,**
> **Jophiel Archangel, cutting all ties.**
> **Jophiel Archangel, clearing the skies,**
> **Jophiel Archangel, the mind truly flies.**

2. Saint Germain, radiate into the collective consciousness the awareness that one problem leads to another, and the problems build upon each other until we have a complexity that seems so overwhelming that most people give up and think conditions could never be changed.

> Jophiel Archangel, your wisdom we hail,
> your sword cutting through duality's veil.
> As you show the way, we know what is real,
> from serpentine doubt, we instantly heal.

7 | Invoking the dynamics of the Golden Age

**Jophiel Archangel, exposing all lies,
Jophiel Archangel, cutting all ties.
Jophiel Archangel, clearing the skies,
Jophiel Archangel, the mind truly flies.**

3. Saint Germain, radiate into the collective consciousness the awareness that the alternative is to reach beyond duality, to reach for the Christ consciousness and thereby allow the Holy Spirit to flow into every aspect of life on earth.

Jophiel Archangel, your reality,
the best antidote to duality.
No lie can remain in your Presence so clear,
with you on our side, no serpent we fear.

**Jophiel Archangel, exposing all lies,
Jophiel Archangel, cutting all ties.
Jophiel Archangel, clearing the skies,
Jophiel Archangel, the mind truly flies.**

4. Saint Germain, radiate into the collective consciousness the awareness that the imbalance of the human consciousness has created animal species whose populations must be regulated by carnivores or diseases.

Jophiel Archangel, God's mind in in me,
and through your clear light, its wisdom we see.
Divisions all vanish, as we see the One,
and truly, the wholeness of mind we have won.

**Jophiel Archangel, exposing all lies,
Jophiel Archangel, cutting all ties.
Jophiel Archangel, clearing the skies,
Jophiel Archangel, the mind truly flies.**

5. Saint Germain, radiate into the collective consciousness the awareness that if a critical mass of people would reach for the Christ consciousness, then the Holy Spirit would become the perfect regulating mechanism that could regulate every aspect of the environment.

Jophiel Archangel, now show us the way,
that leads us beyond duality's fray,
we long to discern the truth and the lie,
so we the serpentine knots can untie.

**Jophiel Archangel, exposing all lies,
Jophiel Archangel, cutting all ties.
Jophiel Archangel, clearing the skies,
Jophiel Archangel, the mind truly flies.**

6. Saint Germain, radiate into the collective consciousness the awareness that this would include overcoming earthquakes, volcanic eruptions and disruptive weather patterns. The Holy Spirit can create the perfect climate that allows the growth of the maximum amount of crops that will then feed the maximum amount of people.

Jophiel Archangel, your Presence is here,
and therefore our minds are perfectly clear,
in wisdom's great fount we do take a bath,
and now we withstand the devil's own wrath.

**Jophiel Archangel, exposing all lies,
Jophiel Archangel, cutting all ties.
Jophiel Archangel, clearing the skies,
Jophiel Archangel, the mind truly flies.**

7. Saint Germain, radiate into the collective consciousness the awareness that the Holy Spirit would make it unnecessary to have diseases, parasites, famines or any of the so-called regulatory mechanisms in nature.

Jophiel Archangel, it is your great task,
to raise all mankind, if only we ask,
so now on behalf of those who are blind,
we ask for your help in wisdom to find.

**Jophiel Archangel, exposing all lies,
Jophiel Archangel, cutting all ties.
Jophiel Archangel, clearing the skies,
Jophiel Archangel, the mind truly flies.**

8. Saint Germain, radiate into the collective consciousness the awareness that with the Holy Spirit, there will be no competition for jobs. Only the number of people will apply for a specific education that are needed to fill the jobs that exist.

Jophiel Archangel, your Presence we hail,
your Light cutting through the serpentine veil,
the serpents can no longer people deceive,
for all now your Flame of Wisdom receive.

**Jophiel Archangel, exposing all lies,
Jophiel Archangel, cutting all ties.
Jophiel Archangel, clearing the skies,
Jophiel Archangel, the mind truly flies.**

9. Saint Germain, radiate into the collective consciousness the awareness that the Holy Spirit will make sure that the economy is in a constant state of growth that will give jobs to every person who is willing to work.

Jophiel Archangel, where else can we go,
when we long the highest wisdom to know?
You share with us gladly all that you are,
and now our vision goes ever so far.

**Jophiel Archangel, exposing all lies,
Jophiel Archangel, cutting all ties.
Jophiel Archangel, clearing the skies,
Jophiel Archangel, the mind truly flies.**

Part 2

1. Saint Germain, radiate into the collective consciousness the awareness that the economy and all aspects of human society have become unbalanced because of the dualistic state of consciousness.

Beloved Apollo, with your second ray,
you open our eyes to see a new day,
We see through duality's lies and deceit,
transcending the mindset producing defeat.

7 | Invoking the dynamics of the Golden Age

> Beloved Apollo, thou Elohim Gold,
> your radiant light our eyes now behold,
> as pages of wisdom you gently unfold,
> our planet is free from all that is old.

2. Saint Germain, radiate into the collective consciousness the awareness that members of the power elite have become so trapped in duality and separation that they believe they know better than God how things should be done on earth.

> Beloved Apollo, in your flame we know,
> that your living wisdom is always a flow,
> in your light we see our own highest will,
> immersed in the stream that never stands still.

> Beloved Apollo, thou Elohim Gold,
> your radiant light our eyes now behold,
> as pages of wisdom you gently unfold,
> our planet is free from all that is old.

3. Saint Germain, radiate into the collective consciousness the awareness that in their duality, these people inevitably create imbalances that lead to problems.

> Beloved Apollo, your light makes it clear,
> why we have taken embodiment here,
> exposing all lies causing the fall,
> you help us reclaim the oneness of all.

> Beloved Apollo, thou Elohim Gold,
> your radiant light our eyes now behold,
> as pages of wisdom you gently unfold,
> our planet is free from all that is old.

4. Saint Germain, radiate into the collective consciousness the awareness that we have an ongoing pattern of an established power elite creating a problem and an aspiring power elite claiming that they can solve the problem.

> Beloved Apollo, exposing all lies,
> we hereby surrender all ego-based ties,
> we know our perception is truly the key,
> to transcending the serpentine duality.

> **Beloved Apollo, thou Elohim Gold,**
> **your radiant light our eyes now behold,**
> **as pages of wisdom you gently unfold,**
> **our planet is free from all that is old.**

5. Saint Germain, radiate into the collective consciousness the awareness that because members of the aspiring elite are still in the consciousness of duality, they inevitably create another imbalance that leads to another problem, and so on indefinitely.

> Beloved Apollo, we heed now your call,
> drawing us into Wisdom's Great Hall,
> working to raise our own cosmic sphere,
> together we form the tip of the spear.

> **Beloved Apollo, thou Elohim Gold,**
> **your radiant light our eyes now behold,**
> **as pages of wisdom you gently unfold,**
> **our planet is free from all that is old.**

6. Saint Germain, radiate into the collective consciousness the awareness that those who are loyal to the cause of freedom need to awaken to who we are and decide to hold the spiritual balance for the awakening of humankind.

Beloved Apollo, your wisdom so clear,
in oneness with you, no serpent we fear,
the beam in our eye we willingly see,
we're free from the serpent's own duality.

**Beloved Apollo, thou Elohim Gold,
your radiant light our eyes now behold,
as pages of wisdom you gently unfold,
our planet is free from all that is old.**

7. Saint Germain, radiate into the collective consciousness the awareness that holding the balance has an Alpha aspect where we raise our consciousness. It has an Omega aspect where we speak the truth that we know and demand change in society.

Beloved Apollo, you help us to see
through your knowing eyes we truly are free,
we willingly stand in your piercing gaze,
empowered, we exit duality's maze.

**Beloved Apollo, thou Elohim Gold,
your radiant light our eyes now behold,
as pages of wisdom you gently unfold,
our planet is free from all that is old.**

8. Saint Germain, radiate into the collective consciousness the awareness that the ascended masters are not allowing the members of the power elite to reincarnate, humankind is allowing this because people are not willing to listen to the teacher and therefore must learn the hard way.

> Beloved Apollo, our vision we raise,
> we see that the earth is in a new phase,
> for nothing can stop the knowledge you bring,
> exposing that there's no separate thing.
>
> **Beloved Apollo, thou Elohim Gold,**
> **your radiant light our eyes now behold,**
> **as pages of wisdom you gently unfold,**
> **our planet is free from all that is old.**

9. Saint Germain, radiate into the collective consciousness the awareness that if we are not willing to listen to the true teacher, then we lose contact with the teacher, and then the false teachers become our teacher.

> Beloved Apollo, in wisdom's great mirth,
> we all are together uplifting the earth,
> as you now the true Flame of Wisdom reveal,
> all of earth's people can see what is real.
>
> **Beloved Apollo, thou Elohim Gold,**
> **your radiant light our eyes now behold,**
> **as pages of wisdom you gently unfold,**
> **our planet is free from all that is old.**

Part 3

1. Saint Germain, radiate into the collective consciousness the awareness that if people are willing to listen to the ascended masters, we can raise people who can take leadership positions and lead from the level of the Christ mind and replace the power elite people who are trapped in duality.

> Master Lanto, golden wise,
> expose in us the ego's lies.
> Master Lanto, will to be,
> we will to win our mastery.

Master Lanto, Wisdom's Fount,
with blessings we can hardly count,
you are for earth a shining light,
your Golden Wisdom oh so bright.

2. Saint Germain, radiate into the collective consciousness the awareness that people need to be able to recognize the difference between those who lead from the consciousness of Christ and those who lead from the consciousness of anti-christ.

> Master Lanto, balance all,
> for wisdom's balance we do call.
> Master Lanto, help us see,
> that balance is the Golden Key.

Master Lanto, Wisdom's Fount,
with blessings we can hardly count,
you are for earth a shining light,
your Golden Wisdom oh so bright.

3. Saint Germain, radiate into the collective consciousness the awareness that will help people see that there is a higher reality and that not everything is a matter of argument and counter-argument.

> Master Lanto, from Above,
> we call forth discerning love.
> Master Lanto, love's not blind,
> through love, God vision we do find.
>
> **Master Lanto, Wisdom's Fount,**
> **with blessings we can hardly count,**
> **you are for earth a shining light,**
> **your Golden Wisdom oh so bright.**

4. Saint Germain, radiate into the collective consciousness the awareness that when the people are not willing to reach for something beyond the consciousness of duality, then the fallen beings, who are trapped in duality, become the teachers of the people by default.

> Master Lanto, we are sure
> as Christic lamb intentions pure.
> Master Lanto, we'll transcend,
> acceleration is our truest friend.
>
> **Master Lanto, Wisdom's Fount,**
> **with blessings we can hardly count,**
> **you are for earth a shining light,**
> **your Golden Wisdom oh so bright.**

5. Saint Germain, radiate into the collective consciousness the awareness that when lifestreams who are stuck in duality ascend to positions of power, they will inevitably misuse that power. When that abuse of power becomes severe enough, people will wake up.

> Master Lanto, we are whole,
> no more division in the soul.
> Master Lanto, healing flame,
> all balance in your sacred name.
>
> **Master Lanto, Wisdom's Fount,**
> **with blessings we can hardly count,**
> **you are for earth a shining light,**
> **your Golden Wisdom oh so bright.**

6. Saint Germain, radiate into the collective consciousness the awareness that we who are in embodiment are the ones who determine what is allowed to occur and continue to occur on earth. We must wake up and say: "Enough is enough!"

> Master Lanto, serve all life,
> as we transcend all inner strife.
> Master Lanto, peace you give,
> to all who want to truly live.
>
> **Master Lanto, Wisdom's Fount,**
> **with blessings we can hardly count,**
> **you are for earth a shining light,**
> **your Golden Wisdom oh so bright.**

7. Saint Germain, radiate into the collective consciousness the awareness that there is a top 10 percent and a bottom 10 percent, but what really determines the fate of the planet is whether the 80 percent of the general population will follow the blind leaders in the bottom 10 percent or whether they will wake up and follow the leaders in the top 10 percent.

Master Lanto, free to be,
in balanced creativity.
Master Lanto, we employ,
your balance as the key to joy.

Master Lanto, Wisdom's Fount,
with blessings we can hardly count,
you are for earth a shining light,
your Golden Wisdom oh so bright.

8. Saint Germain, radiate into the collective consciousness the awareness that in past Golden Ages there was a higher state of consciousness than we see today, but it was not a society in which all people had reached Christhood.

Master Lanto, balance all,
the seven rays upon our call.
Master Lanto, we take flight,
the threefold flame a blazing light.

Master Lanto, Wisdom's Fount,
with blessings we can hardly count,
you are for earth a shining light,
your Golden Wisdom oh so bright.

9. Saint Germain, radiate into the collective consciousness the awareness that in a Golden Age there is a critical mass of people among the top 10 percent who have reached the level of Christhood where they can consciously and knowingly lead by reaching up for a higher truth, coming from their higher selves and the ascended masters.

Lanto dear, your Presence here,
filling up the inner sphere.
Life is now a sacred flow,
God Wisdom we on all bestow.

**Master Lanto, Wisdom's Fount,
with blessings we can hardly count,
you are for earth a shining light,
your Golden Wisdom oh so bright.**

Part 4

1. Saint Germain, radiate into the collective consciousness the awareness that when we are in embodiment, we are still seeing everything through the physical body and the mind. We are inside the energy system of earth, looking at the earth from the inside.

O Saint Germain, you do inspire,
my vision raised forever higher,
with you I form a figure-eight,
your Golden Age I co-create.

**O Saint Germain, what love you bring,
it truly makes all matter sing,
your violet flame does all restore,
with you we are becoming more.**

2. Saint Germain, radiate into the collective consciousness the awareness that this cannot give us the same perspective as ascended beings, looking at the big picture—not only of the earth but of the entire universe.

O Saint Germain, what Freedom Flame,
released when we recite your name,
acceleration is your gift,
our planet it will surely lift.

**O Saint Germain, what love you bring,
it truly makes all matter sing,
your violet flame does all restore,
with you we are becoming more.**

3. Saint Germain, radiate into the collective consciousness the awareness that when we are in embodiment, we can receive this vision from the ascended masters, but we cannot come up with it on our own.

O Saint Germain, in love we claim,
our right to bring your violet flame,
from you Above, to us below,
it is an all-transforming flow.

**O Saint Germain, what love you bring,
it truly makes all matter sing,
your violet flame does all restore,
with you we are becoming more.**

4. Saint Germain, radiate into the collective consciousness the awareness that the law of God is continual, ongoing growth. This is expressed in the physical equivalent, the second law of thermodynamics, which says that if a system is not growing, it will self-destruct.

O Saint Germain, I love you so,
my aura filled with violet glow,
my chakras filled with violet fire,
I am your cosmic amplifier.

**O Saint Germain, what love you bring,
it truly makes all matter sing,
your violet flame does all restore,
with you we are becoming more.**

5. Saint Germain, radiate into the collective consciousness the awareness that a system cannot grow unless it is connected to a higher reality outside itself and thus receives input from that higher reality. This causes it to transcend itself and come closer to manifesting the thoughtforms that exist in the etheric realm.

O Saint Germain, I am now free,
your violet flame is therapy,
transform all hang-ups in my mind,
as inner peace I surely find.

**O Saint Germain, what love you bring,
it truly makes all matter sing,
your violet flame does all restore,
with you we are becoming more.**

6. Saint Germain, radiate into the collective consciousness the awareness that some among the leaders of humankind must be willing to rise up and say: "I can of my own self do nothing, it is the I AM Presence within me who is doing the work."

O Saint Germain, my body pure,
your violet flame for all is cure,
consume the cause of all disease,
and therefore I am all at ease.

**O Saint Germain, what love you bring,
it truly makes all matter sing,
your violet flame does all restore,
with you we are becoming more.**

7. Saint Germain, radiate into the collective consciousness the awareness that today many leaders are not willing to say this, for they believe that they are smart and powerful enough to do all things on their own.

O Saint Germain, I'm karma-free,
the past no longer burdens me,
a brand new opportunity,
I am in Christic unity.

**O Saint Germain, what love you bring,
it truly makes all matter sing,
your violet flame does all restore,
with you we are becoming more.**

8. Saint Germain, radiate into the collective consciousness the awareness that many leaders believe they have the solution to every problem. They believe they can bring forth paradise on earth, even if it requires them to exterminate millions of people that seem to stand in the way of that goal.

O Saint Germain, we are now one,
I am for you a violet sun,
as we transform this planet earth,
your Golden Age is given birth.

**O Saint Germain, what love you bring,
it truly makes all matter sing,
your violet flame does all restore,
with you we are becoming more.**

9. Saint Germain, radiate into the collective consciousness the awareness that a critical mass of people need to say: "There is an alternative to the kind of leaders we have had in recorded history—those who are ego-centered, those who are stuck in duality. There is something beyond the duality consciousness, and we demand leadership that is beyond duality and we are willing to play our roles in taking up that leadership."

O Saint Germain, the earth is free,
from burden of duality,
in oneness we bring what is best,
your Golden Age is manifest.

**O Saint Germain, what love you bring,
it truly makes all matter sing,
your violet flame does all restore,
with you we are becoming more.**

Part 5

1. Saint Germain, radiate into the collective consciousness the awareness that as those in the top 10 percent dare to come out and express Christhood, many will be awakened and say: "Oh but this is true, this is self-evident. Suddenly, we see that we want those kind of leaders in all aspects of society."

Gautama, show my mental state
that does give rise to love and hate,
your exposé I do endure,
so my perception will be pure.

**Gautama, Flame of Cosmic Peace,
unruly thoughts do hereby cease,
we radiate from you and me
the peace to still Samsara's Sea.**

2. Saint Germain, radiate into the collective consciousness the awareness that there is a higher truth. Everything is not relative and we cannot allow the duality consciousness to manipulate everything and turn it into a relativistic truth where those who are in a privileged position can define a "truth" that allows them to maintain or expand their power and privilege, at the cost of the general population living as virtual slaves of the elite.

7 | *Invoking the dynamics of the Golden Age*

Gautama, in your Flame of Peace,
the struggling self I now release,
the Buddha Nature I now see,
it is the core of you and me.

**Gautama, Flame of Cosmic Peace,
unruly thoughts do hereby cease,
we radiate from you and me
the peace to still Samsara's Sea.**

3. Saint Germain, radiate into the collective consciousness the awareness that the key to the establishment of a Golden Age is people who are willing to reach beyond the material world, to reach beyond duality and demonstrate an entirely new form of leadership.

Gautama, I am one with thee,
Mara's demons do now flee,
your Presence like a soothing balm,
my mind and senses ever calm.

**Gautama, Flame of Cosmic Peace,
unruly thoughts do hereby cease,
we radiate from you and me
the peace to still Samsara's Sea.**

4. Saint Germain, radiate into the collective consciousness the awareness that in past Golden Ages those who were not the power elite, but the spiritual elite, still developed, or never overcame, certain attachments that caused them to start seeing themselves as an elite that were better than the people.

> Gautama, I now take the vow,
> to live in the eternal now,
> with you I do transcend all time,
> to live in present so sublime.
>
> **Gautama, Flame of Cosmic Peace,**
> **unruly thoughts do hereby cease,**
> **we radiate from you and me**
> **the peace to still Samsara's Sea.**

5. Saint Germain, radiate into the collective consciousness the awareness that when you think you belong to an elite, you deny the most fundamental reality of the world of form, namely that the Christ and the Christ potential is in every human being, no matter how lowly they might seem in their present state of consciousness.

> Gautama, I have no desire,
> to nothing earthly I aspire,
> in non-attachment I now rest,
> passing Mara's subtle test.
>
> **Gautama, Flame of Cosmic Peace,**
> **unruly thoughts do hereby cease,**
> **we radiate from you and me**
> **the peace to still Samsara's Sea.**

6. Saint Germain, radiate into the collective consciousness the awareness that the higher we rise in Christhood, the more we see the Christ in everyone and the more we work to free that Christ, to help people recognize their Christhood. It becomes a goal to raise up all life, rather than raising up an elite.

7 | Invoking the dynamics of the Golden Age

> Gautama, I melt into you,
> my mind is one, no longer two,
> immersed in your resplendent glow,
> Nirvana is all that I know.
>
> **Gautama, Flame of Cosmic Peace,**
> **unruly thoughts do hereby cease,**
> **we radiate from you and me**
> **the peace to still Samsara's Sea.**

7. Saint Germain, radiate into the collective consciousness the awareness that there can only be elitism when there is someone who is not part of the elite. Members of the elite want to hold back those who are not in the elite, creating a dualistic system of the haves and the have-nots where the population is divided into groups and it is believed that it is impossible to ascend from the lowest to the highest.

> Gautama, in your timeless space,
> I am immersed in Cosmic Grace,
> I know the God beyond all form,
> to world I will no more conform.
>
> **Gautama, Flame of Cosmic Peace,**
> **unruly thoughts do hereby cease,**
> **we radiate from you and me**
> **the peace to still Samsara's Sea.**

8. Saint Germain, radiate into the collective consciousness the awareness that a Golden Age is not a state of perfection that, once reached, will be maintained for a thousand years.

Gautama, I am now awake,
I clearly see what is at stake,
and thus I claim my sacred right
to be on earth the Buddhic Light.

**Gautama, Flame of Cosmic Peace,
unruly thoughts do hereby cease,
we radiate from you and me
the peace to still Samsara's Sea.**

9. Saint Germain, radiate into the collective consciousness the awareness that a Golden Age can only continue if society continues to transcend itself, which means that both the top 10 percent and a critical mass of the middle 80 must transcend themselves.

Gautama, with your thunderbolt,
we give the earth a mighty jolt,
I know that some will understand,
and join the Buddha's timeless band.

**Gautama, Flame of Cosmic Peace,
unruly thoughts do hereby cease,
we radiate from you and me
the peace to still Samsara's Sea.**

Sealing

In the name of the Divine Mother, I call to all ascended masters for the sealing of myself and all people in my circle of influence in the creative flow of the Divine Mother, the River of Life. I call for the multiplication of my calls by all ascended masters so that we form the perfect figure-eight flow of "As Above, so below." Thus, I accept that this is fully manifest, because the mouth of the Lord, the Divine Mother that I AM, has spoken it. Amen.

8 | THE GRAND ILLUSION OF THE SCARCITY OF RESOURCES

My beloved, I Saint Germain come to give you the next installment of my discourses for this conference. What then is the next thing that needs to be reconsidered? As I said yesterday, in order to bring the Golden Age, you need to rethink everything that has been part of life in the old age, which we might call the dark age of Pisces. We are about to shine a light on this planet so that there will be no shadows left. There will be no one and nothing that can hide, there will be no illusion and no lie that could possibly hide from the light – the Christ Light of Aquarius – that will shine upon this planet through those who are willing to re-think everything in their own lives, and therefore be the catalysts for an awakening in the mass consciousness.

One of the things that needs to be rethought is the entire concept of scarcity of resources. From very early on, you have been programmed to believe that planet earth has only limited resources and therefore can sustain only a limited number of people. This is a one hundred percent lie. It has no reality to it whatsoever.

This planet does not have a scarcity of material resources. It has a scarcity of the love of the heart, which has enabled some people to form an elite who are the haves, as opposed to those who are the have-nots.

This is what they have desired to create on this planet from the very moment they were allowed to embody here. Namely a planet where they can form a privileged elite who have abundance, privileges and power beyond the majority of the population so that they can feel that they are special. It is the selfishness – and the self-centeredness that kills the love of the heart – that is directly responsible for what seems to be a lack of physical resources. My beloved, there is a saying in some of the old countries that if there is room in the heart, there is room in the house. Well, if there is room in the heart, then there is room on the planet.

Scarcity is not inevitable

If the consciousness changed and we saw the spreading of the consciousness of Aquarius – as I have full confidence will happen – then you will see that suddenly, the scarcity of resources that today seems inevitable and insurmountable will simply evaporate like the dew when the morning sun rises. There is no scarcity of resources, there is only an illusion of scarcity put upon the people by the elite. They need to have scarcity so that they can have more than others.

Do you see the inevitability of this? You cannot have an elite who has more than the population if there is an abundance of resources. You must create an artificial situation where the people are prevented from reaping the just reward of their labor. The elite has managed to steal the fruits of the people's labor, concentrating it in their own hands instead of allowing it

8 | The grand illusion of the scarcity of resources

to remain in the hands of those who are doing the work, those who are putting the seeds in the ground and are therefore entitled to reap the harvest. This is a state of consciousness that needs to be challenged before the Golden Age can manifest. I can assure you that in the Golden Age there will not be a scarcity of resources, nor will you have the majority of the population on this planet living below the so-called poverty level, which I, by the way, consider to be a completely artificial construct. I can tell you that I want everyone on earth to have the abundant life, materially and spiritually. This means an entirely different consideration than what they currently consider the border between poverty and non-poverty.

Nevertheless, the reality that needs to dawn upon the people is that scarcity is a complete illusion; abundance is the reality—the real potential for planet earth. Did not Christ say: "Fear not little flock, for it is the Father's good pleasure to give you the kingdom." Truly, it is so. The people can only fail to have the kingdom if they reject that kingdom. They will only reject the kingdom if they have come to believe in the lie – promoted by the elite – that there is not room in the inn, there is not room in the kingdom, for them to sit at the same table as the elite.

The Bible states clearly: "God is no respecter of persons." You can see – when you look back at history – that the entire idea of elitism is out of touch with the reality of God. God *is* in everything and in everyone. Every single person on this planet has infinite value in the eyes of God. God wants *everyone* to have the abundant life. This does not mean that there will not be some who are willing to work harder and therefore have a little more than others. It does mean a society in which you simply cannot have a state where there are a few people that are so unnecessarily affluent while many people live in abject poverty. This is one of the things that needs to change.

Why change is more likely in the West than the East

I have a great hope that the change in consciousness can begin right here in this state. When you stay for too long in any one place, you begin to build a habit pattern, an attachment, a desire to keep things the way they are so you can remain comfortable. After all, familiarity breeds comfort, so you are reluctant to change, to change your perspective, your viewpoint, your state of mind. There needs to be a certain change, a certain movement, before people will be willing to rise higher.

That is precisely why this Western part of the United States has a greater potential to change than the Eastern part. It has not had as long to grow comfortable in the old ways. Consider that there is a big city on the east coast called *New* York, as opposed to the old York. There is an entire region called *New* England. The people who settled that region were people who had left England, not because they wanted to create an entirely new world – a better world – but because they wanted to get away from the injustice and poverty in the old world. They wanted to carry as much with them from the old world as they could, to retain what was familiar and comfortable.

In the North East of the United States, you see an entire establishment, a power elite of old money, who want to keep the entire nation in a certain gridlock where they have control of the economy. This was precisely one of the underlying forces behind the civil war. The Southern states had come to challenge the economic dominance of the North East, and thus they had to be beaten down so that the old elite could maintain control.

Certainly, I am not hereby condoning or defending slavery in any way. Nor am I denying that part of the reason for the economic boom in the South was slavery. I am simply pointing out the fact that there is an elite in the North East who are

8 | The grand illusion of the scarcity of resources

reluctant to change. Therefore, we look to the opposite corner of these United States, to the state that has not the same rigidity because it has not been in existence for so long. Nor does it have the same consciousness, for from the very beginning of this state of California, there has been a different state of consciousness of the people who came here. This is not just because of the people but very much because the people were magnetized here. The state of California has, for a very long time, been the anchor of a certain shade, a certain aspect, of the Freedom Flame.

You might know, beloved, that for a long time we of the ascended masters maintained a focus at Mount Shasta. Well, we no longer have a focus at Mount Shasta for the simple reason that we have now expanded the Freedom Flame to cover this entire state. You see, it is a Piscean concept that you need to go to a certain physical location, to climb a certain mountain, in order to find a spiritual experience, or a spiritual flame.

Did not Christ say the kingdom of God is within you? What sense does it make that you think you have to travel to some physical, remote location in order to discover what is already within you? It makes no sense whatsoever, and thus I have expanded the Freedom Flame to this entire state, and even a little bit beyond this state, so that the people everywhere have the opportunity to tune in to that Freedom Flame.

The need for people to pass their tests under Jesus

I must tell you that for this state of California to have an awakening to the consciousness of freedom, the critical mass of the people need to recognize that you cannot ascend to the consciousness of Aquarius unless you have mastered the lessons of the age of Pisces. You cannot even apply to the master of

Aquarius if you have not been willing to learn from the master of Pisces.

It is necessary for the people of this state to realize that the very essence of the message that Jesus came to bring is Christ discernment, discernment between what is real and unreal, what is of God and what is of the duality consciousness. What is it that will enable the people to take back their power (as I spoke about earlier) and stand up to the elite, realizing that they do not need an elite to govern them, rule them or give them access to heaven? Well, it is only that the people recognize the very fact that the elite has ruled through illusions and lies that spring from the serpentine mind, the duality consciousness. There is an alternative to that consciousness, namely the discernment of the Christ mind whereby you can know what is ultimately real and what is ultimately unreal.

Another of the subtle beliefs, the subtle mindsets, that you have been brought up to accept without question is that there is nothing beyond what human beings define as truth. You have been brought up to not question the basic paradigms of the authority figures of your society, be they in church, state, media or wherever. As Jesus has so eloquently explained on his website, for 2,000 years the Christian Church, the official Christian Church, has been a tool for the power elite to pervert the teachings of Christ. Instead of setting the people free, they have been used to oppress the people even more.

This then is the state that must be acknowledged and addressed by the people in this age. As I have already said, there are enough people in embodiment who know the reality of what I am saying at inner levels that they can wake up and demand change, not only in the religious life but also in the political life and in all aspects of society. What needs to be recognized is simply this: There is Christ truth beyond the dualistic so-called truth. Every human being has the potential to acknowledge that truth in their hearts, if they are willing to seek that truth in the only place it can be found, namely in the kingdom within. Thereby, they find the key of knowledge that allows them to divide the real from the unreal.

Those who are the forerunners, those in the top ten percent, need to awaken to this reality. They must dare to begin to exercise their Christ discernment, and dare to express that discernment by stating the truth that they see (even if it is not the highest truth, it still will be a higher truth than what is promoted by the elite). When you dare to express that truth, you will see the beginning of a chain reaction that will spread. All the foundations have been built; it is simply a matter of providing the final push that creates the breakthrough.

Saint Germain reminds people of their vows

I speak to all those, whether they will ever hear me or read these words. I speak to them at inner levels and I say: "I, Saint Germain, remind you of the vows you took before you came into embodiment at this time. It is time, my beloved, to awaken to your spiritual mission and start manifesting that mission so that we can have the breakthrough that we have all planned for so long!"

Everything needs to be challenged, but there are certain things that must be challenged first, one of them certainly the consciousness of scarcity and lack. This state of California has such an abundance of resources that there is absolutely no reason why a substantial portion of the people of this state should live in poverty. This has many ramifications. Again, one of these ramifications is that you need to consider how the consciousness of the elite has created these very subtle divisions in the population between the haves and the have-nots. As one example of this, is it realistic, is it God-like, is it Christ-like that there are millions of people in this state who live as illegal immigrants, illegal aliens, where they do not have the rights that are guaranteed by the constitution? They do not have the right to vote, they do not have health care or benefits of any kind.

The reality of the matter is that it is the consciousness of scarcity, the consciousness of the power elite, that has given rise to the very subtle belief that there should only be a certain amount of people in these United States. What does it say in the old poem: "Give me your tired, your poor, your huddled masses yearning to breathe free." Does it put a number on how many of the huddled masses can be allowed to enter this country? Do you think I, Saint Germain, who has sponsored this nation from the very beginning has put a number on this? Nay, my beloved. Once again, these United States have plenty of resources to sustain a much greater population than we have today.

There are those who believe that we of the ascended masters are republicans who support the republican party and support an anti-immigration agenda. As I have said before, this is not reality. Thus, I hurl the challenge at this state of California to become the forerunner for change in the federal laws whereby you allow the people who are here – and that no one has any serious intent of removing from this nation – to have the same rights and privileges as any other citizen so that you do not have this division of the population into normal citizens and an underclass.

What sense does it make that the richest country in the world has a class of untouchables that do not have the rights of the rest of the population? This is surely an outdated idea, as anyone who will think about this can see in their hearts. I am not thereby saying that you need to open up the floodgates to anyone who will come here. I am saying that if you will put a little greater trust in the Holy Spirit, then the Holy Spirit will regulate the influx of immigrants from around the world so that only the amount arrive here that are meant to be here.

There is, of course, a certain reality to the fear that some people have that if the United States allowed more immigration, there would be a scarcity of jobs and resources in this country. That reality is there, but it is a temporary reality brought about by the fact that this nation has become so controlled by the power elite that they have again created the scarcity. The economy currently would have a hard time sustaining greater numbers of immigrants. If the immigrants came here anyway, that would bring an impetus for changing the basic economic dynamic. I can assure you that for the Golden Age to be brought in, there needs to be far more equal economic opportunity in this nation.

Out-innovating the multi-national corporations

Once again, there is the potential for this state of California to bring forth a shift in the way you look at the economy and you look at the major players in the economy, first of all the big multi-national corporations who now have an iron grip on the economy of the United States. If you will look of the history of this state of California, you will see that what brought most of the immigrants to this state was the gold rush. What was the driving force behind that? Well, there is always a positive and a lower potential. The lowest potential was the dream of easy money so that you could just walk out in the woods and pick up gold nuggets so that you could live the rest of your life without working. Beyond that was a positive potential of equal opportunity for everyone. Whether you were rich or poor, educated or not, you had the opportunity to find gold. It sort of equalled the playing field where no one was particularly better at it than others, at least in the very beginning.

This is the positive dream upon which California is built, the dream that everyone has the potential to make a go of it, so to speak, to create something—a business, bring forth a new idea, a new innovation that makes the old economic order obsolete. Do you not see that it is no coincidence that the major growth of the computer industry has happened here in this state? Do you not see that this was an entirely new level of economic activity that at first the old established corporations could not quite fathom—because it was so different from their paradigm, their business model, that they saw no value in it.

Did you not see it again with the whole dot-com cycle that also was centered in this state, again an entirely new way to look at wealth, an entirely new way to approach the economy. Surely, I know that the power elite is quick to move in and seek to establish control, but that is precisely what this state has the potential to challenge by rewarding innovation over control.

Recently, the legislators in this state have seen the potential of the research in alternative energy and have taken certain measures to stimulate that research. They see that this would be a boon to this state that could potentially create an entirely new industry, an entirely new growth sector. What you always see in a new sector is many small companies that spring up because they have an innovative idea. Then, my beloved, after a time the big corporations and banks move in and take over and start consolidating.

What I am telling you is that there is enough Freedom Flame in this state that you can simply keep outrunning the control by continued innovation. True innovation is an expression of the Freedom Flame, and the Freedom Flame cannot be put in a box, it cannot be controlled. If you keep innovating, you can out-run those who are seeking to stop innovation in order to maintain their grip on the market or the economy.

Do you not see this outplayed in the company Microsoft who from its very beginning has been more concerned about destroying competition than allowing new innovation? Innovation is the key to breaking up the old patterns, the old mold, that keeps the economy and all aspects of life in a society stagnant so that you stop innovation, you stop growth.

Rethinking corporations

There is no better example of this than the feudal societies of Europe where the power elite of the time – the king, the noble class and the churches – had clamped down on innovation by controlling peoples' thoughts as well as their outer situation. No one dared to come up with new ideas because they would probably contradict some Catholic doctrine and thereby send them to hell. Nobody had the time, the energy or the resources to make a new idea become a reality, for they had to slave to make a living and sustain their physical bodies.

My beloved, this is the total opposite of a free society. I tell you that the Freedom Flame that is anchored in this state has the potential to bring out so much new innovation in all fields that the old established power elite will not be able to control it or to hold it back.

It is not a matter of only innovating in terms of bringing forth new products and new technology. It is also a matter of innovating in terms of bringing forth new concepts, new ideas, new ways to look at the old perspectives, new ways to look at business.

As I said, everything needs to be rethought. Well, do we not need to rethink the basic element of the United States' economy, namely the corporate entity that has become bigger than any human being can control? It therefore becomes a beast in itself that has no respect for the value of human life, no respect for the overall purpose of this nation, no respect for human rights. It will mindlessly override all human rights in order to make a bigger profit for the shareholders, who are not part of producing the goods that are produced by the corporation.

There is a great need to rethink corporate ownership, to rethink the stock market. Is it right that you can have a stock market where people buy based on speculation rather than the actual value of the company whose stock they are buying? Is this not a complete disconnect that once again gives an unfair advantage to those who have, and makes it impossible for those who have not to ever come up. You know that over the last decade or more there has been a change where many more people have begun to invest in the stock market through pension funds. I still would like to remind you that even though there are more middle class people that have greater wealth, you will still see that the gap between rich and poor in this nation has increased more in that period than at any previous time.

You still have a bigger gap between the rich and poor, and you still have an underclass who will never – under the current system – have any opportunity to become part of the economic growth. There is a great need for a rethinking of the entire structure, the foundation, of the economy. Again, I can assure you that I have already put in place those who have the expertise to know how the economy works and what needs to happen.

Once again, although they might never hear or read this, I speak into the mass consciousness to awaken them to the reality that: "You are not here to live the good life. You are here to help bring forth the Golden Age of Saint Germain. That is your reason for being, the reason that you chose before you came into embodiment. It is acceptable to me that you have forgotten this mission and have focused on doing what you have been doing, but it is not acceptable to me that you keep being forgetful of this mission. I tell you that it is time to awaken and bring forth a new day, a new era of economic opportunity and equality in opportunity!"

Obviously, I am not here talking about socialism or communism. I am talking about an entirely new economy where there is neither state control nor corporate control. Innovation is the driving force, the innovation that comes through the agency of the Holy Spirit. I will remind you – precisely – that the role of the Holy Spirit is to break up the old patterns that keep people trapped and prevent them from moving on with the River of Life that is the ongoingness of God's consciousness.

My beloved, I thank you once again for your attention, and I shall return again to give you the next installment in this series. I seal you again in the Freedom Flame, the particular Freedom Flame devoted to innovation in all aspects of life. Do not forget to be innovative in your own lives, for the path of Christhood is not about being comfortable. The path of Christhood is about growth. When you accept this, you can find peace in growth instead of seeking peace in still-stand, the peace that can never be a true peace but is a house built on sand that will eventually be overturned by the inevitability of the forward movement of life itself.

9 | INVOKING THE ABUNDANCE CONSCIOUSNESS

In the name I AM THAT I AM, Jesus Christ, I call to all ascended masters working on manifesting the Golden Age, especially Archangel Chamuel, Elohim Heros, Paul the Venetian, Saint Germain and Sanat Kumara to radiate into the collective consciousness the certainty that earth has unlimited resources. Help people see that we can build a new future by working with the ascended masters and letting go of the old way of looking at life, including…

[Make personal calls.]

Part 1

1. Saint Germain, radiate into the collective consciousness the awareness that in order to bring the Golden Age, we need to rethink everything that has been part of life in the old age.

Chamuel Archangel, in ruby ray power,
we know we are taking a life-giving shower.
Love burning away all perversions of will,
we suddenly feel our desires falling still.

Chamuel Archangel, descend from Above,
Chamuel Archangel, with ruby-pink love,
Chamuel Archangel, so often thought-of,
Chamuel Archangel, o come Holy Dove.

2. Saint Germain, radiate into the collective consciousness the awareness that you will shine a light on this planet so that there will be no shadows left, there will be no one and nothing that can hide, there will be no illusion and no lie that could possibly hide from the light.

Chamuel Archangel, a spiral of light,
as ruby ray fire now pierces the night.
All forces of darkness consumed by your fire,
consuming all those who will not rise higher.

Chamuel Archangel, descend from Above,
Chamuel Archangel, with ruby-pink love,
Chamuel Archangel, so often thought-of,
Chamuel Archangel, o come Holy Dove.

3. Saint Germain, radiate into the collective consciousness the awareness that the entire concept of scarcity of resources, that planet earth has only limited resources and therefore can sustain only a limited number of people, is a one hundred percent lie. It has no reality whatsoever.

9 | Invoking the abundance consciousness

Chamuel Archangel, your love so immense,
with clarified vision, our lives now make sense.
The purpose of life you so clearly reveal,
immersed in your love, God's oneness we feel.

**Chamuel Archangel, descend from Above,
Chamuel Archangel, with ruby-pink love,
Chamuel Archangel, so often thought-of,
Chamuel Archangel, o come Holy Dove.**

4. Saint Germain, radiate into the collective consciousness the awareness that this planet does not have a scarcity of material resources. It has a scarcity of the love of the heart, which has enabled some people to form an elite who are the haves, as opposed to those who are the have-nots.

Chamuel Archangel, what calmness you bring,
we see now that even death has no sting.
For truly, in love there can be no decay,
as love is transcendence into a new day.

**Chamuel Archangel, descend from Above,
Chamuel Archangel, with ruby-pink love,
Chamuel Archangel, so often thought-of,
Chamuel Archangel, o come Holy Dove.**

5. Saint Germain, radiate into the collective consciousness the awareness that from the moment they were allowed to embody here, the fallen beings have desired to create a planet where they can form a privileged elite who have abundance, privileges and power beyond the majority of the population.

> Chamuel Archangel, God't Love Flame bestow,
> on all those longing God's true love to know,
> conditions we know can never be real,
> and this is the love you always reveal.
>
> **Chamuel Archangel, descend from Above,**
> **Chamuel Archangel, with ruby-pink love,**
> **Chamuel Archangel, so often thought-of,**
> **Chamuel Archangel, o come Holy Dove.**

6. Saint Germain, radiate into the collective consciousness the awareness that it is the selfishness – and the self-centeredness that kills the love of the heart – that is directly responsible for what seems to be a lack of physical resources.

> Chamuel Archangel, love's seed you have sown,
> in hearts of all those who don't seek to own,
> for love that possesses is nothing but fear,
> that pierces the heart with duality's spear.
>
> **Chamuel Archangel, descend from Above,**
> **Chamuel Archangel, with ruby-pink love,**
> **Chamuel Archangel, so often thought-of,**
> **Chamuel Archangel, o come Holy Dove.**

7. Saint Germain, radiate into the collective consciousness the awareness that as the consciousness of Aquarius spreads, then the scarcity of resources that today seems inevitable and insurmountable will simply evaporate.

Chamuel Archangel, we don't want control,
for this is the devil's hold on the soul,
your love will now break the serpentine chain,
so we are set free God's love to reclaim.

**Chamuel Archangel, descend from Above,
Chamuel Archangel, with ruby-pink love,
Chamuel Archangel, so often thought-of,
Chamuel Archangel, o come Holy Dove.**

8. Saint Germain, radiate into the collective consciousness the awareness that there is no scarcity of resources, there is only an illusion of scarcity put upon the people by the elite. They need to have scarcity so that they can have more than others.

Chamuel Archangel, you are so adept,
at helping us God's true love to accept,
we know that the love for which we so yearn,
is not something we on earth have to earn.

**Chamuel Archangel, descend from Above,
Chamuel Archangel, with ruby-pink love,
Chamuel Archangel, so often thought-of,
Chamuel Archangel, o come Holy Dove.**

9. Saint Germain, radiate into the collective consciousness the awareness that there cannot be an elite who has more than the population if there is an abundance of resources. They must create an artificial situation where the people are prevented from reaping the just reward of their labor.

Chamuel Archangel, for love to accept,
we do not need to be so perfect,
for love is not static but always a flow,
demanding only we're willing to grow.

Chamuel Archangel, descend from Above,
Chamuel Archangel, with ruby-pink love,
Chamuel Archangel, so often thought-of,
Chamuel Archangel, o come Holy Dove.

Part 2

1. Saint Germain, radiate into the collective consciousness the awareness that the elite has managed to steal the fruits of the people's labor, concentrating it in their own hands instead of allowing it to remain in the hands of those who are doing the work.

O Heros-Amora, in your love so pink,
we care not what others about us may think,
in oneness with you, we claim a new day,
as innocent children, we frolic and play.

O Heros-Amora, we reap what we sow,
yet this is Plan B for helping us grow,
for truly, Plan A is that we join the flow,
immersed in the Infinite Love you bestow.

2. Saint Germain, radiate into the collective consciousness the awareness that this state of consciousness needs to be challenged before the Golden Age can manifest. In the Golden Age there will not be a scarcity of resources, nor will the majority of the population be living below the poverty level.

> O Heros-Amora, a new life begun,
> we laugh at the devil, the serious one,
> the serpent is stuck in his duality,
> but we are set free by Love's reality.
>
> **O Heros-Amora, we reap what we sow,**
> **yet this is Plan B for helping us grow,**
> **for truly, Plan A is that we join the flow,**
> **immersed in the Infinite Love you bestow.**

3. Saint Germain, radiate into the collective consciousness the awareness that scarcity is a complete illusion; abundance is the reality—the real potential for planet earth.

> O Heros-Amora, awakened we see,
> in true love is no conditionality,
> we bathe in your glorious Ruby-Pink Sun,
> knowing our God allows life to be fun.
>
> **O Heros-Amora, we reap what we sow,**
> **yet this is Plan B for helping us grow,**
> **for truly, Plan A is that we join the flow,**
> **immersed in the Infinite Love you bestow.**

4. Saint Germain, radiate into the collective consciousness the awareness that God wants all people to have the abundant life. People can only fail to have abundance if they reject it.

O Heros-Amora, life is such a joy,
we see that the world is like a great toy,
whatever the mind into it projects,
the mirror of life exactly reflects.

**O Heros-Amora, we reap what we sow,
yet this is Plan B for helping us grow,
for truly, Plan A is that we join the flow,
immersed in the Infinite Love you bestow.**

5. Saint Germain, radiate into the collective consciousness the awareness that people will only reject abundance if they have come to believe in the lie – promoted by the elite – that there are not enough resources for them to have the same as the elite.

O Heros-Amora, conditions you burn,
we know we are free to take a new turn,
Immersed in the stream of infinite Love,
we know that the Spirit came from Above.

**O Heros-Amora, we reap what we sow,
yet this is Plan B for helping us grow,
for truly, Plan A is that we join the flow,
immersed in the Infinite Love you bestow.**

6. Saint Germain, radiate into the collective consciousness the awareness that God is no respecter of persons. The entire idea of elitism is out of touch with the reality of God. God is in everything and in everyone.

9 | Invoking the abundance consciousness

O Heros-Amora, we feel that at last,
we've risen above the trap of the past,
in true love we claim our freedom to grow,
forever we're one with Love's Infinite Flow.

O Heros-Amora, we reap what we sow,
yet this is Plan B for helping us grow,
for truly, Plan A is that we join the flow,
immersed in the Infinite Love you bestow.

7. Saint Germain, radiate into the collective consciousness the awareness that every single person on this planet has infinite value in the eyes of God. God wants everyone to have the abundant life.

O Heros-Amora, conditions are ties,
forming a net of serpentine lies,
but you have the antidote setting us free,
you take us beyond conditionality.

O Heros-Amora, we reap what we sow,
yet this is Plan B for helping us grow,
for truly, Plan A is that we join the flow,
immersed in the Infinite Love you bestow.

8. Saint Germain, radiate into the collective consciousness the awareness that those who are willing to work harder can have a little more than others. But we cannot have a state where there are a few people that are so unnecessarily affluent while many people live in abject poverty.

O Heros-Amora, your love is no bond,
for love only wants to take us beyond,
your love has no bounds, forever it flies,
raising all life into Ruby-Pink skies.

O Heros-Amora, we reap what we sow,
yet this is Plan B for helping us grow,
for truly, Plan A is that we join the flow,
immersed in the Infinite Love you bestow.

9. Saint Germain, radiate into the collective consciousness the awareness that we cannot ascend to the consciousness of Aquarius unless we have mastered the lessons of the age of Pisces. We cannot even apply to the master of Aquarius if we have not been willing to learn from the master of Pisces.

O Heros-Amora, love bathing the earth,
filling all people with infinite mirth,
for fear and despair there is no more room,
as all are awakened by love's sonic boom.

O Heros-Amora, we reap what we sow,
yet this is Plan B for helping us grow,
for truly, Plan A is that we join the flow,
immersed in the Infinite Love you bestow.

Part 3

1. Saint Germain, radiate into the collective consciousness the awareness that the very essence of the message that Jesus came to bring is Christ discernment, discernment between what is real and unreal, what is of God and what is of the duality consciousness.

Master Paul, venetian dream,
your love for beauty's flowing stream.
Master Paul, in love's own womb,
your power shatters ego's tomb.

Master Paul, your love so true,
and therefore we apply to you,
to set all free in the great love,
that you are shining from Above.

2. Saint Germain, radiate into the collective consciousness the awareness that the elite has ruled through illusions and lies that spring from the serpentine mind, the duality consciousness. There is an alternative to that consciousness, namely the discernment of the Christ mind whereby you can know what is ultimately real and what is ultimately unreal.

Master Paul, your counsel wise,
our minds are raised to lofty skies.
Master Paul, in wisdom's love,
such beauty flowing from Above.

**Master Paul, your love so true,
and therefore we apply to you,
to set all free in the great love,
that you are shining from Above.**

3. Saint Germain, radiate into the collective consciousness the awareness that there is something beyond what human beings define as truth. We need to question the basic paradigms of the authority figures of society, be they in church, state or the media.

Master Paul, love is an art,
it opens up the secret heart.
Master Paul, love's rushing flow,
our hearts awash in sacred glow.

**Master Paul, your love so true,
and therefore we apply to you,
to set all free in the great love,
that you are shining from Above.**

4. Saint Germain, radiate into the collective consciousness the awareness that for 2,000 years the official Christian Church has been a tool for the power elite to pervert the teachings of Christ. Instead of setting the people free, they have been used to oppress the people even more.

Master Paul, accelerate,
upon pure love we meditate.
Master Paul, intentions pure,
our self-transcendence will ensure.

**Master Paul, your love so true,
and therefore we apply to you,
to set all free in the great love,
that you are shining from Above.**

5. Saint Germain, radiate into the collective consciousness the awareness that there is Christ truth beyond the dualistic so-called truth. Every human being has the potential to acknowledge that truth in their hearts, if they are willing to seek that truth in the only place it can be found, namely in the kingdom within.

Master Paul, your love will heal,
our inner light you do reveal.
Master Paul, all life console,
with you we're being truly whole.

**Master Paul, your love so true,
and therefore we apply to you,
to set all free in the great love,
that you are shining from Above.**

6. Saint Germain, radiate into the collective consciousness the awareness that those who are the forerunners, those in the top ten percent, need to awaken to this reality. We must exercise our Christ discernment and express it by stating the truth that we see.

Master Paul, you serve the All,
by helping us transcend the fall.
Master Paul, in peace we rise,
as ego meets its sure demise.

**Master Paul, your love so true,
and therefore we apply to you,
to set all free in the great love,
that you are shining from Above.**

7. Saint Germain, radiate into the collective consciousness the awareness that we need to remember the vows we took before we came into embodiment at this time. It is time to awaken to our spiritual mission so that we can have the breakthrough that we have all planned for so long.

Master Paul, love all life free,
your love is for eternity.
Master Paul, you are the One,
to help us make the journey fun.

**Master Paul, your love so true,
and therefore we apply to you,
to set all free in the great love,
that you are shining from Above.**

8. Saint Germain, radiate into the collective consciousness the awareness that the consciousness of the elite has created subtle divisions in the population between the haves and the have-nots.

Master Paul, you balance all,
the seven rays upon our call.
Master Paul, you paint the sky,
with colors that delight the I.

**Master Paul, your love so true,
and therefore we apply to you,
to set all free in the great love,
that you are shining from Above.**

9. Saint Germain, radiate into the collective consciousness the awareness that the consciousness of scarcity, the consciousness of the power elite, has given rise to the very subtle belief that there should only be a certain amount of people in the United States or the world.

Master Paul, your Presence here,
filling up the inner sphere.
Life is now a sacred flow,
God Love we do on all bestow.

**Master Paul, your love so true,
and therefore we apply to you,
to set all free in the great love,
that you are shining from Above.**

Part 4

1. Saint Germain, radiate into the collective consciousness the awareness that the United States has plenty of resources to sustain a much greater population than we have today.

O Saint Germain, you do inspire,
my vision raised forever higher,
with you I form a figure-eight,
your Golden Age I co-create.

> **O Saint Germain, what love you bring,**
> **it truly makes all matter sing,**
> **your violet flame does all restore,**
> **with you we are becoming more.**

2. Saint Germain, radiate into the collective consciousness the awareness that there needs to be a shift in the way we look at the economy and the major players in the economy, first of all the big multi-national corporations who now have an iron grip on the economy of the United States.

> O Saint Germain, what Freedom Flame,
> released when we recite your name,
> acceleration is your gift,
> our planet it will surely lift.

> **O Saint Germain, what love you bring,**
> **it truly makes all matter sing,**
> **your violet flame does all restore,**
> **with you we are becoming more.**

3. Saint Germain, radiate into the collective consciousness the awareness that when a new economic opportunity is created, many small companies spring up because they have an innovative idea. After a time, the big corporations and banks move in and take over and start consolidating.

> O Saint Germain, in love we claim,
> our right to bring your violet flame,
> from you Above, to us below,
> it is an all-transforming flow.

**O Saint Germain, what love you bring,
it truly makes all matter sing,
your violet flame does all restore,
with you we are becoming more.**

4. Saint Germain, radiate into the collective consciousness the awareness that we need to outrun the control by continued innovation. True innovation is an expression of the Freedom Flame.

O Saint Germain, I love you so,
my aura filled with violet glow,
my chakras filled with violet fire,
I am your cosmic amplifier.

**O Saint Germain, what love you bring,
it truly makes all matter sing,
your violet flame does all restore,
with you we are becoming more.**

5. Saint Germain, radiate into the collective consciousness the awareness that the Freedom Flame cannot be put in a box, it cannot be controlled. If we keep innovating, we can out-run those who are seeking to stop innovation in order to maintain their grip on the market or the economy.

O Saint Germain, I am now free,
your violet flame is therapy,
transform all hang-ups in my mind,
as inner peace I surely find.

> **O Saint Germain, what love you bring,**
> **it truly makes all matter sing,**
> **your violet flame does all restore,**
> **with you we are becoming more.**

6. Saint Germain, radiate into the collective consciousness the awareness that innovation is the key to breaking up the old patterns that keep the economy and all aspects of life in a society stagnant so that it stops innovation and growth.

> O Saint Germain, my body pure,
> your violet flame for all is cure,
> consume the cause of all disease,
> and therefore I am all at ease.

> **O Saint Germain, what love you bring,**
> **it truly makes all matter sing,**
> **your violet flame does all restore,**
> **with you we are becoming more.**

7. Saint Germain, radiate into the collective consciousness the awareness that it is not a matter of only innovating in terms of bringing forth new products and new technology. It is also a matter of innovating in terms of bringing forth new concepts, new ideas, new ways to look at the old perspectives, new ways to look at business.

> O Saint Germain, I'm karma-free,
> the past no longer burdens me,
> a brand new opportunity,
> I am in Christic unity.

**O Saint Germain, what love you bring,
it truly makes all matter sing,
your violet flame does all restore,
with you we are becoming more.**

8. Saint Germain, radiate into the collective consciousness the awareness that we need to rethink the basic element of the United States' economy, namely the corporate entity that has become bigger than any human being can control.

O Saint Germain, we are now one,
I am for you a violet sun,
as we transform this planet earth,
your Golden Age is given birth.

**O Saint Germain, what love you bring,
it truly makes all matter sing,
your violet flame does all restore,
with you we are becoming more.**

9. Saint Germain, radiate into the collective consciousness the awareness that a large corporation becomes a beast in itself that has no respect for the value of human life, no respect for the overall purpose of a nation, no respect for human rights.

O Saint Germain, the earth is free,
from burden of duality,
in oneness we bring what is best,
your Golden Age is manifest.

**O Saint Germain, what love you bring,
it truly makes all matter sing,
your violet flame does all restore,
with you we are becoming more.**

Part 5

1. Saint Germain, radiate into the collective consciousness the awareness that a corporation will mindlessly override all human rights in order to make a bigger profit for the shareholders, who are not part of producing the goods that are produced by the corporation.

> Sanat Kumara, Ruby Fire,
> I seek my place in love's own choir,
> with open hearts we sing your praise,
> together we the earth do raise.

> **Sanat Kumara, Ruby Ray,
> bring to earth a higher way,
> light this planet with your fire,
> clothe her in a new attire.**

2. Saint Germain, radiate into the collective consciousness the awareness that there is a great need to rethink corporate ownership, to rethink the stock market. We cannot have a stock market where people buy based on speculation rather than the actual value of the company whose stock they are buying.

9 | Invoking the abundance consciousness

Sanat Kumara, Ruby Fire,
initiations I desire,
I am for you an electrode,
Shamballa is my true abode.

**Sanat Kumara, Ruby Ray,
bring to earth a higher way,
light this planet with your fire,
clothe her in a new attire.**

3. Saint Germain, radiate into the collective consciousness the awareness that speculation is a complete disconnect that gives an unfair advantage to those who have, and makes it impossible for those who have not to ever come up.

Sanat Kumara, Ruby Fire,
I follow path that you require,
initiate me with your love,
the open door for Holy Dove.

**Sanat Kumara, Ruby Ray,
bring to earth a higher way,
light this planet with your fire,
clothe her in a new attire.**

4. Saint Germain, radiate into the collective consciousness the awareness that the United States now has a bigger gap between rich and poor, and we still have an underclass who will never have any opportunity to become part of the economic growth.

Sanat Kumara, Ruby Fire,
your great example all inspire,
with non-attachment and great mirth,
we give the earth a true rebirth.

**Sanat Kumara, Ruby Ray,
bring to earth a higher way,
light this planet with your fire,
clothe her in a new attire.**

5. Saint Germain, radiate into the collective consciousness the awareness that we need to rethink the entire structure and foundation of the economy. We are not here to live the good life. We are here to help bring forth the Golden Age of Saint Germain.

Sanat Kumara, Ruby Fire,
you are this planet's purifier,
consume on earth all spirits dark,
reveal the inner Spirit Spark.

**Sanat Kumara, Ruby Ray,
bring to earth a higher way,
light this planet with your fire,
clothe her in a new attire.**

6. Saint Germain, radiate into the collective consciousness the awareness that our reason for being, the reason we chose before we came into embodiment, is to bring forth the Golden Age. It is time to awaken and bring forth a new day, a new era of economic opportunity, and equality in opportunity!

Sanat Kumara, Ruby Fire,
you are a cosmic amplifier,
the lower forces can't withstand,
vibrations from Venusian band.

**Sanat Kumara, Ruby Ray,
bring to earth a higher way,
light this planet with your fire,
clothe her in a new attire.**

7. Saint Germain, radiate into the collective consciousness the awareness that this does not mean socialism or communism. It means an entirely new economy where there is neither state control nor corporate control.

Sanat Kumara, Ruby Fire,
I am on earth your magnifier,
the flow of love I do restore,
my chakras are your open door.

**Sanat Kumara, Ruby Ray,
bring to earth a higher way,
light this planet with your fire,
clothe her in a new attire.**

8. Saint Germain, radiate into the collective consciousness the awareness that in the golden age economy, innovation is the driving force, the innovation that comes through the agency of the Holy Spirit.

Sanat Kumara, Ruby Fire,
Venusian song the multiplier,
as we your love reverberate,
the densest minds we penetrate.

**Sanat Kumara, Ruby Ray,
bring to earth a higher way,
light this planet with your fire,
clothe her in a new attire.**

9. Saint Germain, radiate into the collective consciousness the awareness that the role of the Holy Spirit is to break up the old patterns that keep people trapped and prevent them from moving on with the River of Life that is the ongoingness of God's consciousness.

Sanat Kumara, Ruby Fire,
you are for all the sanctifier,
the earth is now a holy place,
purified by cosmic grace.

**Sanat Kumara, Ruby Ray,
bring to earth a higher way,
light this planet with your fire,
clothe her in a new attire.**

Sealing

In the name of the Divine Mother, I call to all ascended masters for the sealing of myself and all people in my circle of influence in the creative flow of the Divine Mother, the River of Life. I call for the multiplication of my calls by all ascended masters so that we form the perfect figure-eight flow of "As Above, so below." Thus, I accept that this is fully manifest, because the mouth of the Lord, the Divine Mother that I AM, has spoken it. Amen.

10 | BE MORE THAN NORMAL!

Saint Germain I AM, and I AM real. You too are real, and the greatest gift you can give to humanity is knowing the difference between what is real and what is unreal. Indeed, there are many people on this earth who do not know the difference. I am not only talking about those who may seem to be obviously disturbed and have issues about knowing what is real and unreal from a normal perspective. I would call your attention to the fact that there are many people who seem normal, but yet do not have any clue as to what is real and what is unreal.

In a sense, it is better to be confused about what is real and what is unreal than to be in the state where you are absolutely sure what is real, yet what you think is real is not real at all. Thus, you do not even have an opening to work with—for these people do not think they are facing a spiritual crisis. They do not think they need to change, that they need to learn anything, that they need to change their perspective, that they need to be healed, that they need to rethink what they believe is real. They are unreachable for a spiritual teacher, for they have become so convinced by the false teachers that they are sure that unreality is real. I have prepared you – in this series of discourses – to go with me on the adventure of the millennia, which is to rise higher in consciousness by being willing to re-think everything.

The greatest threat to your freedom

We have now reached the point where I can ask you to consider the greatest threat to your freedom and to the freedom of humankind, the greatest hindrance to the bringing forth of the Golden Age of Aquarius. This, my beloved, is a factor that has always been the greatest obstacle for the spiritual growth of humankind, for the awakening of people. What is the factor I am talking about?

It is the very subtle, very insidious, programming to which you have all been subjected from the very moment you first took embodiment on this planet, and certainly for your entire lifetime. It is the programming that you are supposed to be *normal*, a normal human being. What does it mean to be normal? Is it not an attempt by the dark forces and the power elite to put you in a box? You are so focused on following the norms defined by your society that you do not dare to challenge those norms—and therefore do not dare to challenge the status quo that keeps the elite in control. As long as you fit into the mold of a normal human being, you will not dare to fulfill your Divine plan, and certainly you will not dare to express your Christhood. There has yet to be a society on this planet – at least in recent history – where being the Christ in action was considered normal by the powers that be.

Those who are my own – who have come into embodiment at this time to help bring the Golden Age of Aquarius into manifestation – certainly, part of your Divine plan is to speak out about conditions in society and to challenge the lies and the illusions. The very deepest thing that you can help me with is by being willing to challenge the ultimate illusion, the illusion of normality. If you will look at the life of Christ, you will see that he too was challenged to be normal, even by his own mother and his brothers and sisters who came to him while he was preaching, being disturbed by the fact that he had shattered their conception of what it meant to be normal.

It is so easy to look at those who do not follow the norm of your particular society and label them with some fancy medical term, be it bipolar, insane, schizophrenic, depressed, having boundary issues or this or that. I can assure you that there are people in mental hospitals in this nation who are actually more in touch with reality than the average person. Certainly, there are also people in mental hospitals who are out of touch with reality and do not know what is real and unreal. What I want you to see here is the fact that the average human being on this planet – the "normal" human being – truly has no conception whatsoever of what is real and what is unreal. People have indeed been programmed to think that this material world and the conditions that you see right now are real and normal, and therefore should be preserved.

Dare to go beyond the norms of your society

This, of course, is the programming of the power elite. They want people to uphold the status quo that maintains their privilege and their power. Once they have set themselves up in those positions of privilege and power, their main concern is not to lose it. That is precisely why they seek to stop progress, they seek to stop new inventions, new ideas, new philosophies, new concepts. When they cannot stop the emergence of new ideas, such as new ideas in spirituality and religion, they seek to prevent the population from embracing those ideas by using the weapon that you have to be normal. They say: This new idea is not normal. It is a cult, it is bad, it is dangerous.

The message I want to get across here is that if you are to fulfill your Divine plans, if you are to manifest your Christhood and do what you came here to do – namely help Saint Germain bring in the Golden Age of Aquarius – then you have to take a long, hard look in the mirror and say: "Where am I attached to being normal, to following the norms defined by my society, my family or even by my own outer mind or my ego?" You must evaluate whether you are more concerned about being seen as being normal by society or whether you are concerned about fulfilling your Divine plan. Certainly, I am not talking about manifesting something that is clearly insane, for being the Christ does not mean that you are insane in any sense of the word. It does mean that you are willing to go beyond the norm, even to do things that for "normal" people might appear to be a little bit "out there," as the popular saying goes.

I am not asking you to be "out there," I am actually asking you to be "in here," in your heart where you know what is real for you and for your mission. You do not allow any outside force to cause you to abort that mission, especially not the force of normality. As I explained earlier today, you cannot put the Holy Spirit in a box. It is not easy to come up with a standard for how the Holy Spirit should express itself in this world. Now you see an even deeper understanding, for when the Holy Spirit flows, it seeks to set people free from their mental boxes, and thus it must challenge their standard for what is normal. We have explained many times that you are who you think you are. You are projecting an image based on your current sense of identity into the cosmic mirror, and the Ma-ter Light takes on the physical manifestation that corresponds to your image. When a critical mass of people in a society, or on the entire planet, have come to believe in a certain standard for what is normal human behavior, well, then it will be very difficult for them to go beyond that standard. They need to see someone who is willing to defy the standard of normality, not in an insane, crazy way but by shattering the boundaries, the limitations, that are set up by the norm.

Challenging the concept of a "normal human being"

What does it really mean to be normal? Well, it means that you accept boundaries for who you are, what you can be and how you can express yourself as long as you want to be an accepted member of society. The job of the Living Christ in embodiment is to challenge people's sense of what is normal, which is what you saw Jesus do with his miracles and his words. Look at how, even in the scriptures, it is portrayed how people wanted him to be normal, to follow their standard, to not go too far beyond, to not push the envelope, push the limits for what was considered possible for a human being.

You see, again, the incredible depth in the statement of Christ: "With men this is impossible, but with God all things are possible." With men – with their human consciousness, with a standard for what is normal – when you are in that state of consciousness, you must accept that there are boundaries and limitations for what can be achieved. That is precisely what the power elite uses to maintain status quo by getting people to believe in the lie that there are certain problems that cannot be solved, or even certain conditions (as I explained in my earlier discourses) that you have come to believe are natural, are normal, because nature simply is that way and there is nothing that can change it.

In reality, there is no norm, there is no standard. Why is this so, my beloved? Because the Creator has created billions of expressions of itself, each one of which is unique in God. If everyone is a unique individual with a unique God-given individuality and identity, well, then how can there be a standard? How can there be a norm? How can there be norms in individuality? How can there be a standard in uniqueness?

Your challenge to create a culture without a norm

Even the area of religion has been influenced by this mindset, to the point where most religious and spiritual movements, even most New Age movements, define a standard for how you are supposed to behave in order to be saved—however they define salvation.

This is another thing you need to re-think, for you have the teaching to create an entirely new environment. When someone comes to you for the first time, they do not feel they have to fit themselves into your box in order to be allowed in. On the contrary, they feel that they are welcomed and accepted for who they are right now because you have no standard for what is normal, for what is lovable. You have transcended the conditional love and come to the point where you have unconditional love for all life.

The only way to have unconditional love is, of course, to have no conditions. Meaning, that you have no expectations of how people should or should not behave. You have no standard for what is normal or what is acceptable behavior.

Every human being is – right now – in a certain state of consciousness. You do not know why a particular person is in that state of consciousness. It may be that the person has made certain choices that were based on duality. It may also be that a person, who seems to be very burdened, has actually taken on something from the mass consciousness and is carrying that burden for many other people, thus making it easier for them to make progress. There is no need to judge with the outer mind. You look at a person, and you accept them for who they are right now. Therefore, you welcome them to your heart. You give them unconditional love, and the acceptance that they are welcome as they are.

Then, of course, you also hold the immaculate concept, that they can transcend whatever limitations or burdens they are facing right now. You do not hold the immaculate concept by having in your mind a standard that says: "Ah this is normal for a spiritual seeker, and that person is below the norm, so I must help that person come up to the norm." Again, there may be people who have taken on conditions that they are meant to carry for the rest of their lifetimes—and so a certain condition might not be meant to be healed. The question is then: Can you still love that person unconditionally without having a norm for what should or should not happen?

Virtually every religion on this planet has fallen prey to the dualistic consciousness of setting up a norm for what it means to be a member of that religion. That is why so many people have felt unwelcomed and unaccepted in particular religions. If you will look at society today, you will see that there are many, many people who have rejected religion – whether it be a specific religion or even all religion – precisely because they did not feel welcomed. This is not necessarily because there was anything wrong with these peoples' state of mind. In fact, in many cases these people have the inner attunement of knowing that in the Aquarian Age, religion itself is supposed to transcend itself, to transcend the old judgmental mindset.

Spiritual attainment as a standard for judging

Here is another concept for you to ponder. I have talked about the need to have Christ discernment, and when you discern, you discern between what is real and what is unreal. I must tell you that it is possible, even for people who have obtained some Christ discernment, to fall prey to the very subtle temptations of the serpentine mind, namely to use the Christ discernment to set up a standard whereby you judge other people. Did not Christ say: "Judge not that ye be not judged," my beloved? The reason is, as we have explained before, that we do not judge you, you judge yourself. The way you judge other people is a reflection of your state of consciousness—and that is the state of consciousness that you also use to judge yourself, even if you are not consciously aware of this.

I bring to your attention that at the lower levels of Christhood – where you are beginning to have some Christ discernment (but do not yet have the full openness of the heart, you have not quite attained unconditional love), it is possible that Christ discernment can become tainted by the tendency to judge, based on a standard for what is normal or what is acceptable. That is why I am giving you the teaching so that you have the opportunity to question the norm. You do not carry the norms of your society with you unquestioned whereby you will unconsciously color your Christ discernment by the norms of society.

Knowing what is unreal and what is real in another human being – when you truly know what is real and unreal – will take you beyond human judgment. Here is why. When you truly see the difference between what is real and what is unreal, well you clearly see what is unreal in another human being but you also see beyond what is unreal and you see the deeper reality that might be hidden behind an outer personality or an outer behavior. When you see what is real in another human being, how can you judge that human being? You will know that this person came from the same source from which you came. Therefore, that person is part of the same Body of God of which you are a part, and therefore that person is *you*.

When you see what is real and what is unreal, you see beyond the outer appearances that create differences and conflicts and you see the underlying oneness of all life. You affirm that oneness, and then you can form what Maitreya has talked about, the community of Oneness, the Sphere of Oneness, where you affirm your oneness with other people in Christ. You never reject anyone, but you allow them to make the choice of whether they will come into oneness with you in Christ, or whether they will remove themselves because they cannot yet handle that oneness. They still have some need to experience separation and duality for a while longer, until they have finally had enough of it.

At least you have given them a real choice by being in Oneness and welcoming them into your Oneness so that they can see that there is an alternative to the separation imposed upon them by the standards of society, by the norm. Do you not see that what is considered normal behavior in your present society is the standard that is entirely based on duality? It therefore confirms the lie that all people are separate beings and are therefore beyond being united in oneness.

Expressing your light despite the norm

Again, question the norm, question the unquestionable, think the unthinkable, accept the unacceptable. Be what you are not supposed to be—dare to be here below all that you already are Above. Accept a new norm, which is that you are a spiritual being and that it is normal and right for you to express your spiritual reality in whatever form comes to you from within. Accept that there is no norm in this world that is going to stop you from expressing your spiritual reality, even if it means creating a website or writing books that cause some people to think that you are crazy or insane.

Even if it means speaking out in ways that will challenge other people and therefore cause them to go into the default reaction of the ego—of saying that there must be something wrong with *you*. This then gives them an excuse for ignoring you so that they do not have to change. Thereby, they can ignore the fact that if *you* can be different, *they* can be different as well. They can continue staying where they are comfortable and where they do not need to take responsibility for themselves.

Do you not see that being normal in your society takes away your need to take responsibility for yourself, to discover who you are and to dare to express who you are? You just need to be normal and flow along with the mass consciousness. This is a very easy and comfortable way to live, for you do not really need to think. The norm has done all the thinking for you.

I congratulate you for your willingness to consider and to be unconditional. You can build on this momentum to take this even further and manifest an even higher degree of unconditionality. Certainly, even though it may seem contradictory, there are degrees of unconditionality in the sense that while unconditional love is unconditional, it is possible for people to have attained partial unconditionality but still have some conditions in other areas.

Be willing to look at yourself and consider: "Where do I have conditions in my love?" I assure you that if you will see where you have conditions that prevent you from expressing love to others, well behind it you will find a condition that also prevents you from accepting God's love for yourself. It therefore causes you to judge yourself according to the norm, to the standard. This prevents you from being who you are and achieving that victory of being here below all that you are Above.

My beloved, wear that label of *not* being normal as an honor badge. Surely, when you seek the Kingdom of God within you – and when you seek that Kingdom beyond anything in this world – you will strive for a higher norm. This is the norm of being unique in God, even in this world where everything is arrayed against the expression of your uniqueness. You saw how the forces were arrayed against Jesus and his expression of his Christhood. Yet he had the courage to be, and I know that you too have that courage, and so I look to you to *be*. Thus, in the gratitude of a Father's heart, I seal you in my love.

11 | INVOKING THE WILL TO BE MORE THAN NORMAL!

In the name I AM THAT I AM, Jesus Christ, I call to all ascended masters working on manifesting the Golden Age, especially Archangel Gabriel, Elohim Astrea, Serapis Bey, Saint Germain and Shiva, to radiate into the collective consciousness the will to be more than normal human beings. Help people see that we can build a new future by working with the ascended masters and letting go of the old way of looking at life, including…

[Make personal calls.]

Part 1

1. Saint Germain, radiate into the collective consciousness the awareness that the greatest gift we can give to humanity is knowing the difference between what is real and what is unreal.

Gabriel Archangel, your light we revere,
immersed in your Presence, nothing we fear.
Disciples of Christ, we do leave behind,
the ego's desire for responding in kind.

Gabriel Archangel, of this we are sure,
Gabriel Archangel, Christ light is the cure.
Gabriel Archangel, intentions so pure,
Gabriel Archangel, in you we're secure.

2. Saint Germain, radiate into the collective consciousness the awareness that many people seem normal, but do not have any clue as to what is real and what is unreal.

Gabriel Archangel, we fear not the light,
in purifications' fire, we delight.
With your hand in ours, each challenge we face,
we follow the spiral to infinite grace.

Gabriel Archangel, of this we are sure,
Gabriel Archangel, Christ light is the cure.
Gabriel Archangel, intentions so pure,
Gabriel Archangel, in you we're secure.

3. Saint Germain, radiate into the collective consciousness the awareness that many people are absolutely sure what is real, yet what they think is real is not real at all.

Gabriel Archangel, your fire burning white,
ascending with you, out of the night.
The ego has nowhere to run and to hide,
in ascension's bright spiral, with you we abide.

11 | Invoking the will to be MORE than normal!

**Gabriel Archangel, of this we are sure,
Gabriel Archangel, Christ light is the cure.
Gabriel Archangel, intentions so pure,
Gabriel Archangel, in you we're secure.**

4. Saint Germain, radiate into the collective consciousness the awareness that these people do not think they need to change or learn anything. They are unreachable for a spiritual teacher, for they have become so convinced by the false teachers that they are sure that unreality is real.

Gabriel Archangel, your trumpet we hear,
announcing the birth of Christ drawing near.
In lightness of being, we now are reborn,
rising with Christ on bright Easter morn.

**Gabriel Archangel, of this we are sure,
Gabriel Archangel, Christ light is the cure.
Gabriel Archangel, intentions so pure,
Gabriel Archangel, in you we're secure.**

5. Saint Germain, radiate into the collective consciousness the awareness that the greatest threat to the freedom of humankind, the greatest hindrance to the bringing forth of the Golden Age of Aquarius, is the very subtle programming that we are supposed to be normal human beings.

Gabriel Archangel, the earth is now free,
embracing a nondual reality,
the judgment of Christ upon forces so dark,
who deny that all have a spiritual spark.

**Gabriel Archangel, of this we are sure,
Gabriel Archangel, Christ light is the cure.
Gabriel Archangel, intentions so pure,
Gabriel Archangel, in you we're secure.**

6. Saint Germain, radiate into the collective consciousness the awareness that this is an attempt by the dark forces and the power elite to put us in a box where we are so focused on following the norms defined by our society that we do not dare to challenge those norms.

Gabriel Archangel, with angels so white,
raising our planet out of the dark night,
as we now intone the Word of the Lord,
the beings who fell are bound by your sword.

**Gabriel Archangel, of this we are sure,
Gabriel Archangel, Christ light is the cure.
Gabriel Archangel, intentions so pure,
Gabriel Archangel, in you we're secure.**

7. Saint Germain, radiate into the collective consciousness the awareness that the members of the power elite do not want anyone to challenge the status quo that keeps the elite in control.

Gabriel Archangel, we call now to you,
the astral plane your light burning through,
entities, demons, discarnates are bound,
as you and we intone Sacred Sound.

**Gabriel Archangel, of this we are sure,
Gabriel Archangel, Christ light is the cure.
Gabriel Archangel, intentions so pure,
Gabriel Archangel, in you we're secure.**

8. Saint Germain, radiate into the collective consciousness the awareness that as long as we fit into the mold of a normal human being, we will not dare to fulfill our Divine plans, and certainly not dare to express our Christhood.

Gabriel Archangel, what glorious day,
your radiant angels have come here to stay,
your purifications fire burning white,
intentions so pure, our hearts taking flight.

**Gabriel Archangel, of this we are sure,
Gabriel Archangel, Christ light is the cure.
Gabriel Archangel, intentions so pure,
Gabriel Archangel, in you we're secure.**

9. Saint Germain, radiate into the collective consciousness the awareness that there has yet to be a society where being the Christ in action was considered normal by the powers that be.

Gabriel Archangel, our planet so pure,
in our bright new future we do feel secure,
with your band of light encircling the earth,
Saint Germain's Golden Age is now given birth.

**Gabriel Archangel, of this we are sure,
Gabriel Archangel, Christ light is the cure.
Gabriel Archangel, intentions so pure,
Gabriel Archangel, in you we're secure.**

Part 2

1. Saint Germain, radiate into the collective consciousness the awareness that the very deepest thing we can help you with is by being willing to challenge the ultimate illusion, the illusion of normality.

> Beloved Astrea, your heart is so true,
> your Circle and Sword of white and blue,
> cut all life free from dramas unwise,
> on wings of Purity our planet will rise.

> **Beloved Astrea, in oneness with you,**
> **your circle and sword of electric blue,**
> **with Purity's Light cutting right through,**
> **raising the earth into all that is true.**

2. Saint Germain, radiate into the collective consciousness the awareness that the average human being on this planet – the "normal" human being – has no conception whatsoever of what is real and what is unreal.

> Beloved Astrea, in God Purity,
> accelerate all of our life energy,
> we're rising beyond every impurity,
> as Purity's Light forever we see.

> **Beloved Astrea, in oneness with you,**
> **your circle and sword of electric blue,**
> **with Purity's Light cutting right through,**
> **raising the earth into all that is true.**

3. Saint Germain, radiate into the collective consciousness the awareness that people have been programmed to think that this material world and the conditions that we see right now are real and normal, and therefore should be preserved.

> Beloved Astrea, from Purity's Ray,
> send forth deliverance to all life today,
> acceleration to Purity, we are now free
> from all that is less than love's Purity.
>
> **Beloved Astrea, in oneness with you,**
> **your circle and sword of electric blue,**
> **with Purity's Light cutting right through,**
> **raising the earth into all that is true.**

4. Saint Germain, radiate into the collective consciousness the awareness that this is the programming of the power elite who want people to uphold the status quo that maintains their privilege and power.

> Beloved Astrea, accelerate us all,
> as for your deliverance we fervently call,
> set all life free from vision impure
> beyond fear and doubt, we're rising for sure.
>
> **Beloved Astrea, in oneness with you,**
> **your circle and sword of electric blue,**
> **with Purity's Light cutting right through,**
> **raising the earth into all that is true.**

5. Saint Germain, radiate into the collective consciousness the awareness that once an elite have set themselves up in positions of privilege and power, their main concern is not to lose it. That is why they seek to stop progress, inventions and new ideas.

> Beloved Astrea, we're willing to see,
> all of the lies that keep us unfree,
> we surrender all lies causing the fall,
> forever affirming the oneness of All.

> **Beloved Astrea, in oneness with you,**
> **your circle and sword of electric blue,**
> **with Purity's Light cutting right through,**
> **raising the earth into all that is true.**

6. Saint Germain, radiate into the collective consciousness the awareness that when the elite cannot stop the emergence of new ideas, they seek to prevent the population from embracing those ideas by using the weapon that we have to be normal. They say: This new idea is not normal. It is a cult, it is bad, it is dangerous.

> Beloved Astrea, accelerate life
> beyond all duality's struggle and strife,
> consume all division between God and man,
> accelerate fulfillment of God's perfect plan.

> **Beloved Astrea, in oneness with you,**
> **your circle and sword of electric blue,**
> **with Purity's Light cutting right through,**
> **raising the earth into all that is true.**

7. Saint Germain, radiate into the collective consciousness the awareness that if we are to fulfill our Divine plans, if we are to manifest our Christhood and help Saint Germain bring in the Golden Age, then we have to overcome all attachment to being normal.

> Beloved Astrea, we lovingly call,
> break down separation's invisible wall,
> raising our minds into true unity
> with the Masters of love in Infinity.
>
> **Beloved Astrea, in oneness with you,**
> **your circle and sword of electric blue,**
> **with Purity's Light cutting right through,**
> **raising the earth into all that is true.**

8. Saint Germain, radiate into the collective consciousness the awareness that we must evaluate whether we are more concerned about being seen as normal by society or whether we are concerned about fulfilling our Divine plans.

> Beloved Astrea, help all of us find,
> the secret that we create with the mind,
> and thus what in ignorance we decreate,
> in knowledge we easily can recreate.
>
> **Beloved Astrea, in oneness with you,**
> **your circle and sword of electric blue,**
> **with Purity's Light cutting right through,**
> **raising the earth into all that is true.**

9. Saint Germain, radiate into the collective consciousness the awareness that being the Christ does not mean that we are insane. It does mean that we are willing to go beyond the norm, even to do things that for "normal" people might appear to be abnormal.

> Beloved Astrea, we all do aspire,
> to learning to use your purity's fire,
> to raise every form in infamy sown,
> as Saint Germain makes this planet his own.
>
> **Beloved Astrea, in oneness with you,**
> **your circle and sword of electric blue,**
> **with Purity's Light cutting right through,**
> **raising the earth into all that is true.**

Part 3

1. Saint Germain, radiate into the collective consciousness the awareness that we cannot allow any outside force to cause us to abort our mission, especially not the force of normality.

> Serapis Bey, what power lies,
> behind your purifying eyes.
> Serapis Bey, it is a treat,
> to enter your sublime retreat.
>
> **Serapis Bey, we call to you,**
> **to help us dual lies see through,**
> **come purify our inner sight,**
> **we see the earth in your great light.**

2. Saint Germain, radiate into the collective consciousness the awareness that we cannot put the Holy Spirit in a box. There is no standard for how the Holy Spirit should express itself in this world.

> Serapis Bey, what wisdom found,
> your words are always most profound.
> Serapis Bey, we tell you true,
> our minds have room for naught but you.

Serapis Bey, we call to you,
to help us dual lies see through,
come purify our inner sight,
we see the earth in your great light.

3. Saint Germain, radiate into the collective consciousness the awareness that when the Holy Spirit flows, it seeks to set people free from their mental boxes, and thus it must challenge their standard for what is normal.

> Serapis Bey, what love beyond,
> our hearts do leap, as we respond.
> Serapis Bey, your life a poem,
> that calls us to our starry home.

Serapis Bey, we call to you,
to help us dual lies see through,
come purify our inner sight,
we see the earth in your great light.

4. Saint Germain, radiate into the collective consciousness the awareness that when a critical mass of people in a society have come to believe in a certain standard for what is normal human behavior, they need to see someone who is willing to defy the standard of normality by shattering the boundaries that are set up by the norm.

> Serapis Bey, your guidance sure,
> our base is clear and white and pure.
> Serapis Bey, no longer trapped,
> by soul in which the self was wrapped.

> **Serapis Bey, we call to you,**
> **to help us dual lies see through,**
> **come purify our inner sight,**
> **we see the earth in your great light.**

5. Saint Germain, radiate into the collective consciousness the awareness that being normal means that we accept boundaries for who we are, what we can be and how we can express ourselves as long as we want to be accepted members of society.

> Serapis Bey, what healing balm,
> in mind that is forever calm.
> Serapis Bey, our thoughts are pure,
> your discipline we shall endure.

> **Serapis Bey, we call to you,**
> **to help us dual lies see through,**
> **come purify our inner sight,**
> **we see the earth in your great light.**

6. Saint Germain, radiate into the collective consciousness the awareness that the job of the Living Christ in embodiment is to challenge people's sense of what is normal, which is what Jesus did.

Serapis Bey, what secret test,
for egos who want to be best.
Serapis Bey, expose the "me,"
that takes away our harmony.

**Serapis Bey, we call to you,
to help us dual lies see through,
come purify our inner sight,
we see the earth in your great light.**

7. Saint Germain, radiate into the collective consciousness the awareness that with the human consciousness, with a standard for what is normal, we must accept that there are boundaries and limitations for what can be achieved.

Serapis Bey, what moving sight,
the self ascends to sacred height.
Serapis Bey, forever free,
in sacred synchronicity.

**Serapis Bey, we call to you,
to help us dual lies see through,
come purify our inner sight,
we see the earth in your great light.**

8. Saint Germain, radiate into the collective consciousness the awareness that this is precisely what members of the power elite use to maintain status quo by getting people to believe in the lie that there are certain problems that cannot be solved, or even certain conditions that are natural and normal.

> Serapis Bey, you balance all,
> the seven rays upon our call.
> Serapis Bey, in space and time,
> the pyramid of self, we climb.

> **Serapis Bey, we call to you,**
> **to help us dual lies see through,**
> **come purify our inner sight,**
> **we see the earth in your great light.**

9. Saint Germain, radiate into the collective consciousness the awareness that in reality, there is no norm, there is no standard because the Creator has created billions of expressions of itself, each one of which is unique in God. There are no norms in individuality, no standard in uniqueness.

> Serapis Bey, your Presence here,
> filling up the inner sphere.
> Life is now a sacred flow,
> God Purity we do bestow.

> **Serapis Bey, we call to you,**
> **to help us dual lies see through,**
> **come purify our inner sight,**
> **we see the earth in your great light.**

Part 4

1. Saint Germain, radiate into the collective consciousness the awareness that we need to create a new spiritual movement that does not define a standard for how one is supposed to behave in order to be saved.

> O Saint Germain, you do inspire,
> my vision raised forever higher,
> with you I form a figure-eight,
> your Golden Age I co-create.

> **O Saint Germain, what love you bring,**
> **it truly makes all matter sing,**
> **your violet flame does all restore,**
> **with you we are becoming more.**

2. Saint Germain, radiate into the collective consciousness the awareness that we need to make people feel that they are welcomed and accepted for who they are right now because we have no standard for what is normal, for what is lovable. We have transcended the conditional love and come to the point where we have unconditional love for all life.

> O Saint Germain, what Freedom Flame,
> released when we recite your name,
> acceleration is your gift,
> our planet it will surely lift.

**O Saint Germain, what love you bring,
it truly makes all matter sing,
your violet flame does all restore,
with you we are becoming more.**

3. Saint Germain, radiate into the collective consciousness the awareness that the only way to have unconditional love is to have no conditions, meaning that we have no expectations of how people should or should not behave. We have no standard for what is normal or what is acceptable behavior.

O Saint Germain, in love we claim,
our right to bring your violet flame,
from you Above, to us below,
it is an all-transforming flow.

**O Saint Germain, what love you bring,
it truly makes all matter sing,
your violet flame does all restore,
with you we are becoming more.**

4. Saint Germain, radiate into the collective consciousness the awareness that every human being is in a certain state of consciousness. There is no need to judge with the outer mind. We accept people for who they are right now and give them room to grow.

O Saint Germain, I love you so,
my aura filled with violet glow,
my chakras filled with violet fire,
I am your cosmic amplifier.

**O Saint Germain, what love you bring,
it truly makes all matter sing,
your violet flame does all restore,
with you we are becoming more.**

5. Saint Germain, radiate into the collective consciousness the awareness that virtually every religion on this planet has fallen prey to the dualistic consciousness of setting up a norm for what it means to be a member of that religion.

O Saint Germain, I am now free,
your violet flame is therapy,
transform all hang-ups in my mind,
as inner peace I surely find.

**O Saint Germain, what love you bring,
it truly makes all matter sing,
your violet flame does all restore,
with you we are becoming more.**

6. Saint Germain, radiate into the collective consciousness the awareness that many people have rejected religion because they did not feel welcomed. In the Aquarian Age, religion is supposed to transcend itself, to transcend the old judgmental mindset.

O Saint Germain, my body pure,
your violet flame for all is cure,
consume the cause of all disease,
and therefore I am all at ease.

> **O Saint Germain, what love you bring,**
> **it truly makes all matter sing,**
> **your violet flame does all restore,**
> **with you we are becoming more.**

7. Saint Germain, radiate into the collective consciousness the awareness that it is possible for people who have obtained some Christ discernment, to fall prey to the subtle temptations of the serpentine mind, namely to use the Christ discernment to set up a standard whereby we judge other people.

> O Saint Germain, I'm karma-free,
> the past no longer burdens me,
> a brand new opportunity,
> I am in Christic unity.

> **O Saint Germain, what love you bring,**
> **it truly makes all matter sing,**
> **your violet flame does all restore,**
> **with you we are becoming more.**

8. Saint Germain, radiate into the collective consciousness the awareness that we need to question the norm so we do not carry the norms of our society with us unquestioned, whereby we will unconsciously color our Christ discernment by the norms of society.

> O Saint Germain, we are now one,
> I am for you a violet sun,
> as we transform this planet earth,
> your Golden Age is given birth.

**O Saint Germain, what love you bring,
it truly makes all matter sing,
your violet flame does all restore,
with you we are becoming more.**

9. Saint Germain, radiate into the collective consciousness the awareness that when we see what is real and unreal, we see beyond the outer appearances that create differences and conflicts, and we see the underlying oneness of all life.

O Saint Germain, the earth is free,
from burden of duality,
in oneness we bring what is best,
your Golden Age is manifest.

**O Saint Germain, what love you bring,
it truly makes all matter sing,
your violet flame does all restore,
with you we are becoming more.**

Part 5

1. Saint Germain, radiate into the collective consciousness the awareness that what is considered normal behavior in present society is a standard that is entirely based on duality. It therefore confirms the lie that all people are separate beings and are beyond being united in oneness.

O Shiva, God of Sacred Fire,
It's time to let the past expire,
I want to rise above the old,
a golden future to unfold.

O Shiva, clear the energy,
O Shiva, bring the synergy,
O Shiva, make all demons flee,
O Shiva, bring back peace to me.

2. Saint Germain, radiate into the collective consciousness the awareness that we need to question the norm, question the unquestionable, think the unthinkable, accept the unacceptable. We need to dare to be here below all that we already are Above.

O Shiva, come and set me free,
from forces that do limit me,
with fire consume all that is less,
paving way for my success.

O Shiva, clear the energy,
O Shiva, bring the synergy,
O Shiva, make all demons flee,
O Shiva, bring back peace to me.

3. Saint Germain, radiate into the collective consciousness the awareness that we need to accept a new norm, which is that we are spiritual beings and that it is normal and right for us to express our spirituality. There is no norm in this world that is going to stop us from expressing our spirituality, even if it means that some people think we are crazy.

> O Shiva, Maya's veil disperse,
> clear my private universe,
> dispel the consciousness of death,
> consume it with your Sacred Breath.
>
> **O Shiva, clear the energy,**
> **O Shiva, bring the synergy,**
> **O Shiva, make all demons flee,**
> **O Shiva, bring back peace to me.**

4. Saint Germain, radiate into the collective consciousness the awareness that we need to dare to speak out in ways that will challenge other people and therefore cause them to go into the default reaction of the ego—of saying that there must be something wrong with us.

> O Shiva, I hereby let go,
> of all attachments here below,
> addictive entities consume,
> the upward path I do resume.
>
> **O Shiva, clear the energy,**
> **O Shiva, bring the synergy,**
> **O Shiva, make all demons flee,**
> **O Shiva, bring back peace to me.**

5. Saint Germain, radiate into the collective consciousness the awareness that being normal in our society takes away our need to take responsibility for ourselves, to discover who we are and to dare to express who we are.

O Shiva, I recite your name,
come banish fear and doubt and shame,
with fire expose within my mind,
what ego seeks to hide behind.

**O Shiva, clear the energy,
O Shiva, bring the synergy,
O Shiva, make all demons flee,
O Shiva, bring back peace to me.**

6. Saint Germain, radiate into the collective consciousness the awareness that the members of the power elite want us to be normal and flow along with the mass consciousness. This is a very easy and comfortable way to live, for we do not really need to think. The norm has done all the thinking for us.

O Shiva, I am not afraid,
my karmic debt hereby is paid,
the past no longer owns my choice,
in breath of Shiva I rejoice.

**O Shiva, clear the energy,
O Shiva, bring the synergy,
O Shiva, make all demons flee,
O Shiva, bring back peace to me.**

7. Saint Germain, radiate into the collective consciousness the awareness that if we have conditions that prevent us from expressing love to others, behind it is a condition that also prevents us from accepting God's love for ourselves.

O Shiva, show me spirit pairs,
that keep me trapped in their affairs,
I choose to see within my mind,
the spirits that you surely bind.

O Shiva, clear the energy,
O Shiva, bring the synergy,
O Shiva, make all demons flee,
O Shiva, bring back peace to me.

8. Saint Germain, radiate into the collective consciousness the awareness that this condition causes us to judge ourselves according to the norm, to the standard. This prevents us from being who we are and achieving that victory of being here below all that we are Above.

O Shiva, naked I now stand,
my mind in freedom does expand,
as all my ghosts I do release,
surrender is the key to peace.

O Shiva, clear the energy,
O Shiva, bring the synergy,
O Shiva, make all demons flee,
O Shiva, bring back peace to me.

9. Saint Germain, radiate into the collective consciousness the awareness that when we seek the Kingdom of God within, we will strive for a higher norm. This is the norm of being unique in God, even in this world where everything is arrayed against the expression of our uniqueness.

O Shiva, all-consuming fire,
with Parvati raise me higher,
when I am raised your light to see,
all men I will draw onto me.

O Shiva, clear the energy,
O Shiva, bring the synergy,
O Shiva, make all demons flee,
O Shiva, bring back peace to me.

Sealing

In the name of the Divine Mother, I call to all ascended masters for the sealing of myself and all people in my circle of influence in the creative flow of the Divine Mother, the River of Life. I call for the multiplication of my calls by all ascended masters so that we form the perfect figure-eight flow of "As Above, so below." Thus, I accept that this is fully manifest, because the mouth of the Lord, the Divine Mother that I AM, has spoken it. Amen.

12 | POLITICS AND EDUCATION IN THE GOLDEN AGE

Most gracious ladies and gentlemen, I Saint Germain come today on a lighter note than the previous days. Truly, you have broken through to a higher level of consciousness and you have been instrumental in breaking through the density found here in this area of Los Angeles, and in California as well. Thereby, you are giving the people in this area an opportunity to rise higher, to think more clearly than they have been able to think for a very long time.

I must tell you that there is no power greater – currently available – than the invocations of Mother Mary. There is a power in these invocations that is unsurpassed by any other spiritual technique—for the very reason that they embody the Alpha and the Omega of God. You have both the affirmations and the rhythmic sections that are repeated, thereby invoking the light and directing it through the affirmations to the specific conditions.

The Word will judge the elite

Beyond that is an even more important facet of the invocations. Is it not stated in this latest invocation that the Word itself will judge the power elite and those who are not willing to change their consciousness? You see, there is immense value in someone in the physical octave being willing to speak the Word physically as you do in these invocations. When you speak that Word, the Word will reverberate through the mass consciousness, and it will be a judgment in the sense that people are given an opportunity – even if they are not consciously aware of this – to accept or reject the Word spoken.

You will see that there are rings upon rings, spreading through the waters of the collective consciousness. As people are hit with a wave of the Word spoken, some will wake up and realize that a new day has dawned. Others will become even more anchored in the rigidity of their consciousness by rejecting the new wave, the new ideas, the new energies of Aquarius.

The need to overcome division in society

My beloved, the message that I want to give this morning is to comment further on the potential for the spreading of a new awareness from this area of California. The one area where there needs to be a new awareness in the United States is in the fact that in a Golden Age there is no division in society. In a Golden Age, precisely what makes it golden is that there has been attained a state of oneness in society.

This, of course, has many facets and many aspects. Of particular importance is the realization in the people that the power elite has always used the divide-and-conquer strategy to divide the people into warring groups and set them up against

12 | Politics and education in the Golden Age

each other. This division of society takes many forms, but one of the most important ones to expose and transcend in this age is the division between science and religion—between spirit and matter.

This nation is founded on the principle that all people were given inalienable rights by their Creator. Meaning that there is a higher authority than any authority on earth, be it the President, Congress or the hidden elite that seeks to rule society behind surface appearances. If the respect for a higher authority erodes, well, then the freedoms that are described in the United States' constitution will also be eroded and taken away from the people. There simply is no way around this. It is one of those instances where – even though I am not in black-and-white thinking – I must tell you that the issue is either-or. Either you have respect for an authority beyond any human power or institution, or your freedoms will be eroded, slowly but surely.

Uniting science and religion

How can we, in the current climate of the United States, preserve or rather reinvigorate that respect for some higher authority that cannot be manipulated by the power elite, the human ego, the duality consciousness? Well, it cannot be done as long as science and religion are divided and therefore present two opposing views of the creation of life, the existence of life. It is not a matter of restoring religion to a dominant role in American society. As many people in America are aware, the founding fathers were very aware of the potential that religion could become a factor for control—as they saw that it had been in Europe for centuries. They wanted to set up a constitution where one particular religion could not dominate and control the government. This has led to the emergence of scientific materialism, which denies anything beyond the material universe. By its very nature, it must deny the existence of any higher authority that could give people rights that are beyond being taken away by any institution on earth. Therefore, science is, in its current form of materialism, in direct opposition to the freedoms of the United States' constitution. Even though it must also be said that religion, in its traditional form of being an exclusivist religion claiming to have the only truth, is also in opposition to the freedoms of the U.S. Constitution.

This is the divide-and-conquer strategy of dividing society into those who see themselves as religious in the traditional sense, and those who see themselves as scientifically minded, therefore being materialists or atheists. It is an illusion to believe that you can preserve freedom in an atheistic or materialistic society. There are those who are unwilling to see this truth. They believe that atheists can be moral people and ethical people. While this is true, I must tell you that it is not possible to preserve freedom in an atheistic society. If you want to see proof of this, then look to the Soviet Union or China. Any reasonable person will be willing to admit that in an atheistic philosophy and ideology, freedom *will* be taken away by the state, for there is no higher authority than the state in those societies.

You can also look at history and look at how the Catholic Church in Europe kept that continent in the Dark Ages for centuries through the control of the Pope and the Catholic hierarchy. You can see that you cannot allow one religion to dominate a society, for then suddenly that religion takes the place of the state. Now there is no higher authority than the Catholic Church. Even though it claims to be the church of Christ – claiming that the Pope is the vicar of Christ – any reasonable person willing to look at history will see that this

12 | Politics and education in the Golden Age

clearly was not the case during the Middle Ages. Certainly, Christ could not have condoned the warring, the torture, the Inquisition and the many other abuses of power.

Universal spirituality beyond all religions

What do we do in this day and age to bring forth a society based on a view of life, based on a paradigm, that is neither traditional religion nor materialism? It transcends these two dualistic opposites, and comes into a higher understanding of the origin of life and the purpose of life. The only solution is Christ discernment that leads to the recognition that behind the outer religions is a deeper understanding of spirituality, a deeper approach, that is universal in nature and that runs like an ever-flowing stream. Every once in a while, someone has been able to dip into that stream and bring a teaching into the physical.

Although the teaching came from the stream, and thus has some validity, the teaching could, from the very beginning, be colored by the culture and the mindset of the people to whom it was given. The teaching could also follow the pattern that you see in almost every religion of gradually becoming rigid, therefore not flowing along with the stream. It is necessary that a critical mass of people in this age become able to look beyond the outer religions and see the universal stream flowing behind all surface appearances. These are the people who are already well aware of the weaknesses of traditional religion. They have not yet quite seen that instead of rejecting all spirituality and religion – jumping into the opposite dualistic polarity of materialism – there is an alternative. It is to transcend duality and lock in to the ever-flowing River of Life—thereby bringing forth a universal spirituality that will not violate the separation of church and state that the founding fathers correctly saw as necessary.

In other words, as we have explained before, the separation of church and state does not mean the separation of spirituality and the state. Again, there must be that recognition of a higher authority, a higher truth, which is the Logos, and the truth of the Logos can be brought forth through the Living Word.

Oracles in the Aquarian age

In past ages you have seen societies where there was much more of a unity between spirituality and government, in the sense that even the rulers of the people would listen to certain prophets, oracles or seers, who would bring forth the Living Word from the Logos itself. We are not looking in the Aquarian age to recreate a society like that, in the sense that there was only one or a few oracles or prophets.

We are looking, in the Aquarian age, to establish a society where at least the top 10 percent of the people all have such Christ discernment that they can recognize the Living Word and be the open doors for the Living Word to stream forth. This is not necessarily as you hear it now spoken in a dictation, but many times spoken in situations in life, such as in the Senate, Congress, political debates or the media. You have people who dare to speak out with the power and the truth of the Holy Spirit. You have people who hear this and who recognize the truth and the validity of the Word itself, regardless of whether they understand where it is coming from.

In other words, I Saint Germain am the hierarch of the Aquarian age, but I am not on an ego trip, my beloved. I do not need all people on earth to recognize the existence and the reality of Saint Germain or to worship me as some kind of God. I only need people to tune in to the universal reality, the truth of the Living Word that resonates in their hearts and their inner beings. Therefore, they are willing to bring that truth into the physical and let it be the guideline for every aspect of society and their personal lives. Their personal lives are in alignment with their own higher beings. Society is in alignment with the higher reality that is beyond what any human mind can conceive in its fullness.

This creates a society where there is no single individual or institution that can control society. The power elite can suppress the Living Word, they can distort the dead word that has been created by the suppression of the Living Word, but as long as the Living Word is flowing through a sufficient number of people, they cannot destroy or distort that Word. The Living Word cannot be put in a box, and it will always challenge status quo—and thereby challenge society and individuals to come up higher in consciousness.

Elitism as a driving force in history

Precisely because, as I have explained earlier, there are so many people embodied in the state of California who are close to the level of consciousness that is needed, there is the potential that California can become the forerunner for this new awareness, this new mindset, this new way of looking at life. It can even come in the form of a new analysis of history where you simply look at history and recognize the existence of a power elite whose members are blinded and controlled by the human ego. Therefore, through the outplaying of this psychological mechanism, they have attempted to dominate the population for thousands of years. By the population becoming aware of this mechanism, even that in itself will bring forth a new day where the power elite cannot rule behind the scenes. I tell you that the power elite can only rule when they can stay hidden from the people. Once they are exposed, then the people will no longer accept the elite, will no longer accept the lies that allow the elite to stay in power by manipulating the situation.

A new approach to politics

As a couple of examples of how this can outplay itself, let me start with the political situation. There are people in these United States who have become so attached to a conservative agenda that they see California as a threat because they see it as a liberal state. There are literally people who wish that California would slide into the ocean. They are so threatened in their conservative political beliefs that they are literally willing to see millions of people die so that they can preserve what they believe is the only true politics of the United States. Truly, it is the politics of the elite wanting to maintain status quo.

On the other hand, it must be recognized that liberalism is not the answer, for it is just another dualistic extreme. I do not look to California to secede from the Union. I do look to California to come up higher, to come beyond duality. I look for it to find a new approach to politics that transcends the traditional two-party system, and therefore becomes a catalyst that will spread throughout the nation. By California going beyond the conservative-liberal duality and finding a new balance, well, then California will no longer be seen as a liberal, New Age state. It will be seen as having found a new approach, a balanced approach.

What can be started here in this state can spread, for certainly there are people in every state that are attuned to the new energies and the consciousness of Aquarius. It is my hope that

12 | Politics and education in the Golden Age

California can transcend duality in politics and find its highest potential in a balanced middle-way approach to politics. The middle way is not the midpoint between liberal and conservative; it is transcending the duality of liberalism and conservatism, thereby finding a new approach.

I am not necessarily saying that there needs to be the emergence of a new political party, although this is certainly one way to solve the current gridlock. It can also be possible that the people will take command over their traditional parties and demand that those parties stop being the parties for the elite, and get back to being what they should have been all along—namely the parties of the people.

The need for a new type of politician

My beloved, there is an immense potential for new creative solutions to be brought forth. There are people in embodiment who have the expertise and the intimate knowledge of the political system, the economic system and every aspect of society. Again, we do not look for this to come from one central authority. We do look to you who are the most spiritually aware people to hold the immaculate concept that those who have the expertise will emerge and dare to speak out, dare to go beyond the norm and become a different kind of politician. Politicians who are not following the norms (that have been established now by the power elite for many a decade) for how a politician should behave in order to get along in the political system.

You have seen a few people who have had the courage to go beyond the norm. You have even seen some of the candidates that are now running for President and how the people have responded to those who are willing to go beyond established politics and bring a wave of fresh air. I tell you that there are candidates that are not even in the running right now because the shift in consciousness has not reached the point where they can be recognized or where they will even have the courage to stand out and bring a new form of politics.

You have seen in the state of California how the people rejected a governor who represented everything that was wrong with the old ways of politics – the corruption and the wheeling and dealing – and instead elected a governor who was more of the people because he was not part of the political establishment. Although this governor does not embody everything I am talking about – because he tends to imitate rather than being attuned and being the open door for creative ideas – yet I tell you that it is a step in the right direction.

If the people will keep thinking beyond the traditional extremes, then there are already other candidates who can quickly emerge and bring California to an even higher level of the willingness to go beyond traditional politics. They have the willingness to admit that things are simply not working in the traditional way, and we need new solutions and we need the people who dare to bring forth those solutions.

Education in the Aquarian age

One other area that I wish to comment on is the area of education. My beloved, for a very long time there has been a tendency among spiritual and religious people to think that the only way to renew education is to create private schools that are based on religious or spiritual principles. You have even seen a certain initiative from the Bush administration to give more funding to private schools. I wish to throw an idea into

12 | Politics and education in the Golden Age

your minds. I wish you to consider whether going with private schools is really the way of the Aquarian age?

Can you not see – when you look at history, especially the history of England – how private schools can very easily become a breeding ground for elitism? Those who can afford to send their children to private schools tend to have an elitist attitude. They tend to want their children to be brought up feeling that they are above and beyond the general population. There is a value in a public school system that throws together people from all walks of society. The classroom becomes a miniature of what these United States are supposed to be— namely a melting pot where we mix everyone together so that we can get beyond the rigidity of the elitist systems that we have seen in the past. I point to an alternative to devoting your attention and your creative energy into creating private schools.

I must tell you that there are educators who are familiar with the ascended masters' teachings, and who have some very good ideas for how education can be renewed. Yet if you keep focusing on creating private schools (that quite frankly do not currently have a realistic potential for spreading across the nation), then you are in essence chasing the pot of gold at the end of the rainbow. I must tell you that your energies and your attention could be used in a more constructive – in a more practical, realistic – manner by seeing the private school as a testing ground for ideas that could then be implemented in the public school systems.

This will mean that you will have to create schools that are not based on a particular spiritual belief system, even the ascended master belief system, but have found a more universal approach to spirituality that can eventually become acceptable in the public school system. As I have said, if we need a more universal spirituality in government, well, then we certainly also need it in education. For it to ever become acceptable, it must be universal and not focused on specific people or specific doctrines or dogmas, or even a specific belief system.

Let go of the dream of an ultimate system

Once again, I hurl the challenge at you to be willing to question everything. I tell you that even the spiritual people can have a tendency to become rigid. They are thinking that now we have found the highest expression of truth, and thus we do not really need to dip into the universal stream, the River of Life, to bring forth an even higher expression, or an even higher application of it for practical matters in society.

As I have explained, there is no standing still. The River of Life moves on. There is no ultimate system of government or education that could ever be brought forth on this planet. My beloved, as I attempted to explain yesterday, when those who are the leaders of a Golden Age society begin to believe that they have found some ultimate system – and that they are the elite who are now seeing it as their job to maintain the system – well, at that point the Golden Age society begins to stagnate and the collapse is only a matter of time.

Thus, let go of the dream of an ultimate educational system, an ultimate state of the economy, an ultimate political system! It will never happen on earth! It is a dualistic dream projected onto the people by those who are trapped in the serpentine consciousness and are attempting to take heaven by force and establish paradise on earth. In reality, this cannot happen as a static society, but only by creating a society that is constantly transcending itself. Thereby, we are raising up the earth to become part of the spiritual realm, as the entire material sphere ascends, as described in Maitreya's book. This is a fundamentally different approach than chasing the pipe dream of some static state of perfection in this realm.

My closing thought for this discourse is to hurl at you the challenge to recognize that in a golden age society, nothing stands still. Thus, you cannot be attached to anything. You cannot allow yourself to believe that: "Oh if we only achieve this particular state of education, or this particular state of a religious movement, or this particular political system, then we don't need to be alert anymore."

My beloved, the reality of it is that there is no stillstand in Christhood. There is no getting comfortable in Christhood. Christhood is an ongoing process of flowing with the River of Life. When you accept this, you can find peace in constant self-transcendence, rather than seeking to establish the false peace of stopping the growth and maintaining status quo. You think that status quo can give you peace when in reality it is only by being in – and being one with – the River of Life that you will ever find peace.

Thus, I thank you for your attention and for providing the platform for this release of teachings. They must be spoken in the physical for them to have the maximum impact on the collective consciousness. I seal you for now, until I shall return again shortly.

13 | INVOKING THE POLITICS AND EDUCATION OF THE GOLDEN AGE

In the name I AM THAT I AM, Jesus Christ, I call to all ascended masters working on manifesting the Golden Age, especially Archangel Raphael, Elohim Cyclopea, Master Hilarion, Saint Germain, the Divine Director and Surya, to radiate into the collective consciousness a vision of the politics and education of the Golden Age. Help people see that we can build a new future by working with the ascended masters and letting go of the old way of looking at life, including…

[Make personal calls.]

Part 1

1. Saint Germain, radiate into the collective consciousness the awareness that there is immense value in someone in the physical octave being willing to speak the Word. When we do, the Word will reverberate through the mass consciousness, and it will be a judgment in the sense that people are given an opportunity to accept or reject the Word spoken.

> Raphael Archangel, your light so intense,
> raise us beyond all human pretense.
> Mother Mary and you have a vision so bold,
> to see that our highest potential unfold.
>
> **Raphael Archangel, for vision we pray,**
> **Raphael Archangel, show us the way,**
> **Raphael Archangel, your emerald ray,**
> **Raphael Archangel, our lives a new day.**

2. Saint Germain, radiate into the collective consciousness the awareness that in a Golden Age there is no division in society. What makes it golden is that there has been attained a state of oneness in society.

> Raphael Archangel, in emerald sphere,
> to immaculate vision we always adhere.
> Mother Mary enfolds us in her Sacred Heart,
> from Mother's true love, we're never apart.

**Raphael Archangel, for vision we pray,
Raphael Archangel, show us the way,
Raphael Archangel, your emerald ray,
Raphael Archangel, our lives a new day.**

3. Saint Germain, radiate into the collective consciousness the awareness that the members of the power elite have always used the divide-and-conquer strategy to split the people into warring groups and set them up against each other.

Raphael Archangel, all ailments you heal,
each cell in our bodies in light now you seal.
Mother Mary's immaculate concept we see,
perfection of health our new reality.

**Raphael Archangel, for vision we pray,
Raphael Archangel, show us the way,
Raphael Archangel, your emerald ray,
Raphael Archangel, our lives a new day.**

4. Saint Germain, radiate into the collective consciousness the awareness that it is important to expose and transcend the division between science and religion—between spirit and matter.

Raphael Archangel, your light is so real,
the vision of Christ in us you reveal.
Mother Mary now helps us to truly transcend,
in emerald light with you we ascend.

**Raphael Archangel, for vision we pray,
Raphael Archangel, show us the way,
Raphael Archangel, your emerald ray,
Raphael Archangel, our lives a new day.**

5. Saint Germain, radiate into the collective consciousness the awareness that democracies are founded on the principle that all people were given inalienable rights by an authority that is higher than any authority on earth, be it the President, Congress or the hidden elite that seeks to rule society behind surface appearances.

> Raphael Archangel, diseases are done,
> as you help us see that all life is One,
> we no longer do your true love reject,
> immaculate vision on all we project.

> **Raphael Archangel, for vision we pray,**
> **Raphael Archangel, show us the way,**
> **Raphael Archangel, your emerald ray,**
> **Raphael Archangel, our lives a new day.**

6. Saint Germain, radiate into the collective consciousness the awareness that if the respect for a higher authority erodes, the freedoms that are described in a democratic constitution will also be eroded and taken away from the people.

> Raphael Archangel, we're healing the earth,
> in immaculate vision we give her rebirth,
> a new era has on this day begun,
> your emerald light now shines like a sun.

> **Raphael Archangel, for vision we pray,**
> **Raphael Archangel, show us the way,**
> **Raphael Archangel, your emerald ray,**
> **Raphael Archangel, our lives a new day.**

13 | Invoking the politics and education of the Golden Age

7. Saint Germain, radiate into the collective consciousness the awareness that preserving the respect for a higher authority cannot be done as long as science and religion are divided and therefore present two opposing views of the creation of life.

Raphael Archangel, the fall is behind,
as all of earth's people the Christ path do find,
we call now to you all people to heal,
as four lower bodies in love you do seal.

**Raphael Archangel, for vision we pray,
Raphael Archangel, show us the way,
Raphael Archangel, your emerald ray,
Raphael Archangel, our lives a new day.**

8. Saint Germain, radiate into the collective consciousness the awareness that it is not a matter of restoring religion to a dominant role in society. The founding fathers of democracy were aware of the potential that religion could become a factor for control.

Raphael Archangel, as you bring the light,
the forces of darkness swiftly take flight,
their day is now done as we claim the earth,
spreading to all an innocent mirth.

**Raphael Archangel, for vision we pray,
Raphael Archangel, show us the way,
Raphael Archangel, your emerald ray,
Raphael Archangel, our lives a new day.**

9. Saint Germain, radiate into the collective consciousness the awareness that scientific materialism, by its very nature, must deny the existence of any higher authority that could give people rights that are beyond being taken away by any institution on earth.

> Raphael Archangel, our vision set free,
> as we can now see God's reality,
> as Saint Germain's vision is manifest here,
> the earth is now sealed in immaculate sphere.
>
> **Raphael Archangel, for vision we pray,**
> **Raphael Archangel, show us the way,**
> **Raphael Archangel, your emerald ray,**
> **Raphael Archangel, our lives a new day.**

Part 2

1. Saint Germain, radiate into the collective consciousness the awareness that the current form of scientific materialism is in direct opposition to the freedoms of democratic institutions.

> Cyclopea so dear, the truth you reveal,
> the truth that duality's ailments will heal,
> your Emerald Light is like a great balm,
> our emotional bodies are perfectly calm.
>
> **Cyclopea so dear, in Emerald Sphere,**
> **in raising perception we shall persevere,**
> **as deep in our hearts your truth we revere,**
> **to immaculate vision the earth does adhere.**

13 | Invoking the politics and education of the Golden Age

2. Saint Germain, radiate into the collective consciousness the awareness that religion, in its traditional form of being an exclusivist religion claiming to have the only truth, is also in opposition to the freedoms of democracy.

> Cyclopea so dear, with you we unwind,
> all negative spirals clouding the mind,
> we know pure awareness is truly our core,
> the key to becoming the wide-open door.
>
> **Cyclopea so dear, in Emerald Sphere,**
> **in raising perception we shall persevere,**
> **as deep in our hearts your truth we revere,**
> **to immaculate vision the earth does adhere.**

3. Saint Germain, radiate into the collective consciousness the awareness that this is the divide-and-conquer strategy of dividing society into those who see themselves as religious in the traditional sense, and those who see themselves as scientifically minded, therefore being materialists or atheists.

> Cyclopea so dear, clear our inner sight,
> empowered, we pierce the soul's fearful night,
> we now see our life through your single eye,
> beyond all disease we're ready to fly.
>
> **Cyclopea so dear, in Emerald Sphere,**
> **in raising perception we shall persevere,**
> **as deep in our hearts your truth we revere,**
> **to immaculate vision the earth does adhere.**

4. Saint Germain, radiate into the collective consciousness the awareness that it is an illusion to believe that we can preserve freedom in an atheistic or materialistic society. It is not possible to preserve freedom in an atheistic society.

> Cyclopea so dear, life can only reflect,
> the images that the mind does project,
> the key to our healing is clearing the mind,
> from the images the ego is hiding behind.
>
> **Cyclopea so dear, in Emerald Sphere,**
> **in raising perception we shall persevere,**
> **as deep in our hearts your truth we revere,**
> **to immaculate vision the earth does adhere.**

5. Saint Germain, radiate into the collective consciousness the awareness that in an atheistic philosophy and ideology, freedom will be taken away by the state, for there is no higher authority than the state.

> Cyclopea so dear, we want to aim high,
> to your healing flame we ever draw nigh,
> through veils of duality we now take flight,
> bathed in your penetrating Emerald Light.
>
> **Cyclopea so dear, in Emerald Sphere,**
> **in raising perception we shall persevere,**
> **as deep in our hearts your truth we revere,**
> **to immaculate vision the earth does adhere.**

6. Saint Germain, radiate into the collective consciousness the awareness that we cannot allow one religion to dominate a society, for then that religion takes the place of the state.

13 | Invoking the politics and education of the Golden Age

> Cyclopea so dear, your Emerald Flame,
> exposes every subtle, dualistic power game,
> including the game of wanting to say,
> that truth is defined in only one way.
>
> **Cyclopea so dear, in Emerald Sphere,
> in raising perception we shall persevere,
> as deep in our hearts your truth we revere,
> to immaculate vision the earth does adhere.**

7. Saint Germain, radiate into the collective consciousness the awareness that we need to bring forth a society based on a paradigm that is neither traditional religion nor materialism, but transcends these two dualistic opposites and comes into a higher understanding of the origin of life and the purpose of life.

> Cyclopea so dear, we're feeling the flow,
> as your Living Truth upon us you bestow,
> from all dual vision we are now set free,
> planet earth in immaculate matrix will be.
>
> **Cyclopea so dear, in Emerald Sphere,
> in raising perception we shall persevere,
> as deep in our hearts your truth we revere,
> to immaculate vision the earth does adhere.**

8. Saint Germain, radiate into the collective consciousness the awareness that the only solution is Christ discernment that leads to the recognition that behind the outer religions is a deeper understanding of spirituality that is universal in nature and that runs like an ever-flowing stream.

Cyclopea so dear, the truth is now clear,
we see higher purpose for which we are here
we know truth transcends all systems below,
immersed in your light, we continue to grow.

**Cyclopea so dear, in Emerald Sphere,
in raising perception we shall persevere,
as deep in our hearts your truth we revere,
to immaculate vision the earth does adhere.**

9. Saint Germain, radiate into the collective consciousness the awareness that it is necessary that a critical mass of people become able to look beyond the outer religions and see the universal stream flowing behind all surface appearances.

Cyclopea so dear, we're feeling your joy,
as creative vision we now do employ,
in lifting earth out of serpentine cage,
to manifest Saint Germain's Golden Age.

**Cyclopea so dear, in Emerald Sphere,
in raising perception we shall persevere,
as deep in our hearts your truth we revere,
to immaculate vision the earth does adhere.**

Part 3

1. Saint Germain, radiate into the collective consciousness the awareness that the people who are already aware of the weaknesses of traditional religion need to see that instead of rejecting all spirituality and religion, the alternative is to transcend duality and lock in to the ever-flowing River of Life.

Hilarion, on emerald shore,
we're free from all that's gone before.
Hilarion, we let all go,
that keeps us out of sacred flow.

Hilarion, with light so green,
we see behind the matter screen,
immaculate our inner sight,
we see the earth is taking flight.

2. Saint Germain, radiate into the collective consciousness the awareness that it is possible to bring forth a universal spirituality that will not violate the separation of church and state that the founding fathers correctly saw as necessary.

Hilarion, the secret key,
is wisdom's own reality.
Hilarion, all life is healed,
the ego's face no more concealed.

Hilarion, with light so green,
we see behind the matter screen,
immaculate our inner sight,
we see the earth is taking flight.

3. Saint Germain, radiate into the collective consciousness the awareness that the separation of church and state does not mean the separation of spirituality and the state. There must be the recognition of a higher authority and that truth can be brought forth through the Living Word.

> Hilarion, your love for life,
> helps us surrender inner strife.
> Hilarion, your loving words,
> thrill our hearts like song of birds.

> **Hilarion, with light so green,**
> **we see behind the matter screen,**
> **immaculate our inner sight,**
> **we see the earth is taking flight.**

4. Saint Germain, radiate into the collective consciousness the awareness that we need to establish a society where at least the top 10 percent of the people all have such Christ discernment that they can recognize the Living Word and be the open doors for the Living Word to stream forth.

> Hilarion, invoke the light,
> your sacred formulas recite.
> Hilarion, your secret tone,
> philosopher's most sacred stone.

> **Hilarion, with light so green,**
> **we see behind the matter screen,**
> **immaculate our inner sight,**
> **we see the earth is taking flight.**

5. Saint Germain, radiate into the collective consciousness the awareness that some people need to dare to speak out with the power and the truth of the Holy Spirit, and others need to recognize the truth and the validity of the Word itself.

> Hilarion, with love you greet,
> us in your temple over Crete.
> Hilarion, your emerald light,
> the third eye sees with Christic sight.

> **Hilarion, with light so green,**
> **we see behind the matter screen,**
> **immaculate our inner sight,**
> **we see the earth is taking flight.**

6. Saint Germain, radiate into the collective consciousness the awareness that you do not need all people to recognize the existence and the reality of Saint Germain or to worship you as some kind of God. You need people to tune in to the universal reality, the truth of the Living Word that resonates in their hearts and their inner beings.

> Hilarion, you give us fruit,
> of truth that is so absolute.
> Hilarion, all stress decrease,
> as our ambitions we release.

> **Hilarion, with light so green,**
> **we see behind the matter screen,**
> **immaculate our inner sight,**
> **we see the earth is taking flight.**

7. Saint Germain, radiate into the collective consciousness the awareness that we need to bring that truth into the physical and let it be the guideline for every aspect of society and our personal lives. Our personal lives are in alignment with our own higher beings. Society is in alignment with the higher reality that is beyond what any human mind can conceive in its fullness.

> Hilarion, our chakras clear,
> as we let go of subtlest fear.
> Hilarion, we are sincere,
> as freedom's truth we do revere.
>
> **Hilarion, with light so green,**
> **we see behind the matter screen,**
> **immaculate our inner sight,**
> **we see the earth is taking flight.**

8. Saint Germain, radiate into the collective consciousness the awareness that we can create a society where there is no single individual or institution that can control society.

> Hilarion, you balance all,
> the seven rays upon our call.
> Hilarion, you keep us true,
> as we remain all one with you.
>
> **Hilarion, with light so green,**
> **we see behind the matter screen,**
> **immaculate our inner sight,**
> **we see the earth is taking flight.**

13 | Invoking the politics and education of the Golden Age

9. Saint Germain, radiate into the collective consciousness the awareness that the power elite can suppress the Living Word, they can distort the dead word that has been created by the suppression of the Living Word, but as long as the Living Word is flowing through a sufficient number of people, they cannot destroy or distort that Word.

> Hilarion, your Presence here,
> filling up the inner sphere.
> Life is now a sacred flow,
> God Vision we on all bestow.

> **Hilarion, with light so green,**
> **we see behind the matter screen,**
> **immaculate our inner sight,**
> **we see the earth is taking flight.**

Part 4

1. Saint Germain, radiate into the collective consciousness the awareness that the Living Word cannot be put in a box, and it will always challenge status quo. It will challenge society and individuals to come up higher in consciousness.

> O Saint Germain, you do inspire,
> my vision raised forever higher,
> with you I form a figure-eight,
> your Golden Age I co-create.

**O Saint Germain, what love you bring,
it truly makes all matter sing,
your violet flame does all restore,
with you we are becoming more.**

2. Saint Germain, radiate into the collective consciousness the awareness that we need to look at history and recognize the existence of a power elite that are blinded and controlled by the human ego. Through the outplaying of this psychological mechanism, they have attempted to dominate the population for thousands of years.

O Saint Germain, what Freedom Flame,
released when we recite your name,
acceleration is your gift,
our planet it will surely lift.

**O Saint Germain, what love you bring,
it truly makes all matter sing,
your violet flame does all restore,
with you we are becoming more.**

3. Saint Germain, radiate into the collective consciousness the awareness that by the population becoming aware of this mechanism, this will bring forth a new day where the members of the power elite cannot rule behind the scenes.

O Saint Germain, in love we claim,
our right to bring your violet flame,
from you Above, to us below,
it is an all-transforming flow.

**O Saint Germain, what love you bring,
it truly makes all matter sing,
your violet flame does all restore,
with you we are becoming more.**

4. Saint Germain, radiate into the collective consciousness the awareness that the members of the power elite can only rule when they can stay hidden from the people. Once they are exposed, the people will no longer accept the lies that allow the elite to stay in power by manipulating the situation.

O Saint Germain, I love you so,
my aura filled with violet glow,
my chakras filled with violet fire,
I am your cosmic amplifier.

**O Saint Germain, what love you bring,
it truly makes all matter sing,
your violet flame does all restore,
with you we are becoming more.**

5. Saint Germain, radiate into the collective consciousness the awareness that conservatism and liberalism are simply two dualistic extremes.

O Saint Germain, I am now free,
your violet flame is therapy,
transform all hang-ups in my mind,
as inner peace I surely find.

> O Saint Germain, what love you bring,
> it truly makes all matter sing,
> your violet flame does all restore,
> with you we are becoming more.

6. Saint Germain, radiate into the collective consciousness the awareness that we need to find a new approach to politics that transcends the traditional two-party system and therefore becomes a catalyst for change.

> O Saint Germain, my body pure,
> your violet flame for all is cure,
> consume the cause of all disease,
> and therefore I am all at ease.

> O Saint Germain, what love you bring,
> it truly makes all matter sing,
> your violet flame does all restore,
> with you we are becoming more.

7. Saint Germain, radiate into the collective consciousness the awareness that by going beyond the conservative-liberal duality, we can transcend duality in politics and find a balanced middle-way approach. This is not the midpoint between liberal and conservative; it is transcending the duality of liberalism and conservatism.

> O Saint Germain, I'm karma-free,
> the past no longer burdens me,
> a brand new opportunity,
> I am in Christic unity.

**O Saint Germain, what love you bring,
it truly makes all matter sing,
your violet flame does all restore,
with you we are becoming more.**

8. Saint Germain, radiate into the collective consciousness the awareness that this does not necessarily mean the emergence of a new political party. People can also take command over their traditional parties and demand that they stop being the parties for the elite and get back to being parties of the people.

O Saint Germain, we are now one,
I am for you a violet sun,
as we transform this planet earth,
your Golden Age is given birth.

**O Saint Germain, what love you bring,
it truly makes all matter sing,
your violet flame does all restore,
with you we are becoming more.**

9. Saint Germain, radiate into the collective consciousness the awareness that the most spiritually aware people need to hold the immaculate concept that those who have the expertise will emerge and dare to speak out, dare to go beyond the norm and become a different kind of politician.

O Saint Germain, the earth is free,
from burden of duality,
in oneness we bring what is best,
your Golden Age is manifest.

**O Saint Germain, what love you bring,
it truly makes all matter sing,
your violet flame does all restore,
with you we are becoming more.**

Part 5

1. Saint Germain, radiate into the collective consciousness the awareness that we need politicians who are not following the norms, established by the power elite, for how a politician should behave in order to get along in the political system.

> Divine Director, I now see,
> the world is unreality,
> in my heart I now truly feel,
> the Spirit is all that is real.

> **Divine Director, send the light,
> from blindness clear my inner sight,
> my vision free, my vision clear,
> your guidance is forever here.**

2. Saint Germain, radiate into the collective consciousness the awareness that there needs to be shift so that new candidates can be recognized and have the courage to stand out and bring a new form of politics.

> Divine Director, vision give,
> in clarity I want to live,
> I now behold my plan Divine,
> the plan that is uniquely mine.

**Divine Director, send the light,
from blindness clear my inner sight,
my vision free, my vision clear,
your guidance is forever here.**

3. Saint Germain, radiate into the collective consciousness the awareness that if the people will keep thinking beyond the traditional extremes, then there are already candidates who can quickly emerge and bring society to an even higher level of the willingness to go beyond traditional politics.

Divine Director, show in me,
the ego games, and set me free,
help me escape the ego's cage,
to help bring in the Golden Age.

**Divine Director, send the light,
from blindness clear my inner sight,
my vision free, my vision clear,
your guidance is forever here.**

4. Saint Germain, radiate into the collective consciousness the awareness that we need to admit that things are simply not working in the traditional way. We need new solutions and we need the people who dare to bring forth those solutions.

Divine Director, I'm with you,
my vision one, no longer two,
as karma's veil you do disperse,
I see a whole new universe.

**Divine Director, send the light,
from blindness clear my inner sight,
my vision free, my vision clear,
your guidance is forever here.**

5. Saint Germain, radiate into the collective consciousness the awareness that private schools can very easily become a breeding ground for elitism because those who can afford to send their children to private schools tend to have an elitist attitude.

Divine Director, I go up,
electric light now fills my cup,
consume in me all shadows old,
bestow on me a vision bold.

**Divine Director, send the light,
from blindness clear my inner sight,
my vision free, my vision clear,
your guidance is forever here.**

6. Saint Germain, radiate into the collective consciousness the awareness that there is a value in a public school system that throws together people from all walks of society.

Divine Director, heart of gold,
my sacred labor I unfold,
o blessed Guru, I now see,
where my own plan is taking me.

**Divine Director, send the light,
from blindness clear my inner sight,
my vision free, my vision clear,
your guidance is forever here.**

7. Saint Germain, radiate into the collective consciousness the awareness that we need to see private schools as a testing ground for ideas that could be implemented in the public school systems.

> Divine Director, by your grace,
> in grander scheme I find my place,
> my individual flame I see,
> uniqueness God has given me.
>
> **Divine Director, send the light,**
> **from blindness clear my inner sight,**
> **my vision free, my vision clear,**
> **your guidance is forever here.**

8. Saint Germain, radiate into the collective consciousness the awareness that we need to create schools that are not based on a particular spiritual belief system, but have found a more universal approach to spirituality that can eventually become acceptable in the public school system.

> Divine Director, vision one,
> I see that I AM God's own Sun,
> with your direction so Divine,
> I am now letting my light shine.
>
> **Divine Director, send the light,**
> **from blindness clear my inner sight,**
> **my vision free, my vision clear,**
> **your guidance is forever here.**

9. Saint Germain, radiate into the collective consciousness the awareness that we need a more universal spirituality in education. It must be universal and not focused on specific people or specific doctrines or dogmas, or even a specific belief system.

> Divine Director, what a gift,
> to be a part of Spirit's lift,
> to raise mankind out of the night,
> to bask in Spirit's loving sight.
>
> **Divine Director, send the light,**
> **from blindness clear my inner sight,**
> **my vision free, my vision clear,**
> **your guidance is forever here.**

Part 6

1. Saint Germain, radiate into the collective consciousness the awareness that even spiritual people have a tendency to become rigid, thinking that now we have found the highest expression of truth.

> Surya, cosmic being bright,
> your balance is my pure delight,
> I am in orbit round God Star,
> in perfect unity we are.
>
> **Surya, banish all extremes,**
> **Surya, shatter Serpent's schemes,**
> **Surya, balance to me bring,**
> **Surya, making my heart sing.**

13 | Invoking the politics and education of the Golden Age

2. Saint Germain, radiate into the collective consciousness the awareness that many people think we do not need to dip into the universal stream to bring forth an even higher expression, or an even higher application of it for practical matters in society. In reality, there is no ultimate system of government or education that could ever be brought forth on this planet.

> Surya, there is more to life,
> than human conflict, war and strife,
> your balance gives me inner peace,
> all outer conflicts do now cease.
>
> **Surya, banish all extremes,**
> **Surya, shatter Serpent's schemes,**
> **Surya, balance to me bring,**
> **Surya, making my heart sing.**

3. Saint Germain, radiate into the collective consciousness the awareness that when those who are the leaders of a Golden Age society begin to believe that they have found some ultimate system, society begins to stagnate and the collapse is only a matter of time.

> Surya, what a wondrous sight,
> from Sirius you send the light,
> of one mind, I now call to thee,
> for your apprentice I would be.
>
> **Surya, banish all extremes,**
> **Surya, shatter Serpent's schemes,**
> **Surya, balance to me bring,**
> **Surya, making my heart sing.**

4. Saint Germain, radiate into the collective consciousness the awareness that we need to let go of the dream of an ultimate educational system, an ultimate state of the economy, an ultimate political system.

> Surya, radiate your light,
> with balance you set all things right,
> consuming energetic dross,
> my letting go is not a loss.

> **Surya, banish all extremes,**
> **Surya, shatter Serpent's schemes,**
> **Surya, balance to me bring,**
> **Surya, making my heart sing.**

5. Saint Germain, radiate into the collective consciousness the awareness that the ultimate system will never happen on earth. It is a dualistic dream projected onto the people by those who are trapped in the serpentine consciousness and are attempting to take heaven by force and establish paradise on earth.

> Surya, your light is alive,
> for inner balance I do strive,
> the alchemy is now begun,
> my heart transformed into a sun.

> **Surya, banish all extremes,**
> **Surya, shatter Serpent's schemes,**
> **Surya, balance to me bring,**
> **Surya, making my heart sing.**

6. Saint Germain, radiate into the collective consciousness the awareness that heaven on earth cannot happen as a static society, but only by creating a society that is constantly transcending itself.

> Surya, come enlighten me,
> duality you help me see,
> extremes they cannot pull me in,
> on Middle Way I always win.
>
> **Surya, banish all extremes,**
> **Surya, shatter Serpent's schemes,**
> **Surya, balance to me bring,**
> **Surya, making my heart sing.**

7. Saint Germain, radiate into the collective consciousness the awareness that in a Golden Age, we are raising up the earth to become part of the spiritual realm. This is a fundamentally different approach than chasing the pipe dream of a static state of perfection in this realm.

> Surya, in your cosmic sphere,
> with Cuzco I your light revere,
> from your perspective o so grand,
> life finally I understand.
>
> **Surya, banish all extremes,**
> **Surya, shatter Serpent's schemes,**
> **Surya, balance to me bring,**
> **Surya, making my heart sing.**

8. Saint Germain, radiate into the collective consciousness the awareness that in a golden age society, nothing stands still. We cannot allow ourselves to believe that if we only achieve a particular form of education, religion or political system, then we don't need to be alert anymore.

> Surya, show me God's design,
> I see that God is all benign,
> you calm my feeling body's storm,
> I know the God beyond all form.
>
> **Surya, banish all extremes,**
> **Surya, shatter Serpent's schemes,**
> **Surya, balance to me bring,**
> **Surya, making my heart sing.**

9. Saint Germain, radiate into the collective consciousness the awareness that when we give up the desire for a static state, we can find peace in constant self-transcendence, rather than seeking to establish the false peace of stopping growth and maintaining status quo.

> Surya, I come from afar,
> and as you show me my home star,
> I see now my internal light,
> a star I am in my own right.
>
> **Surya, banish all extremes,**
> **Surya, shatter Serpent's schemes,**
> **Surya, balance to me bring,**
> **Surya, making my heart sing.**

Sealing

In the name of the Divine Mother, I call to all ascended masters for the sealing of myself and all people in my circle of influence in the creative flow of the Divine Mother, the River of Life. I call for the multiplication of my calls by all ascended masters so that we form the perfect figure-eight flow of "As Above, so below." Thus, I accept that this is fully manifest, because the mouth of the Lord, the Divine Mother that I AM, has spoken it. Amen.

14 | I CHALLENGE YOU TO RETHINK THE CONCEPT OF OWNERSHIP

I come again to give you the next chapter in this unfolding series of discourses, continuing with the theme of being willing to question everything. I must now bring to your attention the need to question one of the fundamental institutions of human society, indeed of human life on this planet, namely the very concept of ownership. My beloved, what can you really own on this planet where everything is so fleeting that it can be here today—gone tomorrow? What do you own when you come into this world? What can you take with you when you leave this world?

Well, what you *do* own – or at least what you ideally *should* own – when you come into this world is your own being, your own mind, your own psyche, your own soul. Then, as you spend time in this material realm, you grow in stature. When you leave, you take with you the growth that you have internalized—the wisdom, the love, the power that you have become. *That,* my beloved, is what you can take with you whereas you well know that you cannot take with you any material possessions.

Everything is made of God's light

There are many of you who are spiritual people and therefore are not as attached to money or material possessions as the people of the world, especially the elite. I encourage you to contemplate in your hearts a very simple truth: Everything comes from God, for without him was not anything made that was made.

Everything you could possibly have in this world is made out of the Mother Light, which is God's own light, an aspect of God's Being that the Father has allowed to manifest as the Mother Light that can be trapped in any form. Behind the forms, there is a universal aspect of the Mother Light, which is what we have called the River of Life.

Think about this, my beloved. What you call form is something that has at least a temporary existence. This means that someone has taken a mental image, projected it upon the Ma-ter Light, thereby drawing a portion of the Ma-ter Light out of the River of Life, causing it to stop flowing with that river and instead taking on a material form.

This in itself is not wrong. How could you exist in the material world, unless there was something that had a material form? The problem comes in when people are influenced by the duality consciousness, which causes them to feel a sense of separation from their source and from the River of Life. When they feel that separation, inevitably along with that feeling comes the fear of loss.

The fear of loss is in a polarity with another more subtle feeling, namely the feeling that you (meaning the separate you that now sees itself separated from the Body of God and the River of Life) can actually own something in this world. When you have that sense of ownership, then once you have something, you want to keep it. The fear of loss drives you to clutch what you have and to hold on to it. Do you see, how this very deep-seated, very subtle, psychological mechanism causes you to separate yourself even more from the River of Life?

The world is designed to give you abundance

You have been sent into a world that is very well designed for giving you the abundant life. In fact, God has designed this world to give you anything and everything you want. However, if you seek to own something, you will limit your possessions to that which you can currently conceive instead of flowing with the River of Life.

Do you see that you have been given free will by God? You have been given the ability to impose images upon the Ma-ter Light, causing the light to take on form whereby it will temporarily stagnate in a certain form. As I said, you have the right to do this, to create any form you desire. What God desires to see for you is that you do not settle for the forms that you can currently conceive, but that you are part of the ongoing movement of the River of Life. Instead of holding on to one limited form, you are constantly transcending yourself, constantly transcending your former mental images so they do not become graven images. Therefore, you are not seeking to hold on to one particular form, for you are willing to transcend that form, allowing that form to become more.

This is what the human ego and those who are trapped in the fallen consciousness cannot fathom. They believe that if a particular form is changed, they will lose that form. In a sense this is true. If you have ten dollars in the bank and they accrue interest and now you have twelve dollars, well in a sense you have lost the ten dollars, at least the sense of having ten dollars in the bank. Is it really a loss, or have you received something more?

Challenge the sense of ownership

You who are the spiritual people have the opportunity (not only in your own lives but also in the collective consciousness and even by speaking out about this in society) to challenge the sense of ownership. This is the very subtle programming that has programmed almost everyone, at least in the more affluent nations on this planet, to believe that one of the main purposes in life is to own something and to accumulate what you own. This very subtle programming is the primary factor that prevents the manifestation of the abundant life on this planet. With the abundant life I mean a state where every human being has enough to eat, has a decent place to live and has a standard of living that gives that person free time and energy to pursue spiritual goals.

This planet is perfectly capable of sustaining 10 billion people in a state of affluence. Obviously, it is not doing so right now. The reason is that the bottom 10 percent of the people – the power elite – are so trapped in the sense of ownership and the fear of loss that they have accumulated the world's wealth and resources to themselves, concentrating it in their own hands—thereby taking from someone else.

This is, as I said, partly a completely unconscious drive that springs from the fear of loss and the illusion that the separate self can own anything. It is also a desire to be better than others because they have more gadgets, more things,

14 | I challenge you to rethink the concept of ownership

more possessions. This is what prevents the shift whereby even nature itself would change so that it could produce the abundance that would feed even more people than are currently living here. Again, I look to those in the top 10 percent, those who are the more aware people, to come to a higher understanding of this and to demonstrate it in your own lives. Demonstrate that when you give up the need to own something for the separate self, well, then you become one with the River of Life.

This does not mean that you do not have personal possessions. There is a certain validity in having certain possessions, but you do not have those possessions in order to have them, to have the sense of owning them. You have them as tools for fulfilling your Divine plan. You have now transcended the consciousness whereby owning something has become an end in itself. Instead, you realize that ownership of anything in this world is simply a means to the greater end of fulfilling your Divine plan, helping to manifest God's kingdom on earth.

Overcome your attachments to owning anything

I must tell you that for many of you it will be necessary to take some dramatic steps in order to shed the programming of ownership that has been so ingrained in you over several lifetimes. There is indeed validity in what you see in many spiritual people who give up all material possessions for a time. I am not thereby saying that this is the only way you can overcome the sense of ownership. It is indeed preferable that you give up all *attachments* to your material possessions so that you only have what you need in order to accomplish your divine plan. Everything else that is unnecessary for that particular goal simply falls away from you.

Now, my beloved, it is important for you to understand that there is no absolute law that says that spiritual or religious people have to be poor. You do not have to be a sage wandering around with a robe as his only possession, begging for food. This is not conducive – for most of you – to fulfilling your Divine plan. What you need to understand is that when you give up the sense of ownership for the separate self, then you can merge your desires, your creativity, your needs, with the River of Life. The River of Life will take great pleasure and joy in fulfilling all of your true needs, all of the needs that are necessary for the fulfillment of your Divine plan. Thereby, you help other people, you set them free. You are raising the entire planet to coming closer to manifesting the abundant life.

Challenge the illusion of lack

In order to sell their illusion of ownership – and the false belief that those who own more are better than those who have less – the power elite and the false teachers have had to sell another subtle illusion. It is that the consciousness of lack (and actual lack and limitation) is unavoidable. When you merge with the River of Life, there is no need for lack. When you truly merge with the river, you not only become one with the river, you *become* the river. This means that you are now – through your being – directing a part of the flow of the River of Life. You can direct it – the very Light of God – into manifesting whatever you need to fulfill your Divine plan.

What I am talking about here is not a superficial psychological mechanism that you can easily overcome by giving a few affirmations or going to a psychologist for an hour or two. This is a very deep-seated mechanism that will require you to do some serious contemplation and soul searching so that you

14 | I challenge you to rethink the concept of ownership

can finally come to see it for the illusion that it is. You can come to believe the reality that when you are willing to transcend your expectations of what life should be, when you are willing to confront and overcome your fear of loss, well, then you will not lose anything. The River of Life will gladly give you more—as you become *more*. As you become more, instead of seeking to own and control everything, you will – because you are in the flow of the River of Life – freely give what you have freely received. Thereby, you spread the wealth, you spread the abundance and everyone will have more.

Do you not see that it is only the illusion of the fallen beings that makes it seem as if there is a limited amount of resources? Therefore, it seems that if you spread those resources to every human being on the planet, nobody would have enough. This is what they want you to believe. The reality is, my beloved, that when those who have start freely giving what they have received, well, then everyone will become more affluent. The entire economy will grow to a higher level, and therefore, economic opportunity and the collective amount of wealth in a society will increase dramatically and exponentially.

Equality without socialism

If you compare the society you have in the United States today to the feudal societies of Europe 500 years ago, you will see that the amount of wealth that was present and available in those medieval societies was much, much smaller than the amount of wealth that is available in today's society. Unfortunately, you see that the unequal distribution of wealth has not improved all that much from medieval times to today—at least not as much as I desire to see happen. This brings up another topic. When you begin to question the concept of ownership, well, then you have some considerations that apply to society as a whole. In every Golden Age that has existed on this planet, there has been a different sense of ownership, a more collective sense of ownership. This literally meant that there was a limit to how much wealth or property could be owned and controlled by one single person, or by one single entity, such as a business or an organization.

It is precisely the sense of separation and the desire to gather possessions for the little self that prevents the Golden Age from manifesting, for it stops the flow of the River of Life. When you overcome that sense of personal, separate-self ownership, well, then the floodgates will be opened and abundance will be streaming forth. It will not stream forth for the good of one individual but for the good of the all so that the entire society, eventually the entire planet, can be raised up.

It is indeed necessary to work on two fronts. The most important is, of course, the raising of consciousness, which will set the stage for a reevaluation of ownership. It is also necessary to work on a political level. It is indeed appropriate that a society that is beginning to move into the golden age consciousness – but has not yet fully made the transition – will set up certain limitations for how much wealth or property can be controlled by one individual or by one corporation.

My beloved, I am not here talking about socialism or communism that replaces individual ownership with state ownership. I am talking about a middle way where there is a limit to how much can be concentrated in the hands of the elite – thereby taken out of circulation – and thereby taking the entire society to a lower level, which actually even limits the elite. The members of the elite do not care because they are not really concerned about the amount of wealth they have. They are concerned about the difference between the amount of wealth they have and the amount of wealth that the average person

14 | I challenge you to rethink the concept of ownership 269

has. They want to be better than others, and they are perfectly willing to keep the entire society at a lower level.

I must tell you that there is a power elite on this planet (and they have been reincarnating again and again and again) who, if they could, would have been perfectly content to keep the total amount of wealth available in the Western world at the level that you saw in the feudal societies. They do not care about expanding the total amount of wealth as much as they care about staying ahead of the population. There is, of course, a few members of the power elite who are trapped in another spiral where they are not even concerned about having more than the people. They are only concerned about having more and more and more, for they have been trapped in a never-ending cycle that can never be filled.

Limiting the power of corporate entities

One of the consequences of these thoughts is that it is necessary for a society like the United States, Europe and other nations that are catching up economically, to consider that at some point it becomes necessary to limit the size of corporations. They cannot become so large that they lose touch with the human element. The corporation cannot become an entity that is ready to suppress and control the entire world if it could.

Instead of allowing corporations to enter into this never-ending quest for power and control, a corporation should be a tool for the greater good of raising the abundance for all. When it comes right down to it, which corporation can exist in a vacuum? A corporation must in many cases use raw materials in order to produce goods that can be sold. It must have workers who can produce those goods. Surely, the shareholders are not going to stand on the factory floor and earn a living by the sweat of their brow, are they? I have no problem with a group of shareholders owning a corporation if they are willing to do the work. If they need other people to do the work, well, then can you really say that the shareholders can have and claim full ownership of the corporation? If that corporation uses raw materials found in the environment—well my beloved, who owns these United States? Is it General Motors? Or General Electric? Or Halliburton? Or is it the American people? Is this nation not one nation under God that is supposed to be *of* the people, *by* the people and *for* the people?

The people have a right to stand up and say: "Stop! We question the right of the elite to own and control 90 percent of the wealth of this nation. They have gathered that wealth by using the resources that belong to all of us and by taking advantage of the labor of all of us. Thus, we have ownership and we have a say so that the wealth of these corporations will not be used to increase the wealth of an elite that already has far more than any human being could possibly spend. Instead, we have a right to demand that the wealth of those corporations is spread among all people in society—including the workers of those corporations."

In a golden age society, you will not see these huge monolithic corporations that transcend national borders. You will see many smaller businesses that have a form of ownership where the employees have part ownership or even full ownership of the business itself. This is creating an entirely different dynamic where people do not simply come to work at a certain time and sit there mindlessly doing mind-numbing, mechanical work without feeling any sense of responsibility or even ownership – in a positive way – of what they are doing. Instead, they are invested in the business and they realize that what they do has an impact on the whole and ultimately benefits themselves. There is an entirely new business model and there are already people in embodiment who are aware of this and who have started to bring forth these business models. My beloved, what I ask you to do is to hold the immaculate concept for this transcendence of the concept of ownership into a new and higher understanding.

Revision of the patent laws

Another important topic to consider is the concept of patents. It is not unreasonable that the inventor of a new product can take out a patent for a time in order to reap a benefit of that product. It should not be possible for a new product to be brought forth, the inventor taking out a patent and then some big corporation buying up the patent, burying it in a drawer somewhere so that a new technology that could compete with their existing business is squashed at the outset.

My beloved, can you really say that the person who invented a new product has ownership of it? Does there not come a point where one has to say that there are certain products, certain forms of technology, that are so important for the good of the all that we cannot allow one person or one corporation to control the use of that technology? Imagine that in some distant past a person had taken out a patent on the wheel. You all had to pay a fee to some monstrous corporation for the fact that you have wheels on your cars.

There are certain forms of technology that are given to humankind for the benefit of all. Where do new inventions and technology actually come from? Well, they do not come out of the blue, nor do they come out of the mind of one person. They come from the ascended realm, for we of the ascended masters are the real inventors for earth. The people who supposedly invent something are simply the recipients. They are not *inventing*, they are *tuning in* so that they can receive what is already there in the etheric realm as a fully developed idea. The person who can tune in and bring forth a new invention deserves to be rewarded, but the invention should be seen as a gift to all people, and it should be used for the good of the all.

As just one example of this, is it reasonable that a private corporation – controlled by a very small group of people – can have virtually total control over the software that runs 90 percent of the world's computers? Does there not come a point where one has to say that computers have become too important for the world at large to allow greed and profit to drive development? We cannot allow greed and profit to enable a corporation to control the use of software, the use of computers, to the point of squashing innovation that could threaten their unique position.

I understand that the computer industry is relatively young, and therefore society has been somewhat taken aback by its emergence. Nevertheless, it is never too late to step back and rethink everything. There is a need to rethink so that either society gives Microsoft an ultimatum of changing its control and ownership of the software, or society decides to create a publicly owned, completely transparent entity that will develop new software that can run on all computers.

I can assure you that if you want to avoid computers being used to control every aspect of your life, well, then you, the people, have to claim ownership of computer technology. This means that you have to demand the greatest possible degree of transparency in every aspect of the development of the crucial software that literally makes the world run.

Thus, my beloved, I have spoken my peace for this installment. I thank you for your attention, and I seal you once again in the Freedom Flame that I AM.

15 | INVOKING A NEW VIEW OF OWNERSHIP

In the name I AM THAT I AM, Jesus Christ, I call to all ascended masters working on manifesting the Golden Age, especially Archangel Uriel, Elohim Peace, Master Nada, Saint Germain and Alpha, to radiate into the collective consciousness a new vision of what we can and cannot own in this world. Help people see that we can build a new future by working with the ascended masters and letting go of the old way of looking at life, including...

[Make personal calls.]

Part 1

1. Saint Germain, radiate into the collective consciousness the awareness that we need to question one of the fundamental institutions of human society, indeed of human life on this planet, namely the concept of ownership.

> Uriel Archangel, immense is the power,
> of angels of peace, all war to devour.
> The demons of war, no match for your light,
> consuming them all, with radiance so bright.

> **Uriel Archangel, use your great sword,**
> **Uriel Archangel, consume all discord,**
> **Uriel Archangel, we're of one accord,**
> **Uriel Archangel, we walk with the Lord.**

2. Saint Germain, radiate into the collective consciousness the awareness that we cannot really own anything on this planet where everything is so fleeting that it can be here today; gone tomorrow.

> Uriel Archangel, intense is the sound,
> when millions of angels, their voices compound.
> They build a crescendo, piercing the night,
> life's glorious oneness revealed to our sight.

> **Uriel Archangel, use your great sword,**
> **Uriel Archangel, consume all discord,**
> **Uriel Archangel, we're of one accord,**
> **Uriel Archangel, we walk with the Lord.**

3. Saint Germain, radiate into the collective consciousness the awareness that the only thing we can own and take with us when we leave this world is our own being, mind, psyche or soul.

> Uriel Archangel, from out the Great Throne,
> your millions of trumpets, sound the One Tone.
> Consuming all discord with your harmony,
> the sound of all sounds will set all life free.
>
> **Uriel Archangel, use your great sword,**
> **Uriel Archangel, consume all discord,**
> **Uriel Archangel, we're of one accord,**
> **Uriel Archangel, we walk with the Lord.**

4. Saint Germain, radiate into the collective consciousness the awareness that as we spend time in the material realm, we grow in stature, and when we leave, we take with us the growth that we have internalized.

> Uriel Archangel, all war is now done,
> for you bring a message, from heart of the One.
> The hearts of all men, now singing in peace,
> the spirals of love, forever increase.
>
> **Uriel Archangel, use your great sword,**
> **Uriel Archangel, consume all discord,**
> **Uriel Archangel, we're of one accord,**
> **Uriel Archangel, we walk with the Lord.**

5. Saint Germain, radiate into the collective consciousness the awareness that everything comes from God, for without him was not anything made that was made.

Uriel Archangel, your infinite peace,
from all warring beings our planet release,
war is a prison from which we are free,
embracing the peace of true unity.

Uriel Archangel, use your great sword,
Uriel Archangel, consume all discord,
Uriel Archangel, we're of one accord,
Uriel Archangel, we walk with the Lord.

6. Saint Germain, radiate into the collective consciousness the awareness that everything we could possibly have in this world is made out of the Mother Light, which is God's own light that the Father has allowed to manifest as the Mother Light that can be trapped in any form.

Uriel Archangel, we send forth the call,
reveal now the oneness that unifies all,
help us the vision of peace now to see,
so we from all conflicts and struggles are free.

Uriel Archangel, use your great sword,
Uriel Archangel, consume all discord,
Uriel Archangel, we're of one accord,
Uriel Archangel, we walk with the Lord.

7. Saint Germain, radiate into the collective consciousness the awareness that behind all forms, there is a universal aspect of the Mother Light, which is the River of Life.

15 | Invoking a new view of ownership

> Uriel Archangel, in service to life,
> you give us release from struggle and strife,
> forgetting the self is truly the key,
> to living a life in true harmony.
>
> **Uriel Archangel, use your great sword,**
> **Uriel Archangel, consume all discord,**
> **Uriel Archangel, we're of one accord,**
> **Uriel Archangel, we walk with the Lord.**

8. Saint Germain, radiate into the collective consciousness the awareness that what we call form is something that has a temporary existence. Someone has taken a mental image, projected it upon the Ma-ter Light, thereby drawing a portion of the Ma-ter Light out of the River of Life, causing it to stop flowing with that river and instead taking on a material form.

> Uriel Archangel, the earth now you raise,
> out of duality's death-bringing haze,
> we call now upon your great Flame of Peace,
> commanding that all petty squabbles do cease.
>
> **Uriel Archangel, use your great sword,**
> **Uriel Archangel, consume all discord,**
> **Uriel Archangel, we're of one accord,**
> **Uriel Archangel, we walk with the Lord.**

9. Saint Germain, radiate into the collective consciousness the awareness that this in itself is not wrong. The problem comes in when people are influenced by the duality consciousness, which causes them to feel a sense of separation from their source, leading to the fear of loss.

Uriel Archangel, as peace is the norm,
to your higher vision the earth does conform,
as people have found your peace from within,
a Golden Age is the prize that we win.

**Uriel Archangel, use your great sword,
Uriel Archangel, consume all discord,
Uriel Archangel, we're of one accord,
Uriel Archangel, we walk with the Lord.**

Part 2

1. Saint Germain, radiate into the collective consciousness the awareness that the fear of loss is in a polarity with another more subtle feeling, namely the feeling that our separate selves can actually own something in this world.

O Elohim Peace, in Unity's Flame,
there is no more room for duality's game,
we know that all form is from the same source,
empowering us to plot a new course.

**O Elohim Peace, through your tranquility,
we are free from the chaos of duality,
in oneness with God a new identity,
we are raising the earth into Infinity.**

2. Saint Germain, radiate into the collective consciousness the awareness that this sense of ownership means that once we have something, we want to keep it. The fear of loss drives us to clutch what we have and to hold on to it. What we think we own, now owns us.

> O Elohim Peace, the bell now you ring,
> causing all atoms to vibrate and sing,
> we give up the sense of a separate "me,"
> we're crossing Samsara's turbulent sea.
>
> **O Elohim Peace, through your tranquility,**
> **we are free from the chaos of duality,**
> **in oneness with God a new identity,**
> **we are raising the earth into Infinity.**

3. Saint Germain, radiate into the collective consciousness the awareness that this very deep-seated, very subtle, psychological mechanism causes us to separate ourselves even more from the River of Life.

> O Elohim Peace, you help us to know,
> that Jesus has come your Flame to bestow,
> upon all who are ready to give up the strife,
> by following Christ into infinite life.
>
> **O Elohim Peace, through your tranquility,**
> **we are free from the chaos of duality,**
> **in oneness with God a new identity,**
> **we are raising the earth into Infinity.**

4. Saint Germain, radiate into the collective consciousness the awareness that the world is very well designed for giving us the abundant life. God has designed this world to give us anything and everything we want.

> O Elohim Peace, through your eyes we see,
> that only in oneness will we ever be free,
> we now see that there is no separate thing,
> to the ego-based self we no longer cling.

> **O Elohim Peace, through your tranquility,**
> **we are free from the chaos of duality,**
> **in oneness with God a new identity,**
> **we are raising the earth into Infinity.**

5. Saint Germain, radiate into the collective consciousness the awareness that if we seek to own something, we will limit our possessions to that which we can currently conceive, instead of flowing with the River of Life.

> O Elohim Peace, you show us the way,
> for clearing the mind from duality's fray,
> you pierce the illusions of both time and space,
> separation consumed by your Infinite Grace.

> **O Elohim Peace, through your tranquility,**
> **we are free from the chaos of duality,**
> **in oneness with God a new identity,**
> **we are raising the earth into Infinity.**

6. Saint Germain, radiate into the collective consciousness the awareness that we have been given free will and the ability to impose images upon the Ma-ter Light, causing the light to take on form, whereby it will temporarily stagnate in a certain form.

O Elohim Peace, what beauty your name,
consuming within us duality's shame,
the earth is set free from burden of fear,
accepting your peace is now manifest here.

**O Elohim Peace, through your tranquility,
we are free from the chaos of duality,
in oneness with God a new identity,
we are raising the earth into Infinity.**

7. Saint Germain, radiate into the collective consciousness the awareness that we have the right to create any form we desire. What God desires for us is that we do not settle for the forms that we can currently conceive, but that we are part of the ongoing movement of the River of Life.

O Elohim Peace, with Christ at our side,
no force of duality can evermore hide,
It was through the vibration of your Golden Flame,
that Christ the illusion of death overcame.

**O Elohim Peace, through your tranquility,
we are free from the chaos of duality,
in oneness with God a new identity,
we are raising the earth into Infinity.**

8. Saint Germain, radiate into the collective consciousness the awareness that instead of holding on to one limited form, we can be constantly transcending ourselves, constantly transcending our former mental images so they do not become graven images.

> O Elohim Peace, you bring now to earth,
> the unstoppable flame of Cosmic Rebirth,
> we give up the sense that something is "mine,"
> allowing your Light through our beings to shine.

> **O Elohim Peace, through your tranquility,**
> **we are free from the chaos of duality,**
> **in oneness with God a new identity,**
> **we are raising the earth into Infinity.**

9. Saint Germain, radiate into the collective consciousness the awareness that we are free only when we do not seek to hold on to one particular form, for we are willing to transcend that form, allowing the form and ourselves to become more.

> O Elohim Peace, as peace now we feel,
> all records of war you totally heal,
> the earth is now free from forces of war,
> restoring her purity known from before.

> **O Elohim Peace, through your tranquility,**
> **we are free from the chaos of duality,**
> **in oneness with God a new identity,**
> **we are raising the earth into Infinity.**

Part 3

1. Saint Germain, radiate into the collective consciousness the awareness that the human ego and those who are trapped in the fallen consciousness believe that if a particular form is changed, they will lose that form.

> Master Nada, beauty's power,
> unfolding like a sacred flower.
> Master Nada, so sublime,
> a will that conquers even time.

> **Master Nada, peace you give,**
> **forevermore in peace we live,**
> **our planet has a peaceful morn,**
> **the Golden Age is hereby born.**

2. Saint Germain, radiate into the collective consciousness the awareness that we do lose what is less, but it is not a true loss because we move on to something more.

> Master Nada, you bestow,
> upon us wisdom's rushing flow.
> Master Nada, mind so strong
> rising on your wings of song.

> **Master Nada, peace you give,**
> **forevermore in peace we live,**
> **our planet has a peaceful morn,**
> **the Golden Age is hereby born.**

3. Saint Germain, radiate into the collective consciousness the awareness that the spiritual people have as our task to challenge the sense of ownership, the subtle programming that has made almost everyone believe that one of the main purposes in life is to own something and to accumulate what we own.

> Master Nada, precious scent,
> your love is truly heaven-sent.
> Master Nada, kind and soft
> on wings of love we rise aloft.
>
> **Master Nada, peace you give,**
> **forevermore in peace we live,**
> **our planet has a peaceful morn,**
> **the Golden Age is hereby born.**

4. Saint Germain, radiate into the collective consciousness the awareness that this subtle programming is the primary factor that prevents the manifestation of the abundant life on this planet.

> Master Nada, mother light,
> our hearts are rising like a kite.
> Master Nada, from your view,
> all life is pure as morning dew.
>
> **Master Nada, peace you give,**
> **forevermore in peace we live,**
> **our planet has a peaceful morn,**
> **the Golden Age is hereby born.**

5. Saint Germain, radiate into the collective consciousness the awareness that this planet is perfectly capable of sustaining 10 billion people in a state of affluence.

Master Nada, truth you bring,
as morning birds in love do sing.
Master Nada, we now feel,
your love that all four bodies heal.

**Master Nada, peace you give,
forevermore in peace we live,
our planet has a peaceful morn,
the Golden Age is hereby born.**

6. Saint Germain, radiate into the collective consciousness the awareness that the planet is not doing so right now because the members of the power elite are so trapped in the sense of ownership and the fear of loss that they have accumulated the world's wealth and resources, concentrating it in their own hands by taking from someone else.

Master Nada, serve in peace,
as all emotions we release.
Master Nada, life is fun,
the solar plexus is a sun.

**Master Nada, peace you give,
forevermore in peace we live,
our planet has a peaceful morn,
the Golden Age is hereby born.**

7. Saint Germain, radiate into the collective consciousness the awareness that this is partly an unconscious drive that springs from the fear of loss and the illusion that the separate self can own anything. It is also a desire to be better than others because they have more possessions.

Master Nada, love is free,
conditions we no longer see.
Master Nada, rise above,
all human forms of lesser love.

**Master Nada, peace you give,
forevermore in peace we live,
our planet has a peaceful morn,
the Golden Age is hereby born.**

8. Saint Germain, radiate into the collective consciousness the awareness that this prevents the shift whereby nature would change so that it could produce the abundance that would feed even more people than are currently living here.

Master Nada, balance all,
the seven rays upon our call.
Master Nada, rise and shine,
your radiant beauty most divine.

**Master Nada, peace you give,
forevermore in peace we live,
our planet has a peaceful morn,
the Golden Age is hereby born.**

15 | Invoking a new view of ownership

9. Saint Germain, radiate into the collective consciousness the awareness that when we give up the need to own something for the separate self, we become one with the River of Life.

Nada Dear, your Presence here,
filling up the inner sphere.
Life is now a sacred flow,
God Peace we do on all bestow.

**Master Nada, peace you give,
forevermore in peace we live,
our planet has a peaceful morn,
the Golden Age is hereby born.**

Part 4

1. Saint Germain, radiate into the collective consciousness the awareness that we can still have personal possessions, but we do not have those possessions in order to have them, to have the sense of owning them. We have them as tools for fulfilling our Divine plans.

O Saint Germain, you do inspire,
my vision raised forever higher,
with you I form a figure-eight,
your Golden Age I co-create.

**O Saint Germain, what love you bring,
it truly makes all matter sing,
your violet flame does all restore,
with you we are becoming more.**

2. Saint Germain, radiate into the collective consciousness the awareness that we can transcend the consciousness whereby owning something has become an end in itself. We see ownership of anything in this world as a means to the greater end of fulfilling our Divine plan.

> O Saint Germain, what Freedom Flame,
> released when we recite your name,
> acceleration is your gift,
> our planet it will surely lift.

> **O Saint Germain, what love you bring,**
> **it truly makes all matter sing,**
> **your violet flame does all restore,**
> **with you we are becoming more.**

3. Saint Germain, radiate into the collective consciousness the awareness that we need to take dramatic steps in order to shed the programming of ownership that has been so ingrained in us over lifetimes.

> O Saint Germain, in love we claim,
> our right to bring your violet flame,
> from you Above, to us below,
> it is an all-transforming flow.

> **O Saint Germain, what love you bring,**
> **it truly makes all matter sing,**
> **your violet flame does all restore,**
> **with you we are becoming more.**

15 | Invoking a new view of ownership

4. Saint Germain, radiate into the collective consciousness the awareness that we need to give up all attachments to our material possessions so that we only have what we need in order to accomplish our Divine plan. Everything else that is unnecessary for that particular goal simply falls away from us.

> O Saint Germain, I love you so,
> my aura filled with violet glow,
> my chakras filled with violet fire,
> I am your cosmic amplifier.

> **O Saint Germain, what love you bring,**
> **it truly makes all matter sing,**
> **your violet flame does all restore,**
> **with you we are becoming more.**

5. Saint Germain, radiate into the collective consciousness the awareness that there is no absolute law that says that spiritual or religious people have to be poor. When we give up the sense of ownership for the separate self, then we can merge our desires, creativity and needs with the River of Life.

> O Saint Germain, I am now free,
> your violet flame is therapy,
> transform all hang-ups in my mind,
> as inner peace I surely find.

> **O Saint Germain, what love you bring,**
> **it truly makes all matter sing,**
> **your violet flame does all restore,**
> **with you we are becoming more.**

6. Saint Germain, radiate into the collective consciousness the awareness that the River of Life will take great pleasure and joy in fulfilling all of the needs that are necessary for the fulfillment of our Divine plans. Thereby, we are raising the entire planet to the abundant life.

> O Saint Germain, my body pure,
> your violet flame for all is cure,
> consume the cause of all disease,
> and therefore I am all at ease.

> **O Saint Germain, what love you bring,**
> **it truly makes all matter sing,**
> **your violet flame does all restore,**
> **with you we are becoming more.**

7. Saint Germain, radiate into the collective consciousness the awareness that in order to sell the illusion of ownership, and that those who *have* are better than those who *have not,* the false teachers have had to sell the illusion that lack is unavoidable.

> O Saint Germain, I'm karma-free,
> the past no longer burdens me,
> a brand new opportunity,
> I am in Christic unity.

> **O Saint Germain, what love you bring,**
> **it truly makes all matter sing,**
> **your violet flame does all restore,**
> **with you we are becoming more.**

8. Saint Germain, radiate into the collective consciousness the awareness that when we merge with the River of Life, there is no need for lack. We can direct the Light of God into manifesting whatever we need to fulfill our Divine plans.

O Saint Germain, we are now one,
I am for you a violet sun,
as we transform this planet earth,
your Golden Age is given birth.

**O Saint Germain, what love you bring,
it truly makes all matter sing,
your violet flame does all restore,
with you we are becoming more.**

9. Saint Germain, radiate into the collective consciousness the awareness that the illusion of lack is a very deep-seated mechanism. We need to see that when we transcend our expectations of what life should be, when we confront and overcome our fear of loss, then we will not lose anything.

O Saint Germain, the earth is free,
from burden of duality,
in oneness we bring what is best,
your Golden Age is manifest.

**O Saint Germain, what love you bring,
it truly makes all matter sing,
your violet flame does all restore,
with you we are becoming more.**

Part 5

1. Saint Germain, radiate into the collective consciousness the awareness that the River of Life will gladly give us more—as we become more. When we freely give what we have freely received, we spread the wealth, we spread the abundance and everyone will have more.

> Beloved Alpha, God's great plan,
> in Central Sun it all began,
> what wondrous vision of a world,
> the cosmic spheres were then unfurled.

> **Beloved Alpha, in your light,**
> **I now see God with inner sight,**
> **as man I will no longer live,**
> **my life to God I fully give.**

2. Saint Germain, radiate into the collective consciousness the awareness that it is only the illusion of the fallen beings that makes it seem like there is a limited amount of resources and that if we spread those resources to every person, nobody would have enough.

> Beloved Alpha, serve the All,
> this is Creator's timeless call,
> from out Creator's perfect whole,
> sprang lifestreams with a sacred goal.

15 | Invoking a new view of ownership

**Beloved Alpha, in your light,
I now see God with inner sight,
as man I will no longer live,
my life to God I fully give.**

3. Saint Germain, radiate into the collective consciousness the awareness that when those who have, start freely giving what they have received, then everyone will become more affluent. The entire economy will grow to a higher level, and economic opportunity will increase dramatically and exponentially.

Beloved Alpha, all was one,
as we were sent from Central Sun,
to you we shall in time return,
for cosmic union we do yearn.

**Beloved Alpha, in your light,
I now see God with inner sight,
as man I will no longer live,
my life to God I fully give.**

4. Saint Germain, radiate into the collective consciousness the awareness that the amount of wealth available in medieval societies was much smaller than the amount of wealth available today. Still, the unequal distribution of wealth has not improved enough.

Beloved Alpha, I now see,
you with Omega form the key,
it was from your polarity,
that I received identity.

Beloved Alpha, in your light,
I now see God with inner sight,
as man I will no longer live,
my life to God I fully give.

5. Saint Germain, radiate into the collective consciousness the awareness that in every previous Golden Age, there has been a more collective sense of ownership. There was a limit to how much wealth or property could be owned and controlled by one single person, or by one single entity, such as a business or an organization.

Beloved Alpha, cosmic gate,
the nexus of your figure-eight,
I sprang from Cosmic Cube so bright,
I am at heart a spark of light.

Beloved Alpha, in your light,
I now see God with inner sight,
as man I will no longer live,
my life to God I fully give.

6. Saint Germain, radiate into the collective consciousness the awareness that the sense of separation and the desire to gather possessions for the little self prevents the Golden Age from manifesting, for it stops the flow of the River of Life.

Beloved Alpha, from your womb,
I did descend to matter's tomb,
but buried I will be no more,
my inner vision you restore.

**Beloved Alpha, in your light,
I now see God with inner sight,
as man I will no longer live,
my life to God I fully give.**

7. Saint Germain, radiate into the collective consciousness the awareness that when we overcome that sense of personal, separate-self ownership, then the floodgates will be opened and abundance will be streaming forth. It will not stream forth for the good of one individual but for the good of the all so that the entire society can be raised up.

Beloved Alpha, I now know,
the love you did on me bestow,
a co-creator, I will bring,
the light to make all matter sing.

**Beloved Alpha, in your light,
I now see God with inner sight,
as man I will no longer live,
my life to God I fully give.**

8. Saint Germain, radiate into the collective consciousness the awareness that we need to raise the collective consciousness, which will set the stage for a reevaluation of ownership.

Beloved Alpha, on this earth,
a new age we are giving birth,
for we are here to bring the love,
that you are sending from Above.

**Beloved Alpha, in your light,
I now see God with inner sight,
as man I will no longer live,
my life to God I fully give.**

9. Saint Germain, radiate into the collective consciousness the awareness that it is also necessary to work on a political level so that society sets up limitations for how much wealth or property can be controlled by one individual or by one corporation.

Beloved Alpha, you and me,
we form a true polarity,
as up Above, so here below,
with life's own river I do flow.

**Beloved Alpha, in your light,
I now see God with inner sight,
as man I will no longer live,
my life to God I fully give.**

Sealing

In the name of the Divine Mother, I call to all ascended masters for the sealing of myself and all people in my circle of influence in the creative flow of the Divine Mother, the River of Life. I call for the multiplication of my calls by all ascended masters so that we form the perfect figure-eight flow of "As Above, so below." Thus, I accept that this is fully manifest, because the mouth of the Lord, the Divine Mother that I AM, has spoken it. Amen.

16 | INVOKING A NEW VIEW OF CORPORATIONS

In the name I AM THAT I AM, Jesus Christ, I call to all ascended masters working on manifesting the Golden Age, especially Saint Germain and the Divine Director, to radiate into the collective consciousness a new view of how society can deal with corporations. Help people see that we can build a new future by working with the ascended masters and letting go of the old way of looking at life, including…

[Make personal calls.]

Part 1

1. Saint Germain, radiate into the collective consciousness the awareness that limiting the concentration of welath is not the same as socialism or communism that replaces individual ownership with state ownership. It is a middle way where there is a limit to how much can be concentrated in the hands of the elite, thereby taking the entire society to a lower level, which actually even limits the elite.

> O Saint Germain, you do inspire,
> my vision raised forever higher,
> with you I form a figure-eight,
> your Golden Age I co-create.
>
> **O Saint Germain, what love you bring,**
> **it truly makes all matter sing,**
> **your violet flame does all restore,**
> **with you we are becoming more.**

2. Saint Germain, radiate into the collective consciousness the awareness that the members of the elite are concerned about the difference between the amount of wealth they have and the amount of wealth that the average person has. They want to be better than others, and they are perfectly willing to keep the entire society at a lower level.

> O Saint Germain, what Freedom Flame,
> released when we recite your name,
> acceleration is your gift,
> our planet it will surely lift.

**O Saint Germain, what love you bring,
it truly makes all matter sing,
your violet flame does all restore,
with you we are becoming more.**

3. Saint Germain, radiate into the collective consciousness the awareness that there is a power elite on this planet who would have been perfectly content to keep the total amount of wealth available in the Western world at the level that we saw in the feudal societies.

O Saint Germain, in love we claim,
our right to bring your violet flame,
from you Above, to us below,
it is an all-transforming flow.

**O Saint Germain, what love you bring,
it truly makes all matter sing,
your violet flame does all restore,
with you we are becoming more.**

4. Saint Germain, radiate into the collective consciousness the awareness that many members of this elite do not care about expanding the total amount of wealth as much as they care about staying ahead of the population.

O Saint Germain, I love you so,
my aura filled with violet glow,
my chakras filled with violet fire,
I am your cosmic amplifier.

> **O Saint Germain, what love you bring,**
> **it truly makes all matter sing,**
> **your violet flame does all restore,**
> **with you we are becoming more.**

5. Saint Germain, radiate into the collective consciousness the awareness that some members of the power elite are trapped in a spiral where they are not concerned about having more than the people. They are only concerned about having more and more, for they have been trapped in a desire that can never be filled.

> O Saint Germain, I am now free,
> your violet flame is therapy,
> transform all hang-ups in my mind,
> as inner peace I surely find.

> **O Saint Germain, what love you bring,**
> **it truly makes all matter sing,**
> **your violet flame does all restore,**
> **with you we are becoming more.**

6. Saint Germain, radiate into the collective consciousness the awareness that it is necessary for a developed society to limit the size of corporations. A corporation cannot become so large that it loses touch with the human element, being ready to suppress and control the entire world if it could.

> O Saint Germain, my body pure,
> your violet flame for all is cure,
> consume the cause of all disease,
> and therefore I am all at ease.

**O Saint Germain, what love you bring,
it truly makes all matter sing,
your violet flame does all restore,
with you we are becoming more.**

7. Saint Germain, radiate into the collective consciousness the awareness that instead of allowing corporations to enter this never-ending quest for power and control, a corporation should be a tool for the greater good of raising the abundance for all.

O Saint Germain, I'm karma-free,
the past no longer burdens me,
a brand new opportunity,
I am in Christic unity.

**O Saint Germain, what love you bring,
it truly makes all matter sing,
your violet flame does all restore,
with you we are becoming more.**

8. Saint Germain, radiate into the collective consciousness the awareness that no corporation can exist in a vacuum. It needs society and it needs the people in order to produce and sell its products.

O Saint Germain, we are now one,
I am for you a violet sun,
as we transform this planet earth,
your Golden Age is given birth.

**O Saint Germain, what love you bring,
it truly makes all matter sing,
your violet flame does all restore,
with you we are becoming more.**

9. Saint Germain, radiate into the collective consciousness the awareness that if the shareholders need other people to do the work, then those shareholders cannot have full ownership of the corporation.

O Saint Germain, the earth is free,
from burden of duality,
in oneness we bring what is best,
your Golden Age is manifest.

**O Saint Germain, what love you bring,
it truly makes all matter sing,
your violet flame does all restore,
with you we are becoming more.**

Part 2

1. Saint Germain, radiate into the collective consciousness the awareness that if a corporation uses raw materials found in the environment, then the people have ownership of those resources.

Divine Director, I now see,
the world is unreality,
in my heart I now truly feel,
the Spirit is all that is real.

**Divine Director, send the light,
from blindness clear my inner sight,
my vision free, my vision clear,
your guidance is forever here.**

2. Saint Germain, radiate into the collective consciousness the awareness that the people have a right to stand up and say: "Stop! We question the right of the elite to own and control 90 percent of the wealth of our nation."

Divine Director, vision give,
in clarity I want to live,
I now behold my plan Divine,
the plan that is uniquely mine.

**Divine Director, send the light,
from blindness clear my inner sight,
my vision free, my vision clear,
your guidance is forever here.**

3. Saint Germain, radiate into the collective consciousness the awareness that the people need to say: "The elite has gathered the wealth by using the resources that belong to all of us and by taking advantage of the labor of all of us. Thus, we have ownership."

Divine Director, show in me,
the ego games, and set me free,
help me escape the ego's cage,
to help bring in the Golden Age.

**Divine Director, send the light,
from blindness clear my inner sight,
my vision free, my vision clear,
your guidance is forever here.**

4. Saint Germain, radiate into the collective consciousness the awareness that the people need to say: "We have a say so that the wealth of these corporations will not be used to increase the wealth of an elite that already has far more than any human being could possibly spend. Instead, we have a right to demand that the wealth of those corporations is spread among all people in society—including the workers of those corporations."

Divine Director, I'm with you,
my vision one, no longer two,
as karma's veil you do disperse,
I see a whole new universe.

**Divine Director, send the light,
from blindness clear my inner sight,
my vision free, my vision clear,
your guidance is forever here.**

5. Saint Germain, radiate into the collective consciousness the awareness that in a golden age society, we will not see these huge monolithic corporations that transcend national borders.

Divine Director, I go up,
electric light now fills my cup,
consume in me all shadows old,
bestow on me a vision bold.

**Divine Director, send the light,
from blindness clear my inner sight,
my vision free, my vision clear,
your guidance is forever here.**

6. Saint Germain, radiate into the collective consciousness the awareness that in the Golden Age, we will see many smaller businesses that have a form of ownership where the employees have part or even full ownership of the business itself.

> Divine Director, heart of gold,
> my sacred labor I unfold,
> o blessed Guru, I now see,
> where my own plan is taking me.

**Divine Director, send the light,
from blindness clear my inner sight,
my vision free, my vision clear,
your guidance is forever here.**

7. Saint Germain, radiate into the collective consciousness the awareness that this is creating an entirely different dynamic where people do not come to work at a certain time and do mind-numbing, mechanical work without feeling any sense of responsibility or ownership of what they are doing.

> Divine Director, by your grace,
> in grander scheme I find my place,
> my individual flame I see,
> uniqueness God has given me.

**Divine Director, send the light,
from blindness clear my inner sight,
my vision free, my vision clear,
your guidance is forever here.**

8. Saint Germain, radiate into the collective consciousness the awareness that in the Golden Age people are invested in the business and they realize that what they do has an impact on the whole and ultimately benefits themselves.

Divine Director, vision one,
I see that I AM God's own Sun,
with your direction so Divine,
I am now letting my light shine.

**Divine Director, send the light,
from blindness clear my inner sight,
my vision free, my vision clear,
your guidance is forever here.**

9. Saint Germain, radiate into the collective consciousness the awareness that you have a new business model and there are already people in embodiment who are aware of this and who have started to bring forth these business models.

Divine Director, what a gift,
to be a part of Spirit's lift,
to raise mankind out of the night,
to bask in Spirit's loving sight.

> **Divine Director, send the light,**
> **from blindness clear my inner sight,**
> **my vision free, my vision clear,**
> **your guidance is forever here.**

Part 3

1. Saint Germain, radiate into the collective consciousness the awareness that while it is not unreasonable that the inventor of a new product can take out a patent for a time, it should not be possible for a big corporation to buy the patent and bury it so that a new technology that could compete with their existing business is squashed at the outset.

> O Saint Germain, you do inspire,
> my vision raised forever higher,
> with you I form a figure-eight,
> your Golden Age I co-create.

> **O Saint Germain, what love you bring,**
> **it truly makes all matter sing,**
> **your violet flame does all restore,**
> **with you we are becoming more.**

2. Saint Germain, radiate into the collective consciousness the awareness that the person who invented a new product truly does not have ownership of it. Certain products, certain forms of technology, are so important for the good of the all that we cannot allow one person or one corporation to control the use of that technology.

O Saint Germain, what Freedom Flame,
released when we recite your name,
acceleration is your gift,
our planet it will surely lift.

**O Saint Germain, what love you bring,
it truly makes all matter sing,
your violet flame does all restore,
with you we are becoming more.**

3. Saint Germain, radiate into the collective consciousness the awareness that certain forms of technology are given to humankind for the benefit of all. New inventions and technology actually come from the ascended realm, for the ascended masters are the real inventors for earth.

O Saint Germain, in love we claim,
our right to bring your violet flame,
from you Above, to us below,
it is an all-transforming flow.

**O Saint Germain, what love you bring,
it truly makes all matter sing,
your violet flame does all restore,
with you we are becoming more.**

4. Saint Germain, radiate into the collective consciousness the awareness that the people who supposedly invent something are simply the recipients. They are not inventing, they are tuning in so that they can receive what is already there in the etheric realm as a fully developed idea.

O Saint Germain, I love you so,
my aura filled with violet glow,
my chakras filled with violet fire,
I am your cosmic amplifier.

**O Saint Germain, what love you bring,
it truly makes all matter sing,
your violet flame does all restore,
with you we are becoming more.**

5. Saint Germain, radiate into the collective consciousness the awareness that the person who can tune in and bring forth a new invention deserves to be rewarded, but the invention should be seen as a gift to all people, and it should be used for the good of the all.

O Saint Germain, I am now free,
your violet flame is therapy,
transform all hang-ups in my mind,
as inner peace I surely find.

**O Saint Germain, what love you bring,
it truly makes all matter sing,
your violet flame does all restore,
with you we are becoming more.**

6. Saint Germain, radiate into the collective consciousness the awareness that it is not reasonable that a private corporation can have virtually total control over the software that runs 90 percent of the world's computers.

O Saint Germain, my body pure,
your violet flame for all is cure,
consume the cause of all disease,
and therefore I am all at ease.

**O Saint Germain, what love you bring,
it truly makes all matter sing,
your violet flame does all restore,
with you we are becoming more.**

7. Saint Germain, radiate into the collective consciousness the awareness that there comes a point where we have to say that computers have become too important for the world at large to allow greed and profit to drive development.

O Saint Germain, I'm karma-free,
the past no longer burdens me,
a brand new opportunity,
I am in Christic unity.

**O Saint Germain, what love you bring,
it truly makes all matter sing,
your violet flame does all restore,
with you we are becoming more.**

8. Saint Germain, radiate into the collective consciousness the awareness that we cannot allow greed and profit to enable a corporation to control the use of software, the use of computers, to the point of squashing innovation that could threaten their unique position.

O Saint Germain, we are now one,
I am for you a violet sun,
as we transform this planet earth,
your Golden Age is given birth.

**O Saint Germain, what love you bring,
it truly makes all matter sing,
your violet flame does all restore,
with you we are becoming more.**

9. Saint Germain, radiate into the collective consciousness the awareness that in order to avoid computers being used to control every aspect of our lives, we have to claim ownership of computer technology. We have to demand the greatest possible degree of transparency in every aspect of the development of the crucial software that makes the world run.

O Saint Germain, the earth is free,
from burden of duality,
in oneness we bring what is best,
your Golden Age is manifest.

**O Saint Germain, what love you bring,
it truly makes all matter sing,
your violet flame does all restore,
with you we are becoming more.**

Sealing

In the name of the Divine Mother, I call to all ascended masters for the sealing of myself and all people in my circle of influence in the creative flow of the Divine Mother, the River of Life. I call for the multiplication of my calls by all ascended masters so that we form the perfect figure-eight flow of "As Above, so below." Thus, I accept that this is fully manifest, because the mouth of the Lord, the Divine Mother that I AM, has spoken it. Amen.

17 | IS IT CONSEQUENTIAL FOR BRINGING IN THE GOLDEN AGE?

Thus, my beloved, we have reached the end of this series of discourses from *my* heart to the heart of those who are my own in embodiment, those who have come with Saint Germain to bring the Golden Age into manifestation at this turning point in earth's history.

I have spoken here to different levels of consciousness. As I said, I have placed people in many different locations and in many different areas of society so that they could do their particular work at that particular place in time and space. This last discourse is directed at those who are the most spiritually aware, the most spiritually mature, and therefore are the ones who have the potential to manifest either full Christhood or a high degree of Christhood in this lifetime.

A higher level of Christ discernment

What I desire to give you, and those who are willing to come into alignment with this vision, is the realization that one of the essential elements of Christhood is not only Christ discernment but a higher level of Christ discernment that enables and empowers you to put your priorities straight. You see this exemplified in Jesus at the age of 12 where he disappeared from Mary and I, and when he was found again said: "Wist ye not that I must be about my Father's business?" This is a motto that you might take on as your own as you contemplate your life—as it has unfolded up until now and as it has the potential to unfold in the future.

What is your "Father's business?" Well, it is your Divine plan, my beloved. It, of course, is not imposed upon you from any external authority, but it is the choices of your own conscious self and your higher being—your I AM Presence. You came here with the love of wanting to see that Divine plan unfold. In order to achieve this goal, you need to step up to that higher level of Christ discernment that gives you the sense of what is truly the priority for you to attain in this lifetime.

What I come to call to your attention is that any Aquarian-age movement has one major, overall goal that supersedes all other goals that you could possibly envision. That goal is simply this: To demonstrate the path to personal Christhood in the material world in such a way that it is impossible for anyone to overlook or deny the reality of it. You have so internalized the path that when you stand before people and demonstrate it, well they are seeing the Living Christ in you as they saw the Living Christ in Jesus.

My beloved, fix in your minds – if you feel that this resonates in your heart – that this is very much a goal that is in alignment with your individual Divine plans. The overall goal of the ascended masters in this age – at the end of the Piscean and the transition to the Aquarian age – is that a critical mass of people finally awaken to the lessons of Pisces and embody them so that they can form the platform for the descent of the aquarian-age consciousness.

What I call you to envision (not of course in a prideful manner, but in a manner of practical realism) is that you are the only ones who have this potential. Thus, if you do not do it, who will? If you do not do it now, then when will it be done? You realize that because you have the potential, it is indeed part of your Divine plan to demonstrate that Christhood, both individually and as a community coming together, dedicating your lives to demonstrating that path. The purpose is that the people of the world do not see it demonstrated in just one individual that they can easily idolize. They see it in many people who have come from similar backgrounds as themselves so that it suddenly becomes much more difficult to see all of them as idols, as exceptions. Someone will begin to realize that if this person – who comes from a similar background as myself – can walk the path of Christhood, then perhaps *I* can too.

The overall goal is Christhood

I have given you many goals in my previous discourses of what needs to happen in the world. If you feel strongly that one or more of these goals is part of your Divine plan, then by all means go after it. In going after that goal, still keep in mind that the overall goal is to demonstrate the path of Christhood. There is a need to demonstrate the path of Christhood in every area of life. There is a need for those who will rethink everything and start to think the thoughts that have not been thought on this planet for eons: How will a Christed being behave in the arena of politics? How will a Christed being behave in the area of business? How will a Christed scientist behave? How will a Christed religious person, religious cleric or priest behave?

This is a great calling. I call this to your outer awareness so you can realize that it is indeed extremely important for you not to become trapped in, not to become attached to, particular outer goals. Did I not just speak about ownership, my beloved. It is indeed possible – and this has happened to many sincere spiritual seekers – to become attached to achieving a particular goal in this world, seeking a particular response from other people or the world.

When you have your priorities straight, you realize that the overall goal is to demonstrate the path of Christhood. You can do this with complete independence of how people respond or do not respond to it. You are not here to produce a particular response, but to give them the choice – sometimes for the first time ever – to choose a response to a Christed being. My beloved, keep in mind, always, that the greater goal is to demonstrate the path of Christhood in all activities in which you engage in society.

Do not let the world distract you

I also want you to realize that there are people who are meant to rise above all entanglement with particular aspects of the world and come to demonstrate the true universal River of Life that runs behind all spirituality. Thereby, they serve to bring forth a demonstration of the possibility of having a truly universal spiritual movement with a truly universal vision. Some of you might feel a calling to being a part of this endeavor where you are directly demonstrating the path of Christhood as a spiritual endeavor. You are forming the Alpha polarity to the people I just spoke about, who are demonstrating the Omega of Christhood expressed in particular areas of society.

What will it take for you to demonstrate the path of Christhood? Well, it will take, of course, many things, but one particular element I want to bring to your attention now. You see, my beloved, the fallen beings, those in the fallen consciousness, are well aware that the greatest threat they face is even one person – but even more, a great number of people – who have manifested Christhood and demonstrate it to the world. One of their primary tactics is to distract or divert your attention from the larger goal of demonstrating Christhood so that you become so focused on achieving a particular goal that it takes you away from the overall path to Christhood. This is not to say that you cannot do some good by pursuing a particular activity, yet it is not the greatest good that you have the potential to bring forth in this embodiment.

I want to give you the concept that you are familiar with from cosmology, of a black hole. I want to take that concept further and make you aware that black holes do not only exist in the physical realm, where they are driven by gravity, but also, of course, exist in the emotional, mental and the lower etheric realms. In those realms (especially in the mental and etheric realms) they often take the form of what we might call a dead-end activity that is designed to distract your attention from the goal of Christhood.

This makes you think that something else is either more important or has to be completed first, before you can focus on the path of Christhood. You keep postponing that path indefinitely until it is too late to demonstrate it in this lifetime. There is a myriad of such activities, and you need to keep in the back of your mind your overall priority, realizing that you need to be alert for any activity that distracts you from that overall goal.

Know which people you cannot help

Let me give you one example, my beloved. I spoke yesterday about the need to establish a truly universal community where people can feel welcomed in whatever state of consciousness they are at. I am obviously not saying that you should allow anyone to come in with whatever ego manifestation they have, and then act out that manifestation to the point where they disturb the peace and the balance of the organization—or even take the organization on a sidetrack that takes it away from its overall goal of demonstrating Christhood.

There are people who have such complexity in their psychology that you have no realistic opportunity to help them in this lifetime. If you became attached to actually helping such a person, well it would take you away from your greater goal of Christhood. You might have been exposed to such people who attempted to draw you into an endless cycle of questionings or debates about this or that or the next thing. All of which led to no real change in the people because they were not willing to transcend some particular aspect of their egos.

It can come to a point where you say: "I cannot help you, and thus I must focus my attention on helping those whom I can actually help. If I continue to focus my attention on the people who are black holes, well, then do I not deprive the other people – whom I have a realistic opportunity to help – of the help that they need?"

Pick your causes carefully

This also applies to particular causes in the world. Although I say that there is a need to demonstrate Christhood in all areas of society, I want you to realize that those who have the greatest attainment and potential to demonstrate Christhood must do so in an overall manner—without being tied up in details that are not truly important for the onward progression of society.

You might go out in society and you might say: "Here is a worthy cause, here is a problem that needs to be corrected." I am not disputing that it is a worthy cause, but I desire you to step back and in your heart tune in to your Christ self and my Presence and ask yourself the question: "Would Saint Germain consider this cause to be essential for bringing in the Golden Age? Or would it really only be a minor step forward that is not *consequential* for the overall goal of manifesting the Golden Age and demonstrating the path to Christhood?"

My beloved, consider what is *consequential* for the fulfillment of your Divine plan, for the demonstration of the path to Christhood, for the manifestation of the Golden Age. If you realize that a particular activity is not consequential for either of those three goals – that are truly one and the same – well, then let it go and trust that there will be someone else who will pick up that torch.

Mother Teresa and environmentalism

May I bring to your attention something that might disturb certain people but nevertheless it needs to be spoken. Mother Theresa created a wonderful organization that has taken up a worthy cause that truly is a problem that needs to be solved. Yet I must tell you that this particular activity is not consequential for bringing the Golden Age into manifestation.

I am not saying that it does not contribute to the forward progression of humankind and thus brings the Golden Age closer. I am simply saying that it is not ultimately *consequential*. I must tell you that there are some wonderful people in that organization who have actually set aside their Christhood and their Divine plans because they have become involved in an activity that diverts their attention from their higher goal.

The same can be said about many other activities, one of the primary ones being the environmentalist movement. Again, a worthy cause, but my beloved, currently so entangled with the power elite (who have actually sponsored, financed and programmed that movement from its very inception to enforce their monopolies on natural resources) that it is almost impossible – and certainly inconsequential – to disentangle the subtle web of lies that is infiltrating that movement.

Even though the environment is a worthy goal, it is far more important – it is *consequential* – to focus on the path of Christhood and raising the consciousness of humankind. As I have explained in this series of discourses, it is only by the raising of the consciousness of humankind that you will truly restore balance to the environment. All imbalances are the product of the imbalances in the collective consciousness.

Be willing to surrender everything

My beloved, be willing to rethink everything, even what you thought was important as a result of growing up in a particular environment. It may be that what you think is important truly *is* important, but you will not truly know unless you are willing to step back and say: "I will rethink this. I am willing to let go of this activity."

This messenger has described how he himself was attached to fulfilling his Divine plan, but finally came to the point where he completely and utterly surrendered it—feeling that if he died at that moment (without doing anything to fulfill his Divine plan) he could leave this planet in peace. It was precisely that surrender – that total surrender to the higher vision – that then empowered him to serve as the messenger for Jesus and all of us. Had he not surrendered his former vision of what he thought his Divine plan was, well he would not be standing here and I would not have a messenger to speak through, to give this very high and intricate teaching. [This is not implying that Kim is Saint Germain's only messenger, only that he was the only one who could be the open door for this particular message at this particular time.]

Each one of you has a potential to be part of something that is *consequential* for the bringing forth of the Golden Age. Be willing to rethink your priorities. Let go of certain activities that you understand from within are not consequential for the overall goal for which you came into this world.

I have given you what I desired to give you during this conference. My beloved, you have earned my gratitude, and I pour it upon you now as you are willing to receive it. Feel the gratitude of the heart of the hierarch of the Aquarian age, the master of Freedom for the earth, the Buddha of Freedom for the earth. On that note, I will withdraw for Gautama will seal this conference.

18 | INVOKING THE AWAKENING OF SAINT GERMAIN'S OWN

In the name I AM THAT I AM, Jesus Christ, I call to all ascended masters working on manifesting the Golden Age, especially Archangel Zadkiel, Elohim Arcturus and Saint Germain, to radiate into the collective consciousness the impulses that will awaken those who came into embodiment in order to help manifest Saint Germain's Golden Age. Help people see that we can build a new future by working with the ascended masters and letting go of the old way of looking at life, including…

[Make personal calls.]

Part 1

1. Saint Germain, radiate into the collective consciousness the awareness that will awaken those who are your own in embodiment, those who have come with Saint Germain to bring the Golden Age into manifestation at this turning point in earth's history.

> Zadkiel Archangel, your flow is so swift,
> in your violet light, we instantly shift,
> into a vibration in which we are free,
> from all limitations of the lesser me.
>
> **Zadkiel Archangel, encircle the earth,**
> **Zadkiel Archangel, with your violet girth,**
> **Zadkiel Archangel, unstoppable mirth,**
> **Zadkiel Archangel, our planet's rebirth.**

2. Saint Germain, radiate into the collective consciousness the awareness that will awaken those who are the most spiritually aware and have the potential to manifest either full Christhood or a high degree of Christhood in this lifetime.

> Zadkiel Archangel, we truly aspire,
> to being the master of your violet fire,
> wielding the power, of your alchemy,
> we use Sacred Word, to set all life free.
>
> **Zadkiel Archangel, encircle the earth,**
> **Zadkiel Archangel, with your violet girth,**
> **Zadkiel Archangel, unstoppable mirth,**
> **Zadkiel Archangel, our planet's rebirth.**

3. Saint Germain, radiate into the collective consciousness the awareness that one of the essential elements of Christhood is not only Christ discernment but a higher level of Christ discernment that empowers us to put our priorities straight.

> Zadkiel Archangel, your violet light,
> transforming the earth, with unstoppable might,
> so swiftly our planet, beginning to spin,
> with legions of angels, our victory we win.

> **Zadkiel Archangel, encircle the earth,**
> **Zadkiel Archangel, with your violet girth,**
> **Zadkiel Archangel, unstoppable mirth,**
> **Zadkiel Archangel, our planet's rebirth.**

4. Saint Germain, radiate into the collective consciousness the awareness that we must be about our Father's business, namely our Divine plans.

> Zadkiel Archangel, the earth is now free,
> from burdens put on her by humanity,
> all people are free from their inner strife,
> embracing the freedom to start a new life.

> **Zadkiel Archangel, encircle the earth,**
> **Zadkiel Archangel, with your violet girth,**
> **Zadkiel Archangel, unstoppable mirth,**
> **Zadkiel Archangel, our planet's rebirth.**

5. Saint Germain, radiate into the collective consciousness the awareness that our Divine plan is not imposed upon us from any external authority, but it is the choices of our own conscious selves and our higher beings—our I AM Presences.

Zadkiel Archangel, the earth will now spin,
much faster as we Christ victory win,
for in Christ the captives are truly set free,
bathed in Christ Light the earth now will be.

Zadkiel Archangel, encircle the earth,
Zadkiel Archangel, with your violet girth,
Zadkiel Archangel, unstoppable mirth,
Zadkiel Archangel, our planet's rebirth.

6. Saint Germain, radiate into the collective consciousness the awareness that we came here with the love of wanting to see our Divine plan unfold. In order to achieve this goal, we need to step up to the higher level of Christ discernment that gives us the sense of what is truly the priority for us to attain in this lifetime.

Zadkiel Archangel, the forces of night,
are bound by your penetrating Freedom Light,
the earth is now cleared by forces so dark,
as your Violet Light provides a new spark.

Zadkiel Archangel, encircle the earth,
Zadkiel Archangel, with your violet girth,
Zadkiel Archangel, unstoppable mirth,
Zadkiel Archangel, our planet's rebirth.

7. Saint Germain, radiate into the collective consciousness the awareness that any Aquarian-age movement has one major, overall goal that supersedes all other goals, namely to demonstrate the path to personal Christhood in the material world.

> Zadkiel Archangel, we truly love you,
> and to Saint Germain we will always be true,
> help us now see our plans so Divine,
> so we on this planet our full light can shine.
>
> **Zadkiel Archangel, encircle the earth,**
> **Zadkiel Archangel, with your violet girth,**
> **Zadkiel Archangel, unstoppable mirth,**
> **Zadkiel Archangel, our planet's rebirth.**

8. Saint Germain, radiate into the collective consciousness the awareness that we need to internalize the path so that when we stand before people and demonstrate it, they are seeing the Living Christ in us as they saw the Living Christ in Jesus.

> Zadkiel Archangel, there is no more night,
> a new day is born from your great Violet Light,
> transforming all manifestations of fear,
> we know that the Golden Age is now here.
>
> **Zadkiel Archangel, encircle the earth,**
> **Zadkiel Archangel, with your violet girth,**
> **Zadkiel Archangel, unstoppable mirth,**
> **Zadkiel Archangel, our planet's rebirth.**

9. Saint Germain, radiate into the collective consciousness the awareness that the overall goal of the ascended masters in this age is that a critical mass of people awaken to the lessons of Pisces and embody them so that they can form the platform for the descent of the aquarian-age consciousness.

Zadkiel Archangel, your violet flame,
the earth and humanity, never the same,
Saint Germain's Golden Age, is a reality,
what glorious wonder, we joyously see.

Zadkiel Archangel, encircle the earth,
Zadkiel Archangel, with your violet girth,
Zadkiel Archangel, unstoppable mirth,
Zadkiel Archangel, our planet's rebirth.

Part 2

1. Saint Germain, radiate into the collective consciousness the awareness that we need to envision, not in a prideful way but in a manner of practical realism, that we are the only ones who have this potential.

Beloved Arcturus, release now the flow,
of Violet Flame to help all life grow,
in ever-expanding circles of light,
it pulses within every atom so bright.

Beloved Arcturus, your Violet Flame pure,
is for every ailment the ultimate cure,
against it no darkness could ever endure,
earth's freedom it will forever ensure.

2. Saint Germain, radiate into the collective consciousness the awareness that if we do not do it, who will? If we do not do it now, then when will it be done?

> Beloved Arcturus, thou Elohim Free,
> we open our hearts to your reality,
> we have no attachments to life here on earth,
> we claim a new life in your Flame of Rebirth.
>
> **Beloved Arcturus, your Violet Flame pure,**
> **is for every ailment the ultimate cure,**
> **against it no darkness could ever endure,**
> **earth's freedom it will forever ensure.**

3. Saint Germain, radiate into the collective consciousness the awareness that because we have the potential, it is part of our Divine plan to demonstrate that Christhood, both individually and as a community coming together, dedicating our lives to demonstrating that path.

> Beloved Arcturus, be with us alway,
> reborn, we are ready to face a new day,
> expanding our hearts into Infinity,
> your flame is the key to our God-victory.
>
> **Beloved Arcturus, your Violet Flame pure,**
> **is for every ailment the ultimate cure,**
> **against it no darkness could ever endure,**
> **earth's freedom it will forever ensure.**

4. Saint Germain, radiate into the collective consciousness the awareness that the purpose is that the people do not see it demonstrated in just one individual that they can easily idolize. They see it in many people who have come from similar backgrounds as themselves.

Beloved Arcturus, your bright violet fire,
now fills every atom, raising them higher,
the space in each atom all filled with your light,
as matter itself is shining so bright.

**Beloved Arcturus, your Violet Flame pure,
is for every ailment the ultimate cure,
against it no darkness could ever endure,
earth's freedom it will forever ensure.**

5. Saint Germain, radiate into the collective consciousness the awareness that the overall goal is to demonstrate the path of Christhood. There is a need to demonstrate the path in every area of life.

Beloved Arcturus, your transforming Grace,
empowers us now every challenge to face,
with your Freedom's Song filling the ear,
we know that to God we're ever so dear.

**Beloved Arcturus, your Violet Flame pure,
is for every ailment the ultimate cure,
against it no darkness could ever endure,
earth's freedom it will forever ensure.**

6. Saint Germain, radiate into the collective consciousness the awareness that there is a need for those who will rethink everything and start to think the thoughts that have not been thought on this planet for eons: How will a Christed being behave in the arena of politics, business, science and religion?

Beloved Arcturus, we surrender all fear,
we're feeling your Presence so tangibly near,
as your violet light floods our inner space,
towards the ascension we willingly race.

**Beloved Arcturus, your Violet Flame pure,
is for every ailment the ultimate cure,
against it no darkness could ever endure,
earth's freedom it will forever ensure.**

7. Saint Germain, radiate into the collective consciousness the awareness that it is extremely important for us not to become trapped in, not to become attached to, particular outer goals.

Beloved Arcturus, bring in a new age,
help earth and humanity turn a new page,
your transforming light gives us certainty,
Saint Germain's Golden Age is a reality.

**Beloved Arcturus, your Violet Flame pure,
is for every ailment the ultimate cure,
against it no darkness could ever endure,
earth's freedom it will forever ensure.**

8. Saint Germain, radiate into the collective consciousness the awareness that many sincere spiritual seekers have become attached to achieving a particular goal in this world, seeking a particular response from other people or the world.

Beloved Arcturus, illusions you pierce,
no serpent can stand against angels so fierce,
no forces of darkness can stop Violet Flame,
all discord on earth it will instantly tame.

> **Beloved Arcturus, your Violet Flame pure,**
> **is for every ailment the ultimate cure,**
> **against it no darkness could ever endure,**
> **earth's freedom it will forever ensure.**

9. Saint Germain, radiate into the collective consciousness the awareness that when we have our priorities straight, we realize that the overall goal is to demonstrate the path of Christhood.

> Beloved Arcturus, we love Saint Germain,
> and therefore we call forth again and again,
> your Violet Flame to flood all the earth,
> so Saint Germain's eyes are filling with mirth.

> **Beloved Arcturus, your Violet Flame pure,**
> **is for every ailment the ultimate cure,**
> **against it no darkness could ever endure,**
> **earth's freedom it will forever ensure.**

Part 3

1. Saint Germain, radiate into the collective consciousness the awareness that we can do this with complete independence of how people respond or do not respond to it. We are not here to produce a particular response, but to give people the choice of how to respond to a Christed being.

> Saint Germain, your alchemy,
> with violet fire now sets us free.
> Saint Germain, we ever grow,
> in freedom's overpowering flow.

**O Saint Germain, your Golden Age,
sets people free from psychic cage,
the earth is raised to starry height,
as we project with Freedom's Sight.**

2. Saint Germain, radiate into the collective consciousness the awareness that there are people who are meant to rise above all entanglement with particular aspects of the world and come to demonstrate the true universal River of Life that runs behind all spirituality.

Saint Germain, your mastery,
of violet flame geometry.
Saint Germain, in you we see,
the formulas that set us free.

**O Saint Germain, your Golden Age,
sets people free from psychic cage,
the earth is raised to starry height,
as we project with Freedom's Sight.**

3. Saint Germain, radiate into the collective consciousness the awareness that some people need to bring forth a demonstration of a truly universal spiritual movement with a universal vision.

Saint Germain, in Liberty,
you give the love that sets all free.
Saint Germain, we do adore,
the violet flame that makes all more.

**O Saint Germain, your Golden Age,
sets people free from psychic cage,
the earth is raised to starry height,
as we project with Freedom's Sight.**

4. Saint Germain, radiate into the collective consciousness the awareness that those in the fallen consciousness are well aware that the greatest threat they face is even one person, but even more a great number of people, who have manifested Christhood and demonstrate it to the world.

Saint Germain, in unity,
we will transcend duality.
Saint Germain, the self so pure,
your violet chemistry so sure.

**O Saint Germain, your Golden Age,
sets people free from psychic cage,
the earth is raised to starry height,
as we project with Freedom's Sight.**

5. Saint Germain, radiate into the collective consciousness the awareness that one of their primary tactics is to distract or divert our attention from the larger goal so that we become so focused on achieving a particular goal that it takes us away from the overall path to Christhood.

Saint Germain, reality,
in violet light we are carefree.
Saint Germain, our auras seal,
your violet flame our chakras heal.

**O Saint Germain, your Golden Age,
sets people free from psychic cage,
the earth is raised to starry height,
as we project with Freedom's Sight.**

6. Saint Germain, radiate into the collective consciousness the awareness that while we may do some good by pursuing a particular activity, it is not the greatest good that we have the potential to bring forth in this embodiment.

Saint Germain, your chemistry,
with violet fire set atoms free.
Saint Germain, from lead to gold,
transforming vision we behold.

**O Saint Germain, your Golden Age,
sets people free from psychic cage,
the earth is raised to starry height,
as we project with Freedom's Sight.**

7. Saint Germain, radiate into the collective consciousness the awareness that black holes do not exist only in the physical realm, but also in the emotional, mental and the lower etheric realms.

Saint Germain, transcendency,
as we are always one with thee.
Saint Germain, from soul we're free,
we so delight in knowing thee.

**O Saint Germain, your Golden Age,
sets people free from psychic cage,
the earth is raised to starry height,
as we project with Freedom's Sight.**

8. Saint Germain, radiate into the collective consciousness the awareness that in the higher realms black holes often take the form of a dead-end activity that is designed to distract our attention from the goal of Christhood.

Saint Germain, nobility,
the key to sacred alchemy.
Saint Germain, you balance all,
the seven rays upon our call.

**O Saint Germain, your Golden Age,
sets people free from psychic cage,
the earth is raised to starry height,
as we project with Freedom's Sight.**

9. Saint Germain, radiate into the collective consciousness the awareness that the dark forces want us to think that something else is either more important or has to be completed first, before we can focus on the path of Christhood. We then keep postponing the path indefinitely until it is too late to demonstrate it in this lifetime.

Saint Germain, your Presence here,
filling up the inner sphere.
Life is now a sacred flow,
God Freedom we on all bestow.

**O Saint Germain, your Golden Age,
sets people free from psychic cage,
the earth is raised to starry height,
as we project with Freedom's Sight.**

Part 4

1. Saint Germain, radiate into the collective consciousness the awareness that spiritual people often become attached to helping people who have such complexity in their psychology that we have no realistic opportunity to help them in this lifetime.

O Saint Germain, you do inspire,
my vision raised forever higher,
with you I form a figure-eight,
your Golden Age I co-create.

**O Saint Germain, what love you bring,
it truly makes all matter sing,
your violet flame does all restore,
with you we are becoming more.**

2. Saint Germain, radiate into the collective consciousness the awareness that some people attempt to draw us into an endless cycle of questionings or debates, all of which lead to no real change in the people because they are not willing to transcend their egos.

O Saint Germain, what Freedom Flame,
released when we recite your name,
acceleration is your gift,
our planet it will surely lift.

**O Saint Germain, what love you bring,
it truly makes all matter sing,
your violet flame does all restore,
with you we are becoming more.**

3. Saint Germain, radiate into the collective consciousness the awareness that we sometimes need to say: "I cannot help you, and thus I must focus my attention on helping those whom I can actually help. If I continue to focus my attention on the people who are black holes, then do I not deprive the people whom I have a realistic opportunity to help of the help that they need?"

O Saint Germain, in love we claim,
our right to bring your violet flame,
from you Above, to us below,
it is an all-transforming flow.

**O Saint Germain, what love you bring,
it truly makes all matter sing,
your violet flame does all restore,
with you we are becoming more.**

18 | Invoking the awakening of Saint Germain's own

4. Saint Germain, radiate into the collective consciousness the awareness that although there is a need to demonstrate Christhood in all areas of society, those who have the greatest attainment and potential to demonstrate Christhood must do so in an overall manner—without being tied up in details that are not truly important for the onward progression of society.

> O Saint Germain, I love you so,
> my aura filled with violet glow,
> my chakras filled with violet fire,
> I am your cosmic amplifier.
>
> **O Saint Germain, what love you bring,
> it truly makes all matter sing,
> your violet flame does all restore,
> with you we are becoming more.**

5. Saint Germain, radiate into the collective consciousness the awareness that we need to step back and in our hearts tune in to our Christ selves and your Presence and ask: "Would Saint Germain consider this cause to be essential for bringing in the Golden Age? Or would it only be a minor step forward that is not consequential for the overall goal of manifesting the Golden Age and demonstrating the path to Christhood?"

> O Saint Germain, I am now free,
> your violet flame is therapy,
> transform all hang-ups in my mind,
> as inner peace I surely find.

**O Saint Germain, what love you bring,
it truly makes all matter sing,
your violet flame does all restore,
with you we are becoming more.**

6. Saint Germain, radiate into the collective consciousness the awareness that we need to consider what is consequential for the fulfillment of our Divine plan, for the demonstration of the path to Christhood, for the manifestation of the Golden Age.

O Saint Germain, my body pure,
your violet flame for all is cure,
consume the cause of all disease,
and therefore I am all at ease.

**O Saint Germain, what love you bring,
it truly makes all matter sing,
your violet flame does all restore,
with you we are becoming more.**

7. Saint Germain, radiate into the collective consciousness the awareness that in many cases we need to have a total surrender to the higher vision before we will discover what is the essential element of our Divine plans.

O Saint Germain, I'm karma-free,
the past no longer burdens me,
a brand new opportunity,
I am in Christic unity.

**O Saint Germain, what love you bring,
it truly makes all matter sing,
your violet flame does all restore,
with you we are becoming more.**

8. Saint Germain, radiate into the collective consciousness the awareness that each one of us has a potential to be part of something that is consequential for the bringing forth of the Golden Age.

O Saint Germain, we are now one,
I am for you a violet sun,
as we transform this planet earth,
your Golden Age is given birth.

**O Saint Germain, what love you bring,
it truly makes all matter sing,
your violet flame does all restore,
with you we are becoming more.**

9. Saint Germain, radiate into the collective consciousness the awareness that we need to be willing to rethink our priorities and let go of certain activities that we understand from within are not consequential for the overall goal for which we came into this world.

O Saint Germain, the earth is free,
from burden of duality,
in oneness we bring what is best,
your Golden Age is manifest.

**O Saint Germain, what love you bring,
it truly makes all matter sing,
your violet flame does all restore,
with you we are becoming more.**

Sealing

In the name of the Divine Mother, I call to all ascended masters for the sealing of myself and all people in my circle of influence in the creative flow of the Divine Mother, the River of Life. I call for the multiplication of my calls by all ascended masters so that we form the perfect figure-eight flow of "As Above, so below." Thus, I accept that this is fully manifest, because the mouth of the Lord, the Divine Mother that I AM, has spoken it. Amen.

19 | SAINT GERMAIN IS THE BUDDHA FOR THE AQUARIAN AGE

I, Gautama, am joyful to take on the great privilege of announcing to you that Saint Germain has attained the level of Buddhahood, and has been anointed by me as a Buddha for the earth—as the Buddha holding the Freedom Flame for the earth. My beloved, this is a very significant development, for we now have Jesus – who also attained Buddhahood not that long ago – and we have Saint Germain, both having achieved this level of consciousness. Both the master of the Piscean age and the master of the Aquarian age have reached that level of Buddhahood, which is significantly higher than the level of consciousness at which most beings ascend.

The anointing took place on the 4th of July this year, 2007, in a simple and small ceremony held at my retreat of Shamballa. I desire you to recognize the Buddha of Freedom.

Now then, my beloved, I shall not tire you with a long discourse, for I know you have worked hard and long hours during this conference, holding the balance for this immense release of teachings. I must tell you that even Saint Germain himself could not have released these teachings before his anointing as the Buddha. These are Buddhic-level teachings that, as he said, have not been released for a very long time on this planet.

Thus, you have an understanding that has not been available even to the most spiritually aware people in past Golden Ages, at least for some time. This, my beloved, is another good sign that we – this time – will create and manifest a Golden Age that has the potential not to go into a degenerative spiral after a short period of time.

The Buddha's Presence in California

My beloved, as Saint Germain has talked about the importance of a breakthrough in consciousness that can start here in California, I desire to announce to you that you have earned a reward, a dispensation from me. At the conference in Virginia and at the conference in Ireland, I anchored my Presence, both in Europe and in Washington D.C. Well, due to your work of transcendence, due to the release of light from Saint Germain, I am also anchoring my presence in – or rather throughout – the state of California.

Certainly, the Presence of the Buddha is not limited by time and space, for time and space are not—they are unreal at the level of Buddhahood. I shall anchor my Presence here, again forming an arc from here to Washington, from Washington to Europe, so that we can see a sparking, a fire beginning to burn, in the collective consciousness. People who are attuned to the consciousness of the Buddha will be awakened to the need to step up higher and to bring forth new ideas and to express those ideas in all areas of society.

This is indeed a significant dispensation, for now we span the East and the West coast of the United States as well as the Atlantic ocean. It is even possible that other conferences in the future – held on other continents – could again create a breakthrough that would allow me to anchor my Presence there as well—eventually forming a grid, an antakharana, that spans the entire planet. This will in some instances be some ways off, for the people in those areas need to do more work to prepare for such a dispensation. Yet I give you the vision of what is possible.

I impart to you my infinite peace

My beloved, I wish to impart to you – as much as it can be possibly done through words and vibration – the infinite, unconditional peace of the Buddha. Saint Germain has given you teachings about the ongoingness of the path, the River of Life and the work of the ascended masters. He has talked about the possibility of immersing yourself in the River of Life, thus finding a peace that not only passes understanding but passes all aspects of the human mind. It is so far beyond what can be conceived by the human mind, which always thinks in terms of this world and thus believes that in order for a person or a society to achieve peace, certain outer conditions must be fulfilled.

Seek to step into that peace of flowing with the River of Life, not being attached to any outer conditions, not thinking your peace depends on outer conditions, nor having any expectations of what the future should bring. Be content to flow with the River of Life. If that River brings you a portion of karma for you to transcend – either personally or for the world – then you meet it with peace. Because you are at peace, you can work through it so much faster.

Or if the River brings you circumstances – problems that you have vowed to take on for the world in order to make it easier for other people to solve certain problems and overcome conditions in their psychology – well, then, again, you do not become entangled in it. You keep your overall perspective and you see it as simply a temporary phase in your overall mission. Then you move through it as quickly as possible so that you can get on with the activities that are truly consequential.

Thus, my beloved, receive the Peace of the Buddha, the infinite, unconditional, never-ending, inexhaustible Peace of the Buddha, the peace that can be given out infinitely without being depleted in the least, for it has no quantity and thus no limitations. That which is beyond quantity, that which cannot be quantified by any measurement in this world, obviously cannot be exhausted, no matter how much is given forth of it.

In fact, I will leave you with a riddle that even infinity is not beyond transcendence, for the more of infinity you use or give, the more it becomes. Thus, when you overcome the consciousness of lack – the fear of loss, the desire to own something for the separate self – well, then you will see the reality that the more you give the more you shall receive. Life, my beloved, does not want to stand still. It wants to grow, it wants to expand, it wants to become more than it is now. It wants to continue to become more in the infinite cycles of God's infinite, inexhaustible, incomprehensible Being. Thus, I seal you in the peace of my heart, the heart of the Buddha of Peace for the earth. Be at peace by *being* Peace.

20 | DIVERSITY IS THE MASTER KEY TO THE GOLDEN AGE

I AM the ascended master Saint Germain. I AM the Hierarch for the Golden Age for planet earth and I intend to use this conference to give a series of teaching dictations concerning the topic you have chosen: "The Descent of the Golden Age."

This is a large topic, I am sure you realize, and I cannot cover it all in a series of dictations. I could not even cover it in a thousand dictations because there are many aspects of the descent of the Golden Age that cannot be expressed in words. They are only brought into manifestation through the descent of the Word.

The Word, as it is mentioned in the Gospel of John, is an expression of the Christ Consciousness. Of course, the Word is more than words. The Word can be expressed through words, but it cannot be captured by or confined to words. Words are, of course, of the material realm and that which is of the material can express and outpicture the immaterial, but it does not *define* the immaterial and thus it cannot *confine* the immaterial.

The descent of the Golden Age is first and foremost that a civilization becomes open to the descent of the immaterial into the material world and that a civilization allows the immaterial to determine the material expression in that society in everything from the highest levels of the government, through art, music, culture and even the individual lives; and especially relationships and family relationships of the people.

No centralized worldly government

Let me discourse, in this opening discourse, on one of the more subtle aspects of the descent of the Golden Age, an aspect that few people have even begun to grasp and understand. I wish to extend an opportunity to those who are open. Let me make it clear that what I will say here applies to every nation on earth. Surely, different nations are on different levels. Some may not be quite ready to internalize what I am going to teach, nevertheless all nations have a potential.

We of the ascended masters hold the vision for each nation. We do not see what is currently manifest as permanent or unavoidable, we do not even see it as wrong or bad. We do not judge according to the standard that you see on earth, the standard which we have many times now made you aware is the standard created by the fallen beings and the fallen mindset. Of course, one of the more subtle aspects of the descent of the Golden Age is that humankind must begin to rise above that fallen mindset: the tendency to judge according to a standard that can be expressed in words instead of letting the Living Word be the standard, or rather set a matrix that is beyond any standard on earth. Let me take you back through history. Let us go back and look at some of the civilizations in the past that at least today are considered "great civilizations." You

20 | Diversity is the master key to the Golden Age

have seen many such civilizations around the world even in the brief time span you call recorded history. Of course, all history is recorded; it is just that right now on earth you only have access to a fragment of the total record of past civilizations.

Nevertheless, here in this area of Central Asia you have seen great civilizations of the past, and by "great" I mean civilizations that have had a great level of organization. They were under one or a few rulers and therefore by being so-called "unified" under one command they could also be unified in carrying out certain tasks that could not be carried out by smaller civilizations. This might be building great cities, it might be building great armies and fighting other armies. This, of course, is not what we of the ascended masters call a great task, but my point is to show that in the past you have seen the formation of certain very large civilizations.

These civilizations reached a very high level of organization and a high level of ability to get things done in the physical, the material world. Look at some of these civilizations in China. Look at some in Central and Southeast Asia, in India, in Persia, the Middle East, Sumerians, Egyptians, and the Roman Empire and in Central and South America. You see this tendency that civilizations would arise that would build great cities and great monuments, some of which even stand today.

It is entirely possible that when people hear the concept that there is a potential of the coming of the Golden Age—and possibly even a physical Golden Age that will surpass any of the golden ages seen in the past – then they come to think that somehow the Golden Age will be modeled on the great civilizations of the past, that it will have a great level of organization. The world will, so to speak, be united under one centralized government and this government can issue edicts or things will be done, or they will often be done the same way around the world.

Filtering out diversity kills creativity

Do you see that in the past these "great" civilizations had attained what they attained by having a very centralized structure, a centralized philosophy but also a very centralized standard for how you judged right and wrong, good and bad, how you defined a standard for how people should behave? What these civilizations did in the past was that they would achieve their results by shutting out diversity, by putting down, by destroying by filtering away diversity. They had a centralized structure so that all they had were people that behaved according to a certain set of rules, often defined by a religion but filtering down to the laws of society.

You may take a more recent look, for example, at the Roman Empire. Again, a very centralized structure and a very centralized philosophy, and of course the willingness to use force. In every civilization in the past that has achieved "greatness" there has been a willingness to use force against those who would not follow the leaders of that civilization, those who claimed their right to diversify rather than to "unify." Force through sameness.

Now then, I AM Saint Germain. I AM an ascended being. I have ascended by transcending all of the patterns and matrices on earth. I have transcended the entire fallen mindset. Thus, I tell you with absolute determination: "The Golden Age of Saint Germain that is prophesied to come into physical manifestation in this 2,000-year period of the Age of Aquarius will not be attained by destroying diversity or by creating a centralized world government. There will be centralized governments, there will even be one overseeing government for the entire planet, but it will not use force and it will not destroy diversity. This is not the vision of Saint Germain." My vision is to create a Golden Age based on diversity. Even though there is a need to have a certain outer apparatus of organization that can coordinate around the world, this centralized organization will *coordinate,* it will not *dictate.* It will not use force, it will not even bring forth a centralized religion or philosophy that all must follow. Why will it not do this? Because if there ever is to be a lasting worldwide organization, it will based on the recognition of the principles that I, Saint Germain, will reveal as the founding principles and the sustaining principles of my Golden Age.

No more exclusivity

Such an organization will recognize that there is a level beyond the material world and that there are intelligent beings in that world that can communicate with human beings. More importantly, it will recognize that we of the ascended masters can communicate through any human being, not necessarily any and all, but we do not communicate exclusively through a small elite or one person. We can potentially communicate with any person regardless of their status or position in the earthly organization or civilization. The Golden Age of Saint Germain will be based on the descent of the Word, which is an expression of the Holy Spirit—and the Holy Spirit bloweth where it listeth. Or rather, when it comes to the Golden Age, it bloweth where *I* listeth for I am the overseer of the Golden Age.

You can see the civilizations of the past and how they were all based on exclusivity, which is the idea that only one person could rule or only one person could be the intermediary between God (or the gods) and man. Look at the Roman Empire and how it was based on the idea of one emperor who in certain periods was even seen as God on earth. The spiritual arrogance of certain emperors was such that they defined themselves as gods on earth. Today, no secular ruler does this but you do indeed see people in spiritual and religious movements who have the arrogance to define themselves as the exclusive incarnation of God or a certain God. You see how the Roman Empire took the idea that the Emperor was God on earth, transferred it to Christianity and now created the philosophy that Jesus was the only intermediary between God and the people. At the same time, there was a church that controlled the people's access to what was administered by Jesus. Thus came the whole superstructure of the Catholic Church with the Pope as the Vicar of Christ.

Why does Christ need a Vicar when Christ instituted the tradition of the Comforter, the Holy spirit that could speak through anyone, blowing where it listesth? If you can make sense of this, my beloved, then you can do something I cannot do for I cannot make sense of it. Of course, I do not see through the filter of the fallen consciousness and I realize that many well-meaning people simply have been deceived. They have no evil intent, they only intended to do the best. They thought they were Christ's representatives, they thought they were doing what Christ wanted them to do, but they failed to do the one thing that can manifest the Golden Age, which was to tune in to the Spirit in their own hearts.

There will not be only one messenger

My beloved, this messenger certainly does not have the spiritual pride that makes him think that there will come a day where the secular leaders of the world would look to him or any other messenger in order to tell them how to do everything through a dictation. There will indeed be messengers, and there will be multiple messengers in the Aquarian Age. There will be some that hold a position where society can and will listen to what is given through them, yet do not fall into the trap of thinking that I, Saint Germain, envision a society where at the very top of a hierarchical structure is a messenger of the ascended masters. This is not our plan; this is not our vision at all.

Even if we could get all of the governments and all of the people to listen to one messenger who was sponsored by the ascended masters, this still is not what we desire for the Golden Age. The Golden Age of Saint Germain is a Golden Age of diversity where the Spirit finds expression through millions of people, in a variety of ways, who are the open doors for receiving something: an idea, an expression, art, music what have you.

There are those today who have never heard about ascended masters and do not need to hear about ascended masters in order to be open doors for the matrices of the Golden Age that I am already letting descend upon the material world as a gentle rain of golden, sometimes multicolored, raindrops.

You all are open to the existence of Saint Germain. That means you have the potential to consciously attune yourselves to my Being and to consciously catch some of these raindrops, the raindrops that are falling, as you might envision, from the very intricate matrices that I have set up in the Cave of Symbols, the symbols for the etheric blueprint of the Golden Age. The light streams through these multifaceted, sometimes very complex, symbols and it is then colored and charged and falls with them. The light falls as you might envision raindrops, sparkling drops of rain that reflect the light from which they came.

Expressing ideas in society

My beloved, being consciously aware of the ascended masters is of great value, but it really only is of great value if you express it, as we have said a number of times now. This does not mean that you walk around in society going from door to door like some religious movements that pound on the door and are ready to preach to anyone who will let them in. You do not have to openly seek to convert other people to follow the teachings of the ascended masters, neither through this nor any other messenger. There are many of you who have it in your Divine plans to be the open doors, but it is through expressing ideas in your field of expertise in society.

You can express these ideas in a universal way without ever referring to us, and this is something I wish to mention. In previous ascended master organizations we have seen some of our students who had the best of intentions to help materialize the Golden Age of Saint Germain, but who like many religious people became deceived by their fervor. They expressed their fervor through their own unresolved psychology. There has been a certain number of students who have had the tendency that they wanted to convert other people and that they were attached to outer results. Therefore, they attempted to use us as the ultimate authority so that they could get people to listen.

You will see the same in some Christian groups that use the Bible as the ultimate authority and go around from door to door, knocking on people's doors. If you let them in, they attempt to beat you into submission through the authority, the infallible authority, of the Bible as the only word of God according to the specific interpretation of that word decided upon by the leaders of their church. We have no desire to see ascended master students do this for it is not your highest potential. Your highest potential is to tune in to whichever

20 | Diversity is the master key to the Golden Age

ascended master is closest to you and then become an open door for what that master wants to bring forth—not what your outer mind thinks that this master wants to bring forth or *should* bring forth according to a standard you have created.

I do not even care if you have created a standard based on past ascended master teachings. Whatever standard you have created will be colored by your outer mind for the Holy Spirit bloweth where it listeth. It does not blow through the standard created by the outer mind! Only if you make an effort to make yourself the "open" door with no screen, then can you be the fullness of the expression of the Living Word that you have the potential to be. In many cases, the Holy Spirit will blow where it listeth by expressing an idea through your work, some area of expertise that you have in society.

It is not the goal of the Holy Spirit to convert other people to the ascended masters' teachings. It is the goal to bring forth ideas that can be incorporated into materializing a higher expression of the Golden Age. Does that mean you can never talk about ascended masters? No, it does not, but you need to be sensitive and as a general rule, in many cases when you are out in society, do not talk about ascended masters unless someone asks you in private, one-on-one: "Where do you get these ideas from?" Then you can tell them, but you do not need to use us as an authority.

You need to be willing to be the open door, expressing an idea and letting the idea do its work. It may be that people reject it. Many people will reject the light, but the light will still make a difference. Why will the light make a difference? Because whenever the light is expressed, you give people an opportunity to either choose the light or to choose to continue in their present level of consciousness. You give them the opportunity to accept the light or reject the light. They did not have that opportunity before they encountered the expression of the light through you, before they encountered something that was immaterial or rather not all based on the fallen standard. This is what Jesus did when he walked the earth in a physical body.

There will be no use of force

The people who met him, they all saw something in him that they had never seen in any other human being. By the mere fact that Jesus walked among people as the open door, he did the work that was meant to be done. Due to the light, they became subject to the School of Hard Knocks, the second law of thermodynamics. In the case of those who actively attacked the Living Christ, the light would actually accelerate their downward spiral so that they more quickly came to their point of no return where they could not continue to embody on this planet.

You may see that Jesus himself was killed, and from an outer viewpoint, did Jesus attain anything in that embodiment? Not from an outer viewpoint, but nevertheless he created the spiral that carried humanity through the Piscean Age and that led to the fact that he today can express his true teachings in a more palatable and more easy-to-understand form. It has led to the fact that we of the ascended masters today can openly reveal our Presence through the Spoken Word, which is harder to deny than previous expressions. While we still respect free will and plausible deniability, we have given people a closer contact with us than they could have had 2,000 years ago. I assure you that 2,000 years ago having a sponsored messenger was simply an impossibility due to the level of the collective consciousness. My point here is this: In the Golden Age of Saint Germain you will see diversity, diversification. There will not be one spiritual or religious organization, nor will there be one organization of government that will dominate the Golden Age, that will dictate or that will use force.

There are sometimes ascended master students who have looked at conditions on earth and seen how bad they really are. It is necessary to look at conditions the way they are and to honestly assess: "Yes, there is something we need to overcome. Yes, we have a higher potential and we could do better." When students of the ascended masters have done this, have been awakened to the fact that things are not the highest potential right now, they sometimes become so zealous that they are almost ready to use force.

For example, we recently saw in a previous dispensation that some among the student body supported the use of force to end the Soviet Union. They were ready to go to war even if it was a devastating world-wide war, or at least a war with worldwide consequences, in order to end what they saw as, in the words of a certain President: the Evil Empire. We of the ascended masters certainly saw problems with the Soviet Empire, there is no question about this. We also saw from the ascended realm the hearts of the Russian people. Do you really think that we of the ascended masters were so intent on destroying the Soviet Empire that we were willing to kill millions of the Russian people in order to attain this goal?

How force-based empires vanish

Certainly, you can see – if you are open to these teachings – that we were not willing to do this for we saw the potential that what *did* happen *could* happen. We saw that it could be dissolved by only a few people among the leaders making a decision. They made that decision because there had been a certain raising of the consciousness of the people, not only in Russia but in all of the republics that were part of the Soviet Union.

You realize, do you not, that when one country, such as Russia, suppresses a number of other countries, it may seem as if they have power over those countries, but when you suppress another country by force it is not a one-way street. It is not that you are the only one exercising power. Yes, you may be exercising power, physical power and material power, but there is a return current of the consciousness of the conquered nations to the nation that conquered them. Whatever happened in the outlying Soviet Republics, had an influence on the Soviet power apparatus centered in Moscow.

There was an exchange of consciousness, and it was in the beginning the Soviet Republics that raised their consciousness and demanded more freedom. This created a figure-eight flow that eventually made it possible for certain leaders, even as dense as their consciousness was, so that even in the few moments that they had where they were not completely drunk with vodka, they could still make a realistic assessment and say: "It is time to end this; *it is time to end this.*"

There are indeed situations on earth where you can look at certain power structures and certain civilizations or empires and you can say—you *must* say: "It is time to end this." The manifestation of power is such that if the people do not voluntarily end it, it will become subject to the second law of thermodynamics, the force of Shiva, that breaks down that which is out of touch with the growth in the consciousness of the people. This is why you have seen certain past civilizations that seemed to be indestructible. They had lasted for decades or centuries but suddenly something happened, either from within or without, that caused them to collapse within a very short period of time.

Why violent empires are allowed to rise

Yes, there is sometimes a need to say: "It is time to end this cycle." Be careful and realize a very important principle, a very subtle principle, that I said I wanted to discourse on, and it is this: Free will is such that whatever people desire to outpicture in the material world, they must be allowed to outpicture it for a time. They need to see the physical manifestation of the ideas that they have come to accept, even sometimes subconscious ideas and matrices.

I wish to give you an idea that I know will be shocking to many people around the world, even many of the ascended master students from previous dispensations. The fact is that you can take an empire such as the Nazi Empire, and you can look at the history of the rise of Hitler and how he came to power. You can look at how he took power by force and deceit, by all means possible. You may say that he stole that power or that he forced the Germans people and the German nation into submitting to his reign, but you see, you cannot force any nation against the consciousness of the people. It would not have been possible for Hitler to take power in 1933 unless he had locked in to and ridden the wave of what had been going on in the collective consciousness of the time.

You need to understand that the collective consciousness is driven by individual people, and this means that if you look at a part of the population, such as the Germans in the 1930's, there was a certain percentage among them that were to some degree the open doors for the flow of Spirit. They were not truly the open doors in the sense that they were completely clear, but they had the ability to receive some stream of energy, which filtered through their beings and was then expressed through their outer consciousness. This means that the flow of energy was colored by their beliefs, and even they were to some degree swept up in that collective movement in the German consciousness. They were not always consciously aware of what they were doing, but they did not have enough clarity to recognize just how far out of line Hitler was with the higher spiritual principles and certainly with the ascended masters. Thus, they could not form enough of a counterbalance to prevent that swing where the majority of the people actually started supporting Hitler.

You understand that after this shift had happened, regardless of how it was brought about, then the many people that received some spiritual light, their light became a force – an occult, mystical force such as Hitler was aware of – that supported the rise of the Nazi regime. This was not, of course, what we of the ascended masters would ideally desire to see happen. We did not desire to see the rise of the Nazi regime as we did not desire to see the rise of the communist regime, but once the shift had happened, we had to allow this to happen in order to allow free will to outpicture itself.

Of course, you saw in the very beginning how the Nazi regime seemed to be unstoppable, even after the war had started. It was unstoppable for two reasons. Partly, as we have said before, through the killing and the torture that forced the release of light but also because they were riding the wave of the release of the Holy Spirit through individual people. Now, be careful to recognize that there is no restriction possible of free will and how it outplays itself.

It is only through people in embodiment that the outplaying of free will can be directed in different directions. I wish to make you realize that only when a critical mass of people shift their awareness, can there be intercession from above that can avoid certain physical calamities. There were not enough people in Germany who shifted their consciousness so that the Second World War and the ultimate military defeat of the Nazi regime could be avoided. This could have happened if enough people, the ones who I am talking about who were the open doors, had shifted the light and their consciousness during the 1930's. It could have happened almost up to the very point that the war began, but there were not enough that shifted their consciousness.

Why the Cold War did not become hot

Now, what I wish to bring to your attention is that after the Second World War there was, of course, the Cold War where there was the potential for war between the Soviet Union and the Western Block, primarily the United States and NATO. Why did this not happen? Well, you must first understand why there even was the confrontation between the blocks. This was again because there were certain people, both in the Soviet Union and in the West, who were able to receive light but who supported their respective power structures. It was by no means inevitable that the West would set itself up in such direct confrontation with the Soviet Union. There were other ways that the West could have responded to this situation.

Because there were people in the West, especially in the United States, who had a certain level of spiritual maturity but who were deceived by what we have called the dualistic mindset, the black-and-white thinking, the epic mindset of wanting to fight an epic battle, then there was this confrontation. Of course, there were people with that mindset in the Soviet Union. Tying in to what I said earlier about ascended master students, even among people who were open to ascended master teachings, there were some that were so deceived by this epic mindset that they actually directed the light that they received through the Holy spirit through that mindset. They said: "The Soviet Union is wrong, communism is wrong, communism is bad, it must be destroyed" and so forth and so on.

Now comes the subtle point I wish to get across here. It is necessary to recognize that something is not in accordance with the higher principles, the higher potential. If you go into the black-and-white, dualistic, epic mindset that wants to label it and judge it as wrong (something that must be destroyed), you are not helping the cause of the ascended masters anymore, even if you call yourself an ascended master student. My beloved, we had to give a teaching through a previous dispensation that was deliberately designed for the epic mindset because we saw that it was actually necessary to divert the attention of many spiritual students so that they would decree for the dissolution of the Soviet Union rather than go out and seek to fight it with physical means.

Do you see this, beloved? You might ponder this concept honestly and ask for your own inner direction to see what I am saying. You will not manifest the Golden Age by destroying anything, even if it is out of alignment with the vision and the principles for the Golden Age. You will manifest the Golden Age when, instead of seeking to destroy, you seek to transcend. You seek to help other people transcend instead of labeling and judging them as being subhuman or as being expendable for the cause.

Seeing other people as subhumans

How many people in the United States of America looked at the Russian people not as human beings as themselves but as some kind of non-human? If they had to be killed by the millions in order to destroy communism and the Evil Empire, then that was acceptable to them. Well, as I said it was never

20 | Diversity is the master key to the Golden Age

acceptable to me, as it was, of course, never acceptable to me that many among the Soviet Leaders and even many of the Russian people looked the same way upon people in the West, namely that they were expendable for the glorious cause of spreading world communism around the world.

Do you see that this mindset cannot bring the Golden Age? It does not matter whether you define the most sophisticated religion, philosophy, civilization and governmental apparatus ever seen on this planet, you will not manifest the Golden Age by seeking to make that apparatus destroy all others, destroy diversity. The point of this discourse is simply this: If you wish to be part of the Golden Age of saint Germain, if you wish to be among the forerunners of it, you need to look at this mindset.

Why do you label other people as being subhumans or being expendable? Because you are in the mindset of judging according to the standard defined by the fallen mindset. You do not see that regardless of the outer bodies and whether they look different from you, regardless of the outer personalities that come from culture and upbringing; in the heart all people share a universal bond. This universal bond in the heart can cause people to unite while they still allow their individual, regional, cultural and natural expressions to flourish.

When you see beyond the material and see the immaterial bond between all people, you are not threatened by other material expressions being different from your own. You rejoice in diversity. If you see something that is not the highest potential, then you do not go in and judge and beat people over the head and try to make them feel fearful. You inspire them. You inspire by embodying the principles that you see, by expressing them, by being the light in action, by being your I AM Presence in action, as Sanat Kumara so eloquently explained. This is how you be a forerunner for the Golden Age of Saint Germain. It might be helpful for you to let go of the mindset that wants to label anything as wrong. Look at yourselves and how you have been brought up in almost any society to have this standard of right and wrong. Instead, transcend it and see that you do not actually improve things by saying: "This is wrong, this needs to be destroyed." You improve things by acknowledging the higher vision and saying: "How can we transcend the old? How can we help others transcend the old? How can we all do what is more than we did before?"

Thus, I seal you in my heart—for now.

21 | THE ALPHA AND THE OMEGA OF THE GOLDEN AGE

I AM the Ascended Master Saint Germain, and I come to give you the second installment in my discourses on The Descent of the Golden Age. I previously gave you the overall picture of the consciousness that needs to be embraced in order for the Golden Age to have a chalice through which it can descend. This time I shall strive to be less philosophical, less spherical and perhaps more practical, but whether it is practical or not depends on how you apply the teaching.

No specific plan for the Golden Age

The teaching is, of course, not meant to tell you every detail in the practical, and this was part of my point in the previous discourse. We will not give you every detail for we are not actually interested in seeing you manifest a specific result, a specific plan. As I have said before, I do not have up here a giant model of what the Golden Age in full manifestation will look like on earth.

The reason for this is partly, as I said earlier, that there is plenty of room for diversity, for individual expression. This means by individual people but also by groups of people, including what you now see as nationalities, but which I see will eventually start to dissolve and become more people who realize that they vibrate at the same level in a deeper level of their beings. They magnetize together based on that inner vibration rather than from certain outer physical characteristics, be they race, ethnicity or nationality.

Let me get on with the topic of how to make the Golden Age practical and how to manifest it in the material realm. This very much requires you to understand the Alpha and the Omega of the Golden Age, the Alpha and the Omega of spirituality, the Alpha and the Omega of life. We have, of course, given a number of dictations and teachings on the fact that you are the Divine feminine because you are in embodiment. Therefore, you have the potential to form a feminine polarity with the ascended masters where we are the masculine polarity in the Alpha-Omega flow between us. There are other aspects of this that I wish to make clear to those who are ready to embrace this teaching.

The problem with scientific materialism

Let me, as a starting point, talk about the current state of science. You have today a philosophy, an approach, to science that is very much out of touch with reality, based on a perversion of the Divine Mother and the Divine Father, a perversion of the Alpha and the Omega. An example of this perversion is the fact that you have a scientific establishment that has espoused a particular philosophical framework, which we might call scientific materialism. The prevailing thoughtforms that dominate the scientific community are that there is nothing beyond the material universe.

It is extremely important for many people in the scientific community, for many people in government circles and for many people among the public that science comes up with some ultimate proof of this philosophy. You will therefore see that there are scientific experiments being conducted that are aimed at coming up with such an ultimate proof, as science can currently conceive of this ultimate proof and how to get it.

You may see that there is research into distant galaxies, the birth and the evolution of galaxies, such as what causes the birth of a sun, what causes the dissolution of a sun. Or is there something called black holes? What causes a black hole; are they the doorway to a parallel universe or what are they? There is research done into the cosmic background radiation that supposedly proves that the Big Bang did happen because it is the remnants of the Big Bang, or so the theory goes. There is an attempt to build ever more powerful machines that can accelerate subatomic particles closer and closer to the speed of light. It is assumed that if you can accelerate a particle to the speed of light, you will have the ultimate demonstration of how matter came into being. My beloved, scientists cannot even agree on what a subatomic particle is so how can they actually know what it is they are trying to accelerate?

The current scientific paradigm defines the kind of experiments that scientists can see, and there is another paradigm that says that it is worth any amount of money to confirm the scientific paradigm. What if the very scientific paradigm that is the foundation for these experiments is fundamentally limited or even fundamentally flawed? Would this not mean that these experiments have no chance whatsoever of producing the result that is hoped for because the result that is hoped for is defined from an incomplete or flawed idea?

Would this not mean that all of these billions of dollars that are spent on this expensive research are, in fact (when you are completely honest and straightforward) wasted, completely wasted? I realize you can say that all of the research that is done will increase certain technological capabilities that might have effects that are actually practical or can produce results. What I seek to point out to you is that on the one side you have a scientific establishment that has a desire for an ultimate theory, the Theory of Everything, and on the other side you have a willingness to spend huge amounts of money on research that only seeks to prove the theory.

If you look at the reality, you will see that the people in the scientific and governmental establishments who are making the decisions to carry out these experiments and to allocate billions of dollars, they are sitting in their very comfortable offices, almost like in an ivory tower, or at least in a glass tower. They have huge salaries and secure lives because they feel that their position in the scientific establishment is secure, and so is their income and their retirement. They are living a very comfortable material life while completely ignoring that there are billions of people on this planet who live beneath the poverty level.

There are millions of children who starve to death every year from either lack of food or from malnutrition. There are numerous problems and cases where people live miserable material lives, yet the very same people who sit there in their comfortable material lives completely ignore this and are ready to allocate billions of dollars in research money to research these far-flung theories. Or to research weapons of how to kill people instead of directing their entire attention at solving the very real problems that people face on this earth.

Elitism and science

Would it really be wise to spend billions of dollars to send man back to the moon or send man to Mars, or would it be better to spend the same amount of money on improving life on this planet? I realize there are some who believe that one day humanity will have used up the resources on this planet and they will have to move on to other planets in order to survive. I also see the minds and hearts of these people and I see that there is nobody who envisions that they will be able to build enough spaceships to transport seven billion human beings to another planet. Therefore, they only envision building enough space ships for themselves, for the elite, and this is precisely the problem I wish to discourse on.

The problem is the elitist mindset, which is a perversion of both the Father and the Mother aspect, but especially of the Father aspect. This goes back to what we have talked about before, namely that there is a small group of fallen beings who have been allowed to embody on this planet and who have brought a certain mindset with them. They perverted the Father aspect in a previous sphere before they fell into this sphere and ended up on planet earth. They did not volunteer to come to planet earth, they fell here because they had disqualified themselves from embodying on other planets. This was for most of them their final opportunity to actually embody in the material realm.

We have earlier given many teachings on this so I will not go into depth here [See *Cosmology of Evil*]. Obviously, it was the collective consciousness of the lifestreams embodying on earth that allowed the fallen beings to come here and they partly came here as a testing. Would people follow the fallen beings, would people follow the elite, or would they stand up for themselves?

The fallen beings had perverted the masculine aspect in a previous sphere. They believe they are superior to the human beings on earth, the lifestreams on earth. In some cases, they *are* more sophisticated in their ability to abuse both the Father and the Mother aspect. This is why they can impress people by certain abilities or by their magnetic charisma as the strong leaders, such as you have seen abundantly throughout history.

If you look back at history, you can see what you call the Judeo-Christian tradition or the three great monotheistic religions: Judaism, Christianity and Islam. You will see clearly that these have been ruled by a specific paradigm that actually is in some ways very similar to the paradigm that rules science. There is a belief in an ultimate theory, an ultimate belief system and an ultimate religion. Science and religion are not very different when you strip away all the outer camouflage and look at the psychology, the mindset, the paradigms behind them—which is the desire to define some ultimate truth.

Submission to the ultimate theory

This is the perversion of the Father, but now comes another perversion of the Father that becomes a perversion of the Mother, which says: "Life in the material realm should submit to the ultimate theory. Human beings should submit to the ultimate theory and live their lives accordingly." This is the demand of both the traditional religions and science. It was the demand of communism and it is the demand of capitalism in a slightly round-a-bout, very well-camouflaged way. The individual must submit to the corporation unless you have the old-fashioned corporations that are led by one individual, but then certainly all other individuals must submit, except of course the elite.

You see this, again, as the demand that all must submit, except of course the elite for they are above the law. This is the reason you have seen the three monotheistic religions systematically suppress and put down women, but have they only suppressed and put down women? Nay, they have suppressed and put down men as well, at least those men that are not part of the elite. It is not just a matter of men and women. Yes, there is a greater suppression of women than men and this must be corrected, but you cannot actually look at the issue of women separately and say: "What do we need to do to stop the suppression of women," as some among the feminist leaders have done. You will never actually end the suppression of women until you also end the suppression of men because you end the entire fallen mindset so that it can no longer rule this planet and so that it is exposed for what it is: a perversion of both the Father and the Mother.

Male and female relationships in the Golden Age

What really is the suppression of women? It is not actually to suppress women. The fallen beings, the elite, are not specifically targeting women and seeking to suppress women; their greater goal is to divide human beings. On the outer, they seek to divide men and women so that they cannot form the correct polarity of the figure-eight flow between, for example, husband and wife. On a greater scale they wish to divide all human beings in themselves.

As a man you cannot be a unified being if you follow the model espoused by the monotheistic religions where you deny the feminine aspect of your own being. You cannot be fully a man if you put down women instead of recognizing your potential to become one with a woman in a relationship. Of course, you cannot be whole as a woman if you either deny the masculine aspect of your own nature or if you – as some feminine leaders do – deny the feminine and instead magnify the masculine. In this way, you actually seek to end the suppression of women by forcefully taking power away from the men in society. Such women cannot find wholeness in themselves and therefore cannot enter into a relationship and therefore cannot find balance.

I am not saying here that a man cannot find balance without being in a relationship with a woman or that a woman cannot find balance without being in a relationship with a man. Many yogis and yoginis have proven throughout the ages that this is possible through spiritual attainment, but it is not possible, not desirable, for the majority of the population. They need a male-female relationship in order to find balance within themselves. Indeed, in the Golden Age it will be seen as the primary purpose for a relationship to help each other grow, overcome psychological wounds and limitations, and find the balance where you magnify and support each other, not as perfect beings but you support each other's growth. As we have attempted to say before, there is no such thing as a perfect human being and there is no such thing as a human being who cannot grow and transcend itself as long as it is in embodiment.

Of course, ascended beings are also constantly transcending ourselves and when we have what we have presented as a Twin Flame relationship, such as between Portia and myself, we are seeking to balance and help each other grow. We are seeking to balance and help each other fulfill the mission we have in helping the lifestreams on earth. There are ascended masters who do not work with earth but who vow to move on into other realms where they seek to rise to higher realms in the spiritual spheres. They also need the masculine and feminine balance in order to fulfill that growth.

We here, who are working with earth, need that masculine-feminine balance in order to fulfill our mission in the best possible way. In the ascended realm we are, of course, not bound by these human concerns of ownership. We do not have the sense that you have on earth where you think you own your spouse. I am not here saying that in a relationship on earth you should freely shift partners and go from partner to partner. This is not practical for life on earth. What I am simply saying is that the ownership issue has been transcended by ascended beings. If I need to perform a certain task on earth and Mother Mary has more expertise in that field, then of course I have no hesitation of seeking the help of Mother Mary whereby I form a masculine-feminine polarity and figure-eight flow with Mother Mary that in no way causes Portia to now suddenly feel jealous.

Things are different in the ascended realm and thus you may look at what we have given you that so and so is a Twin Flame of such and such a master, and it is a concept we have given based on a certain level of consciousness of the chelas and students on earth. It is not the final teaching for things are much more fluid up here.

Certainly, you can also have situations on earth where, for example in a work relationship, a man can have a relationship that is professional with women and vice versa and it does not interfere with the people's personal relationships. What I seek to help you see here is that in order for the Golden Age to truly begin to manifest, it is necessary that as many people as possible understand the perversion of the masculine and feminine. They understand that it is a perversion of the Father element if you seek an ultimate and absolute truth that can be expressed in words. The ultimate and absolute truth is the Living Word that bloweth where it listeth and therefore never takes on a final or ultimate form.

Getting out of the linear mindset

There will never be a final, ultimate, absolute ascended master teaching given, neither through this or any other messenger. It never will happen, my beloved. We are, as we have said before, committed to progressive revelation until the last lifestream has ascended from earth. We will find ways to speak to the remaining lifestreams at the level of consciousness that helps them; not take the *ultimate* step but take the *next* step on their path. When they have taken that step, we will bring forth a progressively higher teaching that can take them to the step up.

This is our commitment. You would do well – if you want to be a forerunner for Saint Germain – to simply let go of this dream of being a member of the ultimate organization, having the ultimate teaching. Get over this linear consciousness where you compare one ascended master teaching to another and then you find something that seems like a contradiction from the linear mind. Indeed, it may be a contradiction to the linear mind, but if you are willing to not go into the linear mind – which is a perversion of the Mother where you compare and analyze everything – then you can transcend it. You can reach a higher level of understanding, perhaps even a higher level of understanding of any of the two teachings you think contradict.

It is a matter of choice: Do you want to stay in that linear mindset that really is a perversion of the Mother where you analyze and compare everything. Or perhaps you analyze and compare everything to what you think is the ultimate teaching, which is a perversion of the Father. You then have both the perversion of the Father and the perversion of the Mother.

Therefore, you are not the open door for the teachings that the I AM Presence wants to bring forth through you. If you cannot be the open door for your I AM Presence, how can you be the open door for an ascended master?

Do you not understand that there are students who have had such a desire to work directly with the ascended masters that they have refused to look in the mirror? Do you not understand that the only way to come into oneness with your I AM Presence is to remove the beam in your own eye that prevents you from feeling that oneness with the Presence? This cannot be done unless you look at yourself. There are students who get very enthusiastic about helping the ascended masters. As I said earlier, they are even willing to kill other people in order to manifest what they think is required for bringing about the Golden Age, such as the destruction of some other system.

In this eagerness, they think they can contact us directly even though they have not worked on their relationship with the I AM Presence. This, of course, cannot be done, my beloved. It is again a perversion of both the Father and the Mother if you think there is a shortcut that will somehow propel you into this important position where you are recognized by the ascended masters. Or you seek to get some kind of position in a spiritual movement or even in society that gives you power and then you think you can use that power to do good for the ascended masters.

Stop identifying with outer things

My beloved, we have seen people who have in past lives earned some openness with the flow of the Spirit. We have seen them in this lifetime direct that flow of the Spirit into one of these misunderstood desires to do good by exercising force. It does not help me bring about the Golden Age. What helps me bring about the Golden Age is that you strive to become an open door. This means that you attain the correct polarity between your I AM Presence and your Conscious You, which is the mediator between the Presence and your lower being, your outer mind and physical body. The Conscious You must be in command of the body and the mind so that these are servants of the Conscious You. They do not overpower, overshadow or blind the Conscious You so that you identify with the body, identify with the outer mind, identify with this spirit that you have accepted into your being or that was implanted in your being, or even with some outer thing, such as a religion or even an ascended master teaching.

You cannot identify with these outer things and at the same time be one with the Presence. When you are one with the Presence, you identify as being an extension of the Presence. Therefore, you know that the outer personality and the physical body are just tools through which you express yourself. There may come a point where they are pure enough that whatever remaining human personality you have does not in any way impede the expression of the Spirit through you because it is not perverting it. It is not coloring it beyond what is acceptable.

We are not saying here that when you attain oneness with your I AM Presence, you have no personality. You can come to the point where even though you have remnants of the ego, they do not color the expression of the light. It is simply given a certain coloring by the personality but it is inconsequential for the fulfillment of the work you are meant to do and that the light is meant to do through you.

When you have this correct polarity with the I AM Presence, you realize that you are not the ego and the outer personality. Therefore, you can begin to see through what I talked

21 | The Alpha and the Omega of the Golden Age

about earlier where you have this consciousness that thinks it knows everything, that thinks it has the ultimate teaching, the ultimate theory, the ultimate understanding. Therefore, it actually believes that it can tell the ascended masters how the ascended masters should save the earth and bring the Golden Age.

There are many people who claim to be students of the ascended masters but actually believe they know better than us how we should teach them personally, how we should teach other people, what we should say and what we should not say. I can tell you that I have watched tens of thousands of people find a book that was sponsored and dictated by the ascended masters through any of our sponsored organizations. They have started reading the book, feeling there was something in there but then they came to a particular statement or teaching that their outer mind could not accept, that contradicted what they saw as the highest truth. They have used that as a reason to reject this specific teaching through that specific organization or to reject all ascended master teachings. They do this because the outer mind, the ego, believes it knows better than the ascended masters. This we should say is an expression of the fallen consciousness, which believes it knows better than God how God should shave created the universe.

You can do nothing to bring the Golden Age

When you overcome this, you realize that the Conscious You is exactly what Jesus talked about when he said: "I can of my own self do nothing." When you realize you are the Conscious You, not the outer personality and ego, you see the reality that you can do noting of the outer self. The outer self can do nothing of value. You, as the Conscious You, really can do nothing for there is nothing that can be done in the material world that is worthwhile, that is transcendental, if it is not done through the power of the Spirit and the flow of the light of the Spirit.

All of us who were in embodiment have for many lifetimes identified with the ego and the outer personality. You can then go out and do things in the world, but you are doing them through force. When you come to the recognition that the Conscious You is Pure Awareness, you realize: "I can do nothing worthwhile without the Spirit. When it comes to the Spirit, I am not the originator, I am not the Creator, I am not the director, I am not the one in charge. My I AM Presence doeth the work!"

The work of the Conscious You is to direct the light, but this happens within the framework set by the Presence. You do have choices at the level of the Conscious You. You still have free will but there are those who only think they have free will by rebelling against God's Will through the ego. This is the ultimate perversion through the ego that says humankind can only attain free will through the fall. Nay my beloved, when you fell into duality, you lost your free will. You think you can do anything through force and you *can* do anything you want through force, but what is done through force can never escape the action-reaction of karma, the karmic return. That karmic return will take away your freedom of choice, your ability to choose. You may think you have made a free choice in the past through force but it will come back and limit you in the future.

It is far better to seek to be the open door. When you are in the right polarity with the I AM Presence – when you have truly free will – that is when you can begin to grasp the higher vision that I Saint Germain hold for the Golden Age. Then you can see how you can play your personal, individual part in bringing it into manifestation. Do you see that you are not deciding with the outer personality what should be a particular manifestation of the Golden Age? You are tuning in to my vision, receiving it through the I AM Presence. Then you are deciding the specifics down here according to your choices, your personality, your background and your experience. Whatever you choose is within the overall vision and therefore whatever you do is not done through force. Whatever you do you will not engender this limiting karmic return and it will not hinder the manifestation of the Golden Age.

Individual expression in the Golden Age

As I have said, I do not have a pre-made plan. I do have a pre-made plan for the overall structure of the Golden Age, but within that structure there is much room for individual creativity. Let me give you a concrete example. There may be a certain building and it is in the overall plan that such a building be built for it symbolizes something that is important for the collective consciousness, but the specifics of the actual design are not important. Here is where there is room for individual expression, and this, of course, goes to all levels of society.

There are certain overall ideas, for example for education and how children can be taught even at the kindergarten level, but it does not mean there is only one right way to do this. There are many ways to express these principles in creating specific types of kindergartens, specific types of schools. I do not envision all schools around the world teaching a common curriculum, or being built a certain way or having certain principles. There is much room for individual expression, there is much room for schools that focus on developing the children's technical or scientific abilities or others that focus on sports, others that focus on musical or creative ability and many other things including for example service. Where is there a school, my beloved, that focuses on helping children know how to give service to life?

To avoid complicating this further, my point is this: Alpha and Omega must be in polarity for the Golden Age to manifest. This goes for all levels, from the overall level of a society to your individual psychology and your relationships with your spouses and children. Alpha and Omega, not only vertical but also horizontal. This is the idea, the overall idea, that I wish to put forth in this discourse so that you may ponder it. Ponder how to apply it to all aspects of life and realize that we will never give specific answers to many questions for you have the capacity to contact your I AM Presence. You have attained enough oneness that you can obtain specific answers from within yourself. As we have said before, we have sponsored messengers to give forth overall teachings but a sponsored messenger cannot be an expert in every area of society and therefore cannot have the knowledge, the vocabulary, and the concepts that allow us to give a specific answer in a specific area. That is why I need you to have this knowledge, to have this expertise.

Do not seek a specific answer in your area of expertise through the messenger. Seek to use the messenger as an example and seek perhaps help from the messenger to overcome the blocks in your psychology that stand in the way of oneness with your Presence. You cannot be a sponsored messenger through some mantle that is dropped upon you from us and through some kind of magic where you are now able to take dictations. You can be a sponsored messenger only when you attain a certain degree of oneness with your Presence and dis-identification from the ego and outer personality. You must get the outer personality and ego out of the way of the messages so that we can speak through you in a reasonably pure manner. I am not saying that you have to be perfect, but you have to have reached a certain level of purity and purity of intent where you do not seek to use your messenger-ship to put down other people or even groups of people.

Use the messenger as an inspiration for you to seek the oneness with your Presence. Through that oneness, I can give you, and other masters can give you, the specific answers that apply to your area of expertise. Recognize that you have the knowledge, you have the chalice through which the Spirit can flow, but what you need to do is focus on being the open door for the flow of the Spirit rather than thinking the flow of the Spirit can only flow through someone else who has some special status or mantle that you do not have.

There is only one messenger at a time who carries the Mantle of Messenger of the Great White Brotherhood, but there are many other mantles, quite frankly millions of mantles that people can receive, that they can earn, and that they can continue to live up to so that we can speak through them. Not through a spoken dictation, but when they are at their workplace having a discussion about a specific problem, then they can be the open doors for the idea that comes from the higher realm. This will bring not just a new solution but an entirely new way of looking at this area, an entirely new approach that is transcendental and clearly comes from the immaterial Spirit flowing into the material.

Materialization: matter-realization. Matter realizing itself as Spirit. Matter will never realize itself as Spirit in the sense that matter does not have self-awareness. Because you – the Conscious You – are in embodiment, you can be the matter realizing itself as Spirit, therefore being the bridge between matter and Spirit so that the matrices of Spirit can be realized in matter. This is the alchemical key to the Golden Age. This is true alchemy, not that you seek a secret formula or a secret ingredient that will mechanically produce as a certain result. You seek to be the open door for the Spirit to produce change in matter, as Jesus demonstrated on so many occasions. It is not that you find a magical formula that you turn water into wine or lead into gold; it is that you allow the Spirit to do it. You then recognize and accept that you cannot force the Spirit to mechanically reproduce the same result over and over again for the Spirit bloweth where it listeth.

I will now blow where I listeth and go to somewhere else and give you time to digest this discourse. I shall blow back here in the coming days and give you another installment. Thus, I seal you in my heart for now.

22 | ELITISM IS THE KEY TO UNDERSTANDING HISTORY

I AM the Ascended Master Saint Germain and I wish to discourse on the shift in mindset that will help bring the Golden Age into manifestation. I have, of course, already talked about part of this shift but I wish to take this to a different level.

The attempt to hold back information

If you look back at the last 2,000 years, what most spiritual people see as the Age of Pisces, you will see that the shift that has been happening is not so much in technology and outer achievement but a shift in the raising of awareness. How can you create the kind of sophisticated technology you have today, technology that would have blown the minds of the people of ancient Rome who thought they had the most sophisticated civilization ever to appear on earth? How do you create technology that is so much more sophisticated than what people could even dream about 2,000 years ago? You do so because there has been an increased awareness of how the physical universe works, what scientists call the laws of nature. What I wish to focus on here is the increase in awareness. Truly, what drives progress in society is this increase in awareness.

If you look back at the past 2,000 years, you will see that the increase in awareness has not happened as a deliberate effort to increase awareness. It has actually been a process that has encountered a lot of opposition. If you look back to the Middle Ages, you will see this probably more clearly than most people see it today. Of course, many people today are aware that during the Dark Ages and the Middle Ages the Catholic Church was in the West the major factor that held back the growth in what most people see as knowledge but which I see as a broader awareness.

Most people know that the Catholic Church burned all of the books of the Greek philosophers, suppressed any kind of new knowledge, attempted to suppress science. Therefore, you can see that the Catholic Church was an outer expression of this opposition to the increase in awareness. You now become aware that there is a force that seeks to slow down or even stop, if it could, the increase in awareness.

I do not wish here to focus on the Catholic Church for it is only one example. We have, of course, seen many other examples even in the modern age where we see the communist empire of the Soviet Union seeking to hold back information. We see, for example, that the Soviet Empire could continue to exist only as long as the people were unaware of exactly what was going on, and what was going on both inside and outside of the Soviet Empire. We see even today how the Empire of China is seeking to filter the amount of information available to its citizens on the Internet, which of course is an almost impossible task even for a regime with the intent and the resources of the current Chinese governmental apparatus.

The force that resists growth in awareness

What we see here is that on the one hand there is a force that wants to stop the growth in awareness, but we also see over the past 2,000 years that this force has not been able to hold back the growth in awareness. This is, of course, because we of the ascended masters have released the light, the ideas and teachings that have caused an increase in awareness on an overall level.

Certainly, the force that seeks to hold back the growth in awareness has been successful in slowing down the growth of awareness. Had it not been so, society would have been even further along both technologically and in other ways than it is today. They do have an impact, yet we of the ascended masters do hold the ultimate power to increase awareness on earth. It is, of course, subject to free will, otherwise we could have raised consciousness even more. The fact is that in every age there will always be some individuals that refuse to submit to the force that seeks to limit awareness. They are therefore willing to be the open door for the bringing forth of some ideas that help bring society, civilization, humanity forward.

When you look at the present age, you still see that there is a force that is seeking to hold back the growth in awareness. This is something that unfortunately too many people in the West, in what calls itself the "free world," are not aware of. They are not sufficiently aware of this force because many people have been deceived into thinking that because they have so-called free societies, free democracies and freedom of speech, there is no force holding back the growth in awareness. This is, of course, not true. All people on earth suffer from a lack of awareness of certain facts, therefore all people are affected by a limited awareness. They are held back in their personal lives and all societies are held back in their ability to manifest the Golden Age and let go of the past.

The crucial awareness that is missing

What is the one awareness that is missing, the one missing ingredient? It is first of all the awareness that life has a spiritual side. As I have said before, I am not looking to create one dominant religion in the Golden Age, but I am indeed looking to spread throughout the world a very universal awareness that there is a spiritual realm and reality beyond the material. Human beings are not evolved animals because human beings are lifestreams that were created in the spiritual realm and have descended into physical bodies on earth. They have descended because life on earth gives them an opportunity to raise their consciousness, to expand their awareness. Therefore, life on earth has a purpose.

This purpose reaches beyond the lifetime of one physical body. Therefore, all people have had previous embodiments on earth and they might have future embodiments depending on the growth of their consciousness. In other words, there is a path that people can follow that leads them from whatever level of consciousness they have now to the level of consciousness that allows them to ascend and become permanent residents of the spiritual realm, become ascended masters.

These are very universal ideas that are not confined to any particular religion. They do not need to be defined by a particular religion as doctrines and dogmas. They are ideas that can be spread. Even some existing religions might be able to accept them, otherwise other religions can come forth that will incorporate these ideas in their own ways, clothing them in a certain outer framework or mythology and stories that appeal to specific groups of people.

Once you have this universal awareness that human beings are not "human" beings but psycho-spiritual beings and that their lives have a purpose, then you have the foundation for stepping back, looking at life, looking at history and really asking: "What is the force that is opposing the growth in awareness that will allow civilization to reach a higher level in all ways?"

The universal worth of all human beings

Once you are open to the spiritual side of life, you can then take the next step forward and realize that if all human beings are psycho-spiritual beings that originated in a higher realm, then you can see that there is a universal humanity, a universal worth, that applies to all human beings. This means that the natural way to look at human beings is that all beings on earth have equal value and should have equal rights. These rights should be defined in order to give all people an equal opportunity to expand their awareness on an individual level. All of the laws that guide specific societies should proceed from this foundation of individual growth to then define the parameters for how a particular society wants to grow as a unit, as a whole.

Groups of people who form what you today see as nation-states have a right to define certain laws for how the members of their group interact with each other, what form of government they decide to have and what laws guide the interaction of human beings in that society and also how that group interacts with the larger whole of humanity. When you accept this universal worth of all human beings, you can then step back and see what has been the missing ingredient, the missing link in people's understanding of history. You can begin by realizing that there are some people in every historical period who have obviously and clearly demonstrated that they do not have this respect for the universal worth and value of all human beings.

You can see, in every society in the past, the formation of an elite. Although you may see that they use certain physical means and define certain privileged positions for themselves, what you can really begin to see is the mindset. These people did not have the mindset that all human beings on earth have equal worth and should have equal rights and equal opportunity to grow. They did not respect these universal rights and values; instead they respected only their own rights, only their own value. They did everything they could to set themselves up as an elite who was not only in control of the majority of the population but who had actually suppressed the majority of the population so that they were the worker bees that worked to maintain the privileged lifestyle of the elite.

The hidden influence of elitism

The one ingredient that is missing right now is an awakening to the influence of elitism on the course of humanity. In our spiritual teachings we have explained that the power elites of history are made up of a limited number of lifestreams that are what we have called fallen lifestreams. In a higher sphere than the material realm they decided to rebel against God's plan and purpose for the universe. Nevertheless, it is not even necessary that people in general come to accept this idea, which many people are not ready to accept at this point—although, certainly the top 10 percent of the most spiritually aware people are ready to accept these concepts.

It is not necessary that society at large will accept this, as long as they are awakened to the concept that there is an elite and even that there has always been an elite. Even though the elite is not unified, nevertheless there is a unified intent, movement and force towards suppressing the general population. This means that the elite will resist the awakening, the growth in awareness of the general population.

Even though you have seen a tremendous growth in knowledge and awareness over the past 2,000 years, there is still an elite who is seeking to limit the awareness of the population so that they can continue to suppress the majority of the people through the people's ignorance of what is really going on. It is necessary for people at large to begin to realize that this elite is not made up of lifestreams who are stupid. They are highly intelligent and sophisticated and therefore they will seek to use whatever means are available in a given society. They are willing to adapt, and although most of them are not able to see that they are fighting a losing battle, they are nevertheless willing to adapt to the changing times and to accept that there are certain times where certain ideas cannot be held back.

Democracy and elitism

That is why you will see, for example, that there came a point where the power elites of the world accepted that democracy was inevitable; they could not prevent the birth of many democracies around the world. This does not mean that democratic societies do not have an elite and are not ruled by hidden elites. There is no democratic society that does not have people with the elitist mindset who actually look down on the population and feel that they are entitled to privileges and they are entitled to rule.

If you look at the democratic world, you will see that there are some rather small countries with just a few million people in the population and in such countries you do not find the most sophisticated or power-hungry members of the worldwide elite. The larger a country becomes, the more power it has and the more it will attract the lifestreams that want power and will seek to do anything they can to get this power. That is why, as I have said before, that there is no country in the democratic world that has a stronger power elite than the United States. There is hardly a country in what we call the democratic world that has a more elitist society than the United States where the elite do not openly control the political process but they control it in hidden ways through the money system, the financial system.

This is of course what you see world-wide. You may point to a country like Kazakhstan where many Western nations see that they have a leader who was not elected through the same democratic process as you have in the West, but the fact is that the United States is actually more elitist than a society like Kazakhstan. It is not necessarily a matter of the outer form of government, it is a matter of which kind of lifestreams are truly in charge of that society. I can assure you that there is hardly any population in the democratic world that is more deceived than Americans for they believe they have the most free nation in the world. It is not so, for there is hardly a nation where a small elite has more control. There is hardly a nation where so few have so much control over so many. This then is the awakening that I have worked very hard, for more than century, to bring down through the identity, mental and emotional levels. The fact that I have been able to speak about this through sponsored messengers in embodiment shows that this awareness is beginning to spill into the physical.

Do not try to battle the elite

There are many people around the world who have never heard about Saint Germain or ascended masters but who have nevertheless opened their minds to receive fragments, impulses of this awareness. I ask those of you who are aware of ascended masters to hold the vision and to make the calls that this awareness will begin to break through on a larger and larger scale so that people become aware of the influence of elitism, the existence of the elitist mindset and the existence of an elite.

Now reach back to what I said in my previous discourses where we do not in any way desire to see the spiritual people on earth engage in a battle against the elite, neither do we desire to see the people of the world engage in a physical battle against the elite. We do not desire to see a repetition of the French Revolution or the Bolshevik Revolution or other violent revolutions. We do not desire to see civil wars like we see in Syria and other nations, we do not even desire to see violent uprisings and demonstrations against sitting governments. We have no problem with people demonstrating, but only peacefully.

We desire that you, who are the spiritual people, avoid going into the mindset that I described when I talked about ascended master students adopting a mindset of wanting to fight communism. I am in no way shape or form – *mark my words* – I am in no way encouraging ascended master students to engage in the epic mindset and think they have to destroy the elite for Saint Germain. You do not – you *will* not – further the descent of the Golden Age through force and violence.

You will not help me bring the Golden Age by fighting the power elite. You will help me bring the Golden Age by helping to expose the power elite, by awakening the people to the existence of the power elite and then awakening the people to the mindset that is beyond the epic mindset, beyond the dualistic mindset.

My beloved, we will not manifest the Golden Age as long as the elite rules society, yet we will not overcome the elite through violence and force. We will not overcome the elite by destroying the elite but by transcending the elitist mindset. How can a small power elite rule a nation as large as the United States where there is a free government that is elected by the people, where there is freedom of speech, where there is a so-called free press, even though it is not as free as it claims to be? Nevertheless, there is freedom of the press in the sense that anyone could start a newspaper or a website and spread information and the government could not stop it. Yet how does the elite rule?

It rules because it is taking advantage of the mindset of the majority of the people, and the majority of the people are still stuck in black-and-white thinking and the dualistic mindset, and even in the epic struggle. So many people in the United States believe that it is the duty of the United States to be a bulwark of freedom, a bastion of freedom, and to even spread freedom and democracy around the world.

Overcoming the epic mindset

I realize many Americans are beginning to question this mindset, especially after the Iraq war. Nevertheless, there are still so many that are trapped in this mindset that the elite that rules America can rule because the people cannot even ask the questions—they are so blinded by this mindset. What I need the spiritual people to do is to ask these questions and to be willing to look in the mirror and see where you have remnants of black-and-white thinking, where you have remnants of this epic mindset that portrays the world as an epic struggle between good and evil. We have already given sufficient teachings through this messenger that anyone who claims to be an ascended master student should be able to quickly transcend this epic mindset and realize that the epic struggle between good and evil is a struggle between the two dualistic polarities of the fallen consciousness. It has nothing to do whatsoever with the ascended master consciousness.

You will not ascend as long as you maintain any remnants of this consciousness in your being. You will ascend only by transcending it, you will manifest your Christhood only by transcending it. You will be able to express this Christhood in embodiment and help bring forth the Golden Age only by transcending this dualistic, fallen mindset.

Those of you who are open to the existence of ascended masters, you are open because you have the potential to transcend this mindset in this embodiment. That is how you attain Christhood and qualify for your ascension. There is no other way, as we have now explained so many times that any of you should be able to find one explanation that resonates with your current level of consciousness. You can use it to take the next step up and even become aware that your ultimate goal of the spiritual path is to transcend this fallen mindset. You can demonstrate by example and by your teachings that it is possible for all people to transcend it, that it is necessary to transcend it for the birth of the Golden Age to become reality.

There are many aspects of the Golden Age that are ready to be born, but as you know with a woman who is ready to give birth, there can be a delay for various reasons. I can assure you that the major delay right now is that those who call themselves ascended master students have not been willing to step back and look at the epic mindset and the necessity to transcend it in themselves so that they can help bring about society's transcendence of this state of consciousness.

Thus, this is my installment for now. I shall speak further on what will happen to society in practical terms when it begins to transcend this epic mindset and begins to acknowledge openly that the goal of an enlightened, awakened society is to extend equal opportunity to all people and to respect the humanity and the spirituality of each human being, therefore giving the best possible possibility for people to raise their consciousness on an individual basis. Yet, I shall seal you for now in the heart of Saint Germain.

23 | THE QUESTIONS MOST PEOPLE CANNOT EVEN ASK

Saint Germain I AM, and I wish to continue my discourse from this morning where I talked about the shift in consciousness. You first have the Alpha aspect, which is that people realize that they are more than human beings, that they are spiritual beings and that everything on earth is a schoolroom where they have the opportunity to raise their consciousness. Life has a purpose that reaches beyond the physical body and the pleasures you can encounter here on earth.

The Omega aspect of this realization is that life on earth is not the way it is meant to be because life on earth is not geared towards giving people equal opportunity, equal rights, equal worth. The reason for this is that there is an elite who is always seeking to set itself up to have privileges and power over the population. The elite does not have the mindset that all people have equal worth for they believe they are worth more than the ordinary people.

The power elite and the consciousness of separation

Why do the members of the elite not want people to have this awareness? Well, first of all because they do not want to be exposed, they do not want to be seen for what they are. They know that if people see the elite and see that they actually are like the Emperor who has noting on, then they will not be willing to submit to them. Why would you submit to the elite if you see that the elite has no power? How can you see that the elite has no power? You can see this when you recognize that you are more than a human being. You are a spiritual being, and therefore you do not have to submit to any power on earth.

This is what the Buddha demonstrated, this is what Jesus demonstrated, and this is what other spiritual leaders, such as Padma Sambhava, have demonstrated. You can attain a state of consciousness where you can walk the earth in a physical body, but you will not be subject to any power on earth. You are willing to be the open door for the power of God, and the power of God cannot be controlled by the power elite. They cannot maintain their power over the people when sufficient numbers among the people begin to see themselves as spiritual beings with the potential to be the open door for the power of God.

As we have said before, the last thing the power elite wants on earth is for people to follow Jesus' example so there are suddenly 10,000 people with full Christhood in embodiment and many with a smaller degree of Christhood. Why is it they are actually so afraid of this? Because when there are people who have attained a degree of Christhood, they will not be subject to the consciousness that I have talked about, the consciousness of the elite. The essence of this consciousness is actually that you see yourself as a separate being, separated from God and separated from other people.

23 | The questions most people cannot even ask

The consciousness of inequality

What does this lead to? It leads to the consciousness you see on earth, the consciousness of inequality. Do you see that the essence of the elitist consciousness is the exact opposite of the consciousness I outlined previously? I said that if all people are extensions of spiritual beings in a higher realm, then all people have equal worth and they deserve equal opportunity. The consciousness of elitism is based on a fundamental inequality so that all people are not created equal, they are not all endowed with inalienable rights that no power on earth can take away from them. The power elite can have power, they can have a privileged position, only if they are not equal to a majority of the population. They must find some kind of philosophy that puts people down and divides them into distinct categories. This is what you have seen in all past civilizations and you have seen it today as well.

You see how even the Christian religion, even the teachings given by Christ, were used to create, sustain and support an elitist society where the king, the noble class and the church hierarchy formed a privileged class and the majority of the population were literally the property or the slaves of this privileged class. You have seen this under communism, even though the comment was made that all people would be equal and that there would be no classes in society. Of course, there was a class for those who ran the communist system. As I said, the promise was also made in the democratic nations that all are equal under the law, but as you see in the United States and in other nations, clearly there is an elite who rules through economic power, rules behind the scenes.

As I said, this elite can rule only because the majority of the population are also blinded by this illusion of separation. This is what makes it possible that you can see such incredible inequality on earth between, for example, the rich countries, such as the United States, and some of the poorest countries that you see in Africa, Asia or Southeast Asia.

When you begin to attain a degree of Christ discernment, you first of all have the Alpha realization: "I am not a human being, I am more than a human being, I am more than an evolved animal, I am a spiritual being that descended from above." As you begin to truly integrate this realization, you will come to the point where you look around you and you say: "Well, if I am a spiritual being, then where did all other people on earth come from? Are they not spiritual beings as well?" This leads you to the obvious realization that: "Yes, all human beings originated as spiritual beings."

This leads you to a state of consciousness that is characterized by oneness instead of separation. There is the vertical oneness of you knowing you are one with God instead of separated from God. There is also the horizontal oneness where you know that you are one with all other human beings instead of being separated from them. This is what Jesus expressed when he said: "I and my Father are one" and: "Inasmuch as ye have done it unto the least of these my brethren, ye have done it unto me." This is what you begin to feel when you attain a degree of Christhood.

Asking the unasked questions

When you have this Christ discernment, you can step back and you can begin to ask some of the millions of questions that people who are trapped in the consciousness of separation simply cannot ask because they cannot even conceive of these questions. I already gave an example of how the scientific elite can sit there and spend billions of dollars researching inconsequential theories, seeking to prove inconsequential theories, while millions of people are starving.

You can ask: "How is it possible that you can have these nations that have such a high degree of material welfare – such that truly no one needs more and certainly no one should want more – as long as there are two billion people or more living under the poverty level and millions of people starving?" Only the consciousness of separation can explain the fact that many among the richest nations are completely absorbed in their affluent lifestyle, only focused on getting more and more money, more and more property, bigger houses, bigger cars, more vacations. By the way, when they go on vacations, do they go and see how people really live in other parts of world? Nay, they may travel to a country where there are many poor people but they travel to the protected and exclusive tourist resorts that are set up by the international power elite.

What kind of consciousness fails to have compassion for the fact that not everyone has a lifestyle that is worthy of spiritual beings? Well, only the consciousness of separation. I am not here seeking to blame anyone nor am I seeking to shame anyone into changing their approach. I am simply pointing out that what will bring the Golden Age into manifestation is that millions of people attain a degree of Christ discernment where they naturally begin to ask these questions and ask them publicly, project them out publicly through all means available to them. This ranges from discussing this with their acquaintances to writing about it in any outlet where there is an opening, and even creating outlets where there is no opening, such as creating organizations that seek to raise awareness about these issues. This includes the organization Mother Mary outlined with the purpose of raising awareness of the issues related to women. But there are many other such organizations that can be created to raise awareness of particular issues.

For that matter, it is possible to create a worldwide umbrella organization that has as its goal to raise awareness through all means possible. This, of course, is an endeavor that will require many people with a variety of experience. You may say: "Well, what about the United Nations, is that not one of the purposes behind the United Nations?" Certainly it could be, but right now it is not being fulfilled as I envision it for there are, of course, not enough people who dare to openly acknowledge that life has a spiritual side. Society, civilization cannot fulfill its potential if we do not acknowledge that life has a spiritual side. There is only so far we can go as human beings. Only when we achieve Christ discernment, will we be able to step back and ask the questions that we cannot even ask from the consciousness of separation.

Why do democracies build armies?

Another question to ask: "Why is it that there are democratic nations who continue to build up their armies, such as the United States continuing to create more and more sophisticated weapons even though there truly is no enemy for which they need these weapons?" They are not needed for the national defense, and I would remind you that the constitution specifically says that the Federal Government is to provide for the *national* defense. It does not say that the Federal Government has the obligation to create an armed force that can strike anywhere around the globe at any time and overturn governments or start a war here or there or anywhere that someone desires. National defense, my beloved, does not require nuclear-driven aircraft carriers that can send a strike force anywhere around the world.

Do you see that as long as a nation is in this state of consciousness, it is projecting into the cosmic mirror? What the cosmic mirror will project back is not necessarily an enemy who can threaten the United States but certainly the appearance of such an enemy, and thus seemingly the justification for continuing this completely unnecessary arms race.

Imagine if not only the money that is put into arms but also the research into more arms could be freed up. Imagine that the minds of the scientists who are right now focusing on weapons research could be freed up to do other things, such as alternative forms of energy, eradicating disease, eradicating poverty and hunger. For this to happen, you have to question: "Why has it not already happened?"

Creating an enemy for the arms race

The only answer is, again, that the members of the elite do not want it to happen. They want to maintain their power and their privileges. They want to maintain, first of all, the sense that they are special, that they belong to an elite that has more than the people. Do you see that they do not want equality, they do not want equal opportunity; they want privileged positions that no one can challenge?

This is what they always wanted. They loved the feudal societies of Europe for they were born into a position and stayed in it for a lifetime. They have been trying to recreate this kind of a society under the disguise of democracy and a so-called free-market economy. Of course, hardly any country has had a free economy for the last century where capitalism has managed to spread its tentacles to all of the nations that were not under communism.

As some of you will know, it even spread its tentacles into communism for who financed Lenin and the Bolshevik revolution? Who continued to extend credit to the Soviet Union so that they could continue to build the arms that necessitated the ongoing arms race between East and West? Do you see, my beloved, if you don't have a real enemy, you have to create one? Then you have the dualistic battle between the two sides which is the hallmark of the dualistic consciousness.

How many people on earth can even ask such questions? When you see tens of thousands of people attain a higher degree of Christhood, then they will begin to ask these questions. Some have already started. You who are the spiritual people, who know about the ascended masters, visualize and make calls that these people become even more aware and become even more courageous. Visualize that there is a growing awareness that no society can afford to allow its government and the media to shut down the people who dare to speak out.

How to undermine a democracy

Look at the United States and how they have persecuted one person who dared to leak confidential files to Wikileaks. My beloved, you may say that he was unpatriotic and endangered the nation, but I would say that what truly endangers the nation is when a government does not have transparency. Who is it that does not want transparency? As I said: the power elite. What is it that they have done, my beloved? As I said in my previous discourse, they are not stupid. Do you not realize that when they saw the emergence of the United States as a democratic nation that had attempted to root out elitism, they became very concerned. They became even more concerned when they saw other nations follow the example of the United States and institute democracies.

What is the essence of a democracy? It is that each person in that society has one vote and that all votes count the same. What many do not realize is that each person must cast his or her vote based on what they know. They cannot vote based on what they do not know. What does this mean? It means that a democracy can function at its highest potential only when there is complete transparency in the government, in businesses and in all aspects of society.

Do you think the power elite liked this development? Do you not realize that they saw – decades earlier – what was coming and that democracies would have to become more and more transparent and therefore the power elite could hide less and less? Do you really think it was beyond their capacity to say: "We need to stop this and how can we do it? Ah, we will create an enemy of democracy, namely the Soviet Union."

The Soviet Union would be hostile and it would have spies that go into the West, and it itself would be secretive and try to prevent people in the West from knowing what was going on there. Now, with the creation of this one state apparatus, you suddenly had the justification that made democratic leaders say: "But we cannot allow ourselves to be transparent for then the Soviet Union will know all our secrets and they will be able to destroy us. We need to keep certain things secret for the Soviet Union." Of course, the real issue was that the power elite wanted to keep things secret from the people in democratic nations.

Capitalism financing communism

This is just a brief glimpse into how the more sophisticated members of the power elite think. This is just a brief glimpse into what they can do in terms of one banker in the United States seeing the potential for a revolution in Russia, seeking out the person who might carry it out and then giving Lenin the impetus, the finances to actually start the process. Surely, Morgan and other bankers did not know whether their attempt would be successful. In fact they could not even imagine that it would lead to the creation of the Soviet Union as powerful as it became.

Nevertheless, it shows you how those who are members of the power elite in embodiment, even without knowing the full extent of what they are doing, become tools for the darker forces that are out of embodiment and who see even more of a negative potential than people in embodiment. This is why there is only one force that can counteract this and it is that more and more people in embodiment attain Christ discernment. You can then be the open doors for the ascended masters, which is the only force that really can counteract the dark forces and the embodied power elite that seek to take the earth down into a self-destructive spiral.

The earth is in an upward spiral, but it is in an upward spiral only because some people on earth have dared to be the open door for the spiritual light and higher ideas. Many have done this but many more are ready in this age to awaken to their potential to be the open doors, to have the raised awareness that allows them to go with whatever expertise they have. Or they might even go with expertise they don't have but they suddenly feel the determination: "I need to study this area. I need to understand how the economy works, how politics works, how education works." Then they go out and speak out, then they go out there and ask the questions.

Educating children on basic psychology

Another question that needs to be asked is: "Why hasn't society educated children in how to deal with their own personal psychology, overcome their own personal limitations, so that they themselves can have happier and more fulfilled lives?" Well, there is only one answer: The power elite does not want people to overcome their wounds because it is through the wounds that both the embodied power elite and the dark forces behind them can control people. Do you not see that billions of people on this planet, even in the richest nations of the world, are leading lives of intense suffering? Not because of physical causes but because of their internal psychological wounds, which causes them to live an entire lifetime in a constant state of inner agitation and suffering.

Why haven't the rich nations looked at this and said: "Now that we have provided physical, material welfare, isn't it time we provide psycho-spiritual welfare? If we really want people to overcome these wounds, then we need to recognize they are more than human, they are spiritual beings." That is why they have the potential to overcome their wounds and manifest a state of consciousness where they are not, as Jesus described 2,000 years ago, houses divided against themselves that cannot stand against the elite.

Do you not see that Jesus actually sought to start a movement that could help people attain healing through the power of the Holy Spirit and Christ awareness? People would be willing to look at the beam in their own eye, wrestle with their own psychology and come to that point of inner resolution where they were able to have Christ discernment and express it in society without being emotionally and psychologically destroyed by the forces that be. Do you not see – if you take a look at some of the people in history who have attempted to change things, who have attempted to speak up – that many of them had their own internal psychological issues? Many did not fulfill their missions because of such issues, many did only a small fraction of what they could have done. Many more never even got started on their missions and therefore are not known to the public.

There is such an incredible potential if any nation would make a determined policy to teach children from an early age how to heal their psychology and find inner peace and resolution. Can you imagine the creativity that would be unleashed for that nation? Certainly, some of the smaller affluent nations are ready to make this commitment for they do not have, as I said, so many representatives of the power elite that they can stop this. It is really only a matter of the public awareness making a simple shift so that people begin to say: "Why haven't we done this, it is so obvious that we need to do this?"

The power elite wants to abort Christhood before it can manifest. That is why there are so many things in society that are going on, and are allowed to go on, that are specifically designed to magnify, or at least prevent the resolution of people's psychological limitations. Education truly is one of the most prominent examples of this where you have again the power elite creating a division.

A golden age approach to education

The power elite, seventeen centuries ago, took over the Christian religion. When they became aware that the Christian religion could no longer dominate the intellectual life of Western societies, they instantly started to create the opposite: scientific materialism. This is another dualistic polarity like capitalism and communism.

Since then, they have now managed to create a society that is divided. There are still many people who hold on to traditional Christian values and there are many people who are equally intent on promoting the materialistic life-view. You now have democratic nations who have a complete inconsistency for they cannot decide what kind of people they are ministering to from their governments. They have a Constitution that is based on the idea that all people have rights, but you cannot have rights unless they are given by a higher authority. If rights are given by the state, then whoever runs the state defines the rights that are given to the people. Then you do not have democracy, my beloved, you *cannot* have democracy.

If you have a democratic nation that recognizes that people have rights, yet at the same time this nation will not recognize that people are spiritual beings, then you have an inconsistency. Why will they not recognize that people are spiritual beings? First of all, there is the opposition from scientific materialism, which says there is nothing beyond the material realm so people cannot be spiritual beings. Then there is the fact that you have the opposite polarity, also defined by the power elite, which makes people think that if they do recognize that people are spiritual beings, then we go back to the old days of being dominated by Christianity. No one wants that so society is stuck in a no-gods land where they do not know what to do.

There is an alternative to traditional Christianity and to scientific materialism. It is the universal form of spirituality. When societies begin to recognize this, then they can begin to create an educational system that from a very early age teaches children what kind of beings they are: You are psycho-spiritual beings. You have the potential to overcome the limitations in your own psychology; the limitations that go back many lifetimes. Whatever you have experienced in your childhood in this lifetime, does not determine who you are because you brought a lot with you. Even what you brought with you does not determine who you are for you have the potential to rise above it.

Then you proceed to give children tools to rise above this. When you create and educational establishment like this, within a generation you will have an entirely new approach to society. You will have children who were brought up with an understanding of their own psychology and the potential to master their psychology. In many cases, they will have a sense of purpose and know that one of the purposes of life is to precisely attain self-mastery.

Psycho-spiritual welfare

Just imagine what will happen when those children begin to have children. What we see today is, of course, that most parents export their own unresolved psychology onto their children, which is why you see so many dysfunctional families. Is it really so hard to look at the fact that most affluent nations have more and more psychological, family and social problems, more and more dysfunctional families, more and more divorces, more and more shipwrecked children. Is it really impossible to look at all of this and say: "Why is this happening? We need to understand why this is happening." Then you realize it is because when you have reached a certain level of material affluence, it is necessary for society to step up and look at the psycho-spiritual welfare of its members. This becomes the goal of that society if it is to transcend itself instead of becoming subject to the second law of thermodynamics, starting to disintegrate from within and from without.

Today, you have hardly any child that was not negatively affected by the unresolved psychology of the parents. You have children who grow up with psychological wounds, having no idea how to deal with them and therefore exporting them to their children as well. You see how these psychological wounds are inherited from generation to generation. Over several generations they can actually begin to affect what you call the genetic makeup so that children are born with a predisposition to have mental problems, mental diseases.

Many among the current generation are born with these, what we might call "dangerous" or "explosive" tendencies that predispose them to have attention deficit disorder or some of the many other diseases that are common today, including schizophrenia in many of its subtle forms. Society looks at this and they think that nothing can be done about it, but the reality is that when you are willing to raise your awareness, when you are willing to invoke the light of God, you can rise above your so-called genetic predisposition. You can then reverse the trend so that you can pass on better dispositions to your children. Within three or four generations, all of these explosive predispositions can be completely eradicated from a society so that children now are not born with a predisposition but only have to deal with a psychological makeup that they carry with them in their souls from lifetime to lifetime.

The potential to serve other nations

My beloved, there are thousands of such unusual questions that can be asked, that *must* be asked for the Golden Age to manifest. I am not intent on defining all of them, although I will certainly bring more to your attention in the coming years. Nevertheless, there are already millions of people in embodiment who – with a simple raising of awareness – could suddenly raise their minds above the cloud, above the fog, of the collective consciousness.

People suddenly begin to see these questions and see how in their own life experience they have encountered all of these conditions that in their hearts they know are not right. They could never really see why, and now they see it and now they are ready to speak out and say: "The emperor has nothing on, the members of the power elite have nothing on and it is time that we step up to a higher awareness of this particular problem and even all aspects of society. We need to ask ourselves what is the highest potential for the modern affluent democracies? Is it really enough to continue on the track we are on, or do we have a potential to step up to where we realize that because we have worked ourselves to a higher potential, to a higher situation, we now have the privilege, the joy, the potential to serve other nations, to seek to raise up the whole of the family of nations. Then we can take our own nations to a higher level." When you reach the level that many Western democracies and some nations in other parts of the world have – such as Australia and New Zealand and several countries in Southeast Asia, including Japan – when you reach the level that these nations have reached, then you simply cannot go higher unless you begin to serve others.

My beloved, look at the nation of Japan. Go back to a decade or two ago when it enjoyed unparalleled material prosperity. Because it continued to isolate itself, what has happened since then? The economy has gone down, and you will see the same tendency in all other affluent democracies. For that matter, you are already seeing this to some degree. I tell you that until these nations acquire enough Christ-perspective that they can begin to serve others, even to serve the whole of humanity, then they will go into these downward spirals.

It will seem to them as if there is no way out, but there is a way *up*, my beloved. There is no way *out* for you cannot solve these problems horizontally. You can transcend them by going up and by looking honestly at how you can serve others.

That, then, is the address that I wish to bring forth at this time, in the space-time continuum. Rest assured that I have my own spiritual continuum that I will continue to bring forth. Thus, I seal you for now in the heart of Saint Germain.

24 | INVOKING AN END TO SUPPRESSION BY THE POWER ELITE

In the name I AM THAT I AM, Jesus Christ, I call to all ascended masters working on manifesting the Golden Age, especially Mother Mary and Saint Germain to radiate into the collective consciousness an exposure of how the power elite suppresses people. Help people see that we can build a new future by working with the ascended masters and letting go of the old way of looking at life, including…

[Make personal calls.]

Part 1

1. Saint Germain, radiate into the collective consciousness the awareness that in the Golden Age, civilization will allow the immaterial to determine the material expression in everything from the highest levels of the government, through art, music, culture and the individual lives and relationships of the people.

> O Saint Germain, you do inspire,
> my vision raised forever higher,
> with you I form a figure-eight,
> your Golden Age I co-create.
>
> **O Saint Germain, what love you bring,**
> **it truly makes all matter sing,**
> **your violet flame does all restore,**
> **with you we are becoming more.**

2. Saint Germain, radiate into the collective consciousness the awareness that the Golden Age will *not* be modeled on the so-called "great" civilizations of the past because the world will *not* be united under one centralized government.

> O Saint Germain, what Freedom Flame,
> released when we recite your name,
> acceleration is your gift,
> our planet it will surely lift.
>
> **O Saint Germain, what love you bring,**
> **it truly makes all matter sing,**
> **your violet flame does all restore,**
> **with you we are becoming more.**

3. Saint Germain, radiate into the collective consciousness the awareness that the civilizations of the past destroyed diversity by demanding that all people obey a centralized leadership of the fallen beings.

> O Saint Germain, in love we claim,
> our right to bring your violet flame,
> from you Above, to us below,
> it is an all-transforming flow.

> **O Saint Germain, what love you bring,**
> **it truly makes all matter sing,**
> **your violet flame does all restore,**
> **with you we are becoming more.**

4. Saint Germain, radiate into the collective consciousness the awareness that the Golden Age of Saint Germain will not be attained by destroying diversity or by creating a centralized world government that uses force to suppress creativity.

> O Saint Germain, I love you so,
> my aura filled with violet glow,
> my chakras filled with violet fire,
> I am your cosmic amplifier.

> **O Saint Germain, what love you bring,**
> **it truly makes all matter sing,**
> **your violet flame does all restore,**
> **with you we are becoming more.**

5. Saint Germain, radiate into the collective consciousness the awareness that you envision a Golden Age based on diversity where a centralized organization will coordinate. It will not dictate, use force or bring forth a centralized religion or philosophy that all must follow.

> O Saint Germain, I am now free,
> your violet flame is therapy,
> transform all hang-ups in my mind,
> as inner peace I surely find.

> **O Saint Germain, what love you bring,**
> **it truly makes all matter sing,**
> **your violet flame does all restore,**
> **with you we are becoming more.**

6. Saint Germain, radiate into the collective consciousness the awareness that in the Golden Age, civilization will recognize that there is a level beyond the material world and that there are intelligent beings in that world that can communicate with human beings.

> O Saint Germain, my body pure,
> your violet flame for all is cure,
> consume the cause of all disease,
> and therefore I am all at ease.

> **O Saint Germain, what love you bring,**
> **it truly makes all matter sing,**
> **your violet flame does all restore,**
> **with you we are becoming more.**

7. Saint Germain, radiate into the collective consciousness the awareness that no institution on earth can ever have a monopoly on communication from the ascended masters because the Holy Spirit bloweth where it listeth.

> O Saint Germain, I'm karma-free,
> the past no longer burdens me,
> a brand new opportunity,
> I am in Christic unity.
>
> **O Saint Germain, what love you bring,**
> **it truly makes all matter sing,**
> **your violet flame does all restore,**
> **with you we are becoming more.**

8. Saint Germain, radiate into the collective consciousness the awareness that the Golden Age of Saint Germain is an age of diversity where the Spirit finds expression through millions of people who are the open doors for receiving new ideas.

> O Saint Germain, we are now one,
> I am for you a violet sun,
> as we transform this planet earth,
> your Golden Age is given birth.
>
> **O Saint Germain, what love you bring,**
> **it truly makes all matter sing,**
> **your violet flame does all restore,**
> **with you we are becoming more.**

9. Saint Germain, radiate into the collective consciousness the awareness that it is not your goal to convert all people to the ascended masters' teachings but to bring forth a universal form of spirituality.

> O Saint Germain, the earth is free,
> from burden of duality,
> in oneness we bring what is best,
> your Golden Age is manifest.
>
> **O Saint Germain, what love you bring,**
> **it truly makes all matter sing,**
> **your violet flame does all restore,**
> **with you we are becoming more.**

Part 2

1. Saint Germain, radiate into the collective consciousness the awareness that you do not want to use force to destroy even dictatorial empires. You want a raising of the consciousness so that people come to the realization that: "It is time to end this."

> O blessed Mary, Mother mine,
> there is no greater love than thine,
> as we are one in heart and mind,
> my place in hierarchy I find.

24 | Invoking an end to suppression by the power elite

**O Mother Mary, generate,
the song that does accelerate,
the earth into a higher state,
all matter does now scintillate.**

2. Saint Germain, radiate into the collective consciousness the awareness that free will mandates that whatever people desire to outpicture in the material world, they must be allowed to outpicture it for a time. They need to see the physical manifestation of the ideas that they have come to accept.

I came to earth from heaven sent,
as I am in embodiment,
I use Divine authority,
commanding you to set earth free.

**O Mother Mary, generate,
the song that does accelerate,
the earth into a higher state,
all matter does now scintillate.**

3. Saint Germain, radiate into the collective consciousness the awareness that only when a critical mass of people shift their awareness, can there be intercession from above that can avoid certain physical calamities. This is why the wars of the past century could not be avoided.

I call now in God's sacred name,
for you to use your Mother Flame,
to burn all fear-based energy,
restoring sacred harmony.

> O Mother Mary, generate,
> the song that does accelerate,
> the earth into a higher state,
> all matter does now scintillate.

4. Saint Germain, radiate into the collective consciousness the awareness that the great conflicts of the past were created because some people with spiritual attainment supported their own regimes so that their light was misqualified into upholding dualistic empires.

> Your sacred name I hereby praise,
> collective consciousness you raise,
> no more of fear and doubt and shame,
> consume it with your Mother Flame.

> O Mother Mary, generate,
> the song that does accelerate,
> the earth into a higher state,
> all matter does now scintillate.

5. Saint Germain, radiate into the collective consciousness the awareness that the light is perverted when people go into the epic mindset and believe that a cause is so important that it justifies the killing or forcing of other people.

> All darkness from the earth you purge,
> your light moves as a mighty surge,
> no force of darkness can now stop,
> the spiral that goes only up.

**O Mother Mary, generate,
the song that does accelerate,
the earth into a higher state,
all matter does now scintillate.**

6. Saint Germain, radiate into the collective consciousness the awareness that in a Golden Age, we cannot label other people as subhumans who are expendable for a greater cause. There is no cause that justifies the killing of other people.

All elemental life you bless,
removing from them man-made stress,
the nature spirits are now free,
outpicturing Divine decree.

**O Mother Mary, generate,
the song that does accelerate,
the earth into a higher state,
all matter does now scintillate.**

7. Saint Germain, radiate into the collective consciousness the awareness that regardless of the bodies and outer personalities, in the heart all people share a universal bond. This universal bond in the heart can cause people to unite while they still allow their individual, regional, cultural and natural expressions to flourish.

I raise my voice and take my stand,
a stop to war I do command,
no more shall warring scar the earth,
a golden age is given birth.

O Mother Mary, generate,
the song that does accelerate,
the earth into a higher state,
all matter does now scintillate.

8. Saint Germain, radiate into the collective consciousness the awareness that when we see beyond the material and see the immaterial bond between all people, we are not threatened by other material expressions being different from our own. We rejoice in diversity.

As Mother Earth is free at last,
disasters belong to the past,
your Mother Light is so intense,
that matter is now far less dense.

O Mother Mary, generate,
the song that does accelerate,
the earth into a higher state,
all matter does now scintillate.

9. Saint Germain, radiate into the collective consciousness the awareness that we do not bring the Golden Age by upholding a standard of right and wrong. Instead, we need to focus on improving things by acknowledging the higher vision and saying: "How can we transcend the old? How can we help others transcend the old? How can we all do what is more than we did before?"

In Mother Light the earth is pure,
the upward spiral will endure,
prosperity is now the norm,
God's vision manifest as form.

24 | Invoking an end to suppression by the power elite

O Mother Mary, generate,
the song that does accelerate,
the earth into a higher state,
all matter does now scintillate.

Part 3

1. Saint Germain, radiate into the collective consciousness the awareness that you do not have a giant model of what the Golden Age in full manifestation will look like in every detail. There is plenty of room for diversity and individual expression.

> O Saint Germain, you do inspire,
> my vision raised forever higher,
> with you I form a figure-eight,
> your Golden Age I co-create.

> **O Saint Germain, what love you bring,**
> **it truly makes all matter sing,**
> **your violet flame does all restore,**
> **with you we are becoming more.**

2. Saint Germain, radiate into the collective consciousness the awareness that it is not the golden age mindset that scientists spend billions of dollars seeking to give ultimate proof of the materialistic paradigm while millions of people are starving.

> O Saint Germain, what Freedom Flame,
> released when we recite your name,
> acceleration is your gift,
> our planet it will surely lift.

**O Saint Germain, what love you bring,
it truly makes all matter sing,
your violet flame does all restore,
with you we are becoming more.**

3. Saint Germain, radiate into the collective consciousness the awareness that science is deeply influenced by an elitist mindset that comes from the fallen beings.

O Saint Germain, in love we claim,
our right to bring your violet flame,
from you Above, to us below,
it is an all-transforming flow.

**O Saint Germain, what love you bring,
it truly makes all matter sing,
your violet flame does all restore,
with you we are becoming more.**

4. Saint Germain, radiate into the collective consciousness the awareness that it was the collective consciousness of the people on earth that allowed the fallen beings to come here and they partly came here as a testing. Would people follow the elite, or would they stand up for themselves?

O Saint Germain, I love you so,
my aura filled with violet glow,
my chakras filled with violet fire,
I am your cosmic amplifier.

**O Saint Germain, what love you bring,
it truly makes all matter sing,
your violet flame does all restore,
with you we are becoming more.**

5. Saint Germain, radiate into the collective consciousness the awareness that the fallen beings believe they are superior to the human beings on earth, which is why they try to set themselves up as strong leaders.

O Saint Germain, I am now free,
your violet flame is therapy,
transform all hang-ups in my mind,
as inner peace I surely find.

**O Saint Germain, what love you bring,
it truly makes all matter sing,
your violet flame does all restore,
with you we are becoming more.**

6. Saint Germain, radiate into the collective consciousness the awareness that the three monotheistic religions are ruled by a specific paradigm that is similar to the paradigm that rules science, namely the belief in an ultimate theory or religion.

O Saint Germain, my body pure,
your violet flame for all is cure,
consume the cause of all disease,
and therefore I am all at ease.

**O Saint Germain, what love you bring,
it truly makes all matter sing,
your violet flame does all restore,
with you we are becoming more.**

7. Saint Germain, radiate into the collective consciousness the awareness that the perversion of the Father aspect defines an ultimate truth, and the perversion of the Mother demands that all must submit to the ultimate theory.

O Saint Germain, I'm karma-free,
the past no longer burdens me,
a brand new opportunity,
I am in Christic unity.

**O Saint Germain, what love you bring,
it truly makes all matter sing,
your violet flame does all restore,
with you we are becoming more.**

8. Saint Germain, radiate into the collective consciousness the awareness that the demand of both the traditional religions and science, even communism and capitalism, is that the individual must submit to the leading elite.

O Saint Germain, we are now one,
I am for you a violet sun,
as we transform this planet earth,
your Golden Age is given birth.

**O Saint Germain, what love you bring,
it truly makes all matter sing,
your violet flame does all restore,
with you we are becoming more.**

9. Saint Germain, radiate into the collective consciousness the awareness that the three monotheistic religions have systematically suppressed both men and women. We cannot end the suppression of women until we end the fallen mindset so that it can no longer rule this planet.

O Saint Germain, the earth is free,
from burden of duality,
in oneness we bring what is best,
your Golden Age is manifest.

**O Saint Germain, what love you bring,
it truly makes all matter sing,
your violet flame does all restore,
with you we are becoming more.**

Part 4

1. Saint Germain, radiate into the collective consciousness the awareness that the suppression of women springs from the greater goal of dividing men and women so they cannot form the correct polarity of the figure-eight flow between them.

O blessed Mary, Mother mine,
there is no greater love than thine,
as we are one in heart and mind,
my place in hierarchy I find.

O Mother Mary, generate,
the song that does accelerate,
the earth into a higher state,
all matter does now scintillate.

2. Saint Germain, radiate into the collective consciousness the awareness that there will never be a final, ultimate, absolute spiritual teaching given, and we need to let go of the dream of an ultimate spiritual organization.

I came to earth from heaven sent,
as I am in embodiment,
I use Divine authority,
commanding you to set earth free.

O Mother Mary, generate,
the song that does accelerate,
the earth into a higher state,
all matter does now scintillate.

3. Saint Germain, radiate into the collective consciousness the awareness that the alchemical key to the Golden Age is not a secret formula but that we become open doors for the flow of the Spirit. This cannot happen if we are divided within ourselves or fighting each other.

I call now in God's sacred name,
for you to use your Mother Flame,
to burn all fear-based energy,
restoring sacred harmony.

**O Mother Mary, generate,
the song that does accelerate,
the earth into a higher state,
all matter does now scintillate.**

4. Saint Germain, radiate into the collective consciousness the awareness that what drives progress in society is an increase in awareness. That is why the elite will always oppose this increase in awareness.

Your sacred name I hereby praise,
collective consciousness you raise,
no more of fear and doubt and shame,
consume it with your Mother Flame.

**O Mother Mary, generate,
the song that does accelerate,
the earth into a higher state,
all matter does now scintillate.**

5. Saint Germain, radiate into the collective consciousness the awareness that in every age some individuals will refuse to submit to the force that seeks to limit awareness. They are willing to be the open doors for ideas that help bring society forward.

All darkness from the earth you purge,
your light moves as a mighty surge,
no force of darkness can now stop,
the spiral that goes only up.

**O Mother Mary, generate,
the song that does accelerate,
the earth into a higher state,
all matter does now scintillate.**

6. Saint Germain, radiate into the collective consciousness the awareness that too many people in the West are not sufficiently aware of the power elite because they have been deceived into thinking that because we have so-called free societies, free democracies and freedom of speech, there is no force holding back the growth in awareness.

All elemental life you bless,
removing from them man-made stress,
the nature spirits are now free,
outpicturing Divine decree.

**O Mother Mary, generate,
the song that does accelerate,
the earth into a higher state,
all matter does now scintillate.**

7. Saint Germain, radiate into the collective consciousness the awareness that the missing ingredient is the awareness that life has a spiritual side. Human beings are not evolved animals because we were created in the spiritual realm and descended into physical bodies on earth.

I raise my voice and take my stand,
a stop to war I do command,
no more shall warring scar the earth,
a golden age is given birth.

**O Mother Mary, generate,
the song that does accelerate,
the earth into a higher state,
all matter does now scintillate.**

8. Saint Germain, radiate into the collective consciousness the awareness that there is a path that people can follow that leads them from whatever level of consciousness they have now to the level of consciousness that allows them to ascend and become permanent residents of the spiritual realm.

As Mother Earth is free at last,
disasters belong to the past,
your Mother Light is so intense,
that matter is now far less dense.

**O Mother Mary, generate,
the song that does accelerate,
the earth into a higher state,
all matter does now scintillate.**

9. Saint Germain, radiate into the collective consciousness the awareness that human beings are not "human" beings but psycho-spiritual beings and that our lives have a purpose. This makes it easier to see the force of elitism and its influence throughout history.

In Mother Light the earth is pure,
the upward spiral will endure,
prosperity is now the norm,
God's vision manifest as form.

**O Mother Mary, generate,
the song that does accelerate,
the earth into a higher state,
all matter does now scintillate.**

Part 5

1. Saint Germain, radiate into the collective consciousness the awareness that because all human beings are psycho-spiritual beings that originated in a higher realm, there is a universal humanity, a universal worth, that applies to all human beings.

O Saint Germain, you do inspire,
my vision raised forever higher,
with you I form a figure-eight,
your Golden Age I co-create.

**O Saint Germain, what love you bring,
it truly makes all matter sing,
your violet flame does all restore,
with you we are becoming more.**

2. Saint Germain, radiate into the collective consciousness the awareness that the natural way to look at human beings is that all beings on earth have equal value and should have equal rights. These rights should be defined in order to give all people an equal opportunity to expand their awareness on an individual level.

> O Saint Germain, what Freedom Flame,
> released when we recite your name,
> acceleration is your gift,
> our planet it will surely lift.
>
> **O Saint Germain, what love you bring,**
> **it truly makes all matter sing,**
> **your violet flame does all restore,**
> **with you we are becoming more.**

3. Saint Germain, radiate into the collective consciousness the awareness that all of the laws that guide specific societies should proceed from this foundation of individual growth to then define the parameters for how a particular society wants to grow as a whole.

> O Saint Germain, in love we claim,
> our right to bring your violet flame,
> from you Above, to us below,
> it is an all-transforming flow.
>
> **O Saint Germain, what love you bring,**
> **it truly makes all matter sing,**
> **your violet flame does all restore,**
> **with you we are becoming more.**

4. Saint Germain, radiate into the collective consciousness the awareness that groups of people who form what we see as nation-states have a right to define certain laws for how the members of their group interact with each other and the larger whole of humanity.

> O Saint Germain, I love you so,
> my aura filled with violet glow,
> my chakras filled with violet fire,
> I am your cosmic amplifier.
>
> **O Saint Germain, what love you bring,**
> **it truly makes all matter sing,**
> **your violet flame does all restore,**
> **with you we are becoming more.**

5. Saint Germain, radiate into the collective consciousness the awareness that when we accept the universal worth of all human beings, we can see what has been the missing ingredient, the missing link, in people's understanding of history. It is that some people do not have this respect for the universal worth and value of all human beings.

> O Saint Germain, I am now free,
> your violet flame is therapy,
> transform all hang-ups in my mind,
> as inner peace I surely find.
>
> **O Saint Germain, what love you bring,**
> **it truly makes all matter sing,**
> **your violet flame does all restore,**
> **with you we are becoming more.**

6. Saint Germain, radiate into the collective consciousness the awareness that in every society in the past, we see the formation of an elite. These people do not have the mindset that all human beings on earth have equal worth and should have equal rights and equal opportunity to grow.

> O Saint Germain, my body pure,
> your violet flame for all is cure,
> consume the cause of all disease,
> and therefore I am all at ease.

> **O Saint Germain, what love you bring,**
> **it truly makes all matter sing,**
> **your violet flame does all restore,**
> **with you we are becoming more.**

7. Saint Germain, radiate into the collective consciousness the awareness that members of the elite do not respect universal rights and values; instead they respect only their own rights, only their own value.

> O Saint Germain, I'm karma-free,
> the past no longer burdens me,
> a brand new opportunity,
> I am in Christic unity.

> **O Saint Germain, what love you bring,**
> **it truly makes all matter sing,**
> **your violet flame does all restore,**
> **with you we are becoming more.**

8. Saint Germain, radiate into the collective consciousness the awareness that some people have done everything they could to set themselves up as an elite who is in control of the majority of the population. They have suppressed the majority of the population so that they are the worker bees that work to maintain the privileged lifestyle of the elite.

> O Saint Germain, we are now one,
> I am for you a violet sun,
> as we transform this planet earth,
> your Golden Age is given birth.
>
> **O Saint Germain, what love you bring,
> it truly makes all matter sing,
> your violet flame does all restore,
> with you we are becoming more.**

9. Saint Germain, radiate into the collective consciousness the awareness that the one ingredient that is missing right now is an awakening to the influence of elitism on the course of humanity.

> O Saint Germain, the earth is free,
> from burden of duality,
> in oneness we bring what is best,
> your Golden Age is manifest.
>
> **O Saint Germain, what love you bring,
> it truly makes all matter sing,
> your violet flame does all restore,
> with you we are becoming more.**

Sealing

In the name of the Divine Mother, I call to all ascended masters for the sealing of myself and all people in my circle of influence in the creative flow of the Divine Mother, the River of Life. I call for the multiplication of my calls by all ascended masters so that we form the perfect figure-eight flow of "As Above, so below." Thus, I accept that this is fully manifest, because the mouth of the Lord, the Divine Mother that I AM, has spoken it. Amen.

25 | INVOKING THE EXPOSURE OF THE POWER ELITE

In the name I AM THAT I AM, Jesus Christ, I call to all ascended masters working on manifesting the Golden Age, especially Jesus, Maitreya and Saint Germain to radiate into the collective consciousness an impulse that will awaken people to the existence of the power elite. Help people see that we can build a new future by working with the ascended masters and letting go of the old way of looking at life, including…

[Make personal calls.]

Part 1

1. Saint Germain, radiate into the collective consciousness the awareness that the power elites of history are made up of a limited number of fallen lifestreams. They have rebelled against God's plan and purpose for the universe.

O Saint Germain, you do inspire,
my vision raised forever higher,
with you I form a figure-eight,
your Golden Age I co-create.

**O Saint Germain, what love you bring,
it truly makes all matter sing,
your violet flame does all restore,
with you we are becoming more.**

2. Saint Germain, radiate into the collective consciousness the awareness that even though the elite is not unified, there is a unified intent, movement and force towards suppressing the general population. The elite will resist the growth in awareness of the population.

O Saint Germain, what Freedom Flame,
released when we recite your name,
acceleration is your gift,
our planet it will surely lift.

**O Saint Germain, what love you bring,
it truly makes all matter sing,
your violet flame does all restore,
with you we are becoming more.**

3. Saint Germain, radiate into the collective consciousness the awareness that even though we have seen a tremendous growth in knowledge and awareness over the past 2,000 years, there is still an elite who is seeking to limit the awareness of the population so that they can continue to suppress people through our ignorance of what is going on.

25 | *Invoking the exposure of the power elite*

O Saint Germain, in love we claim,
our right to bring your violet flame,
from you Above, to us below,
it is an all-transforming flow.

**O Saint Germain, what love you bring,
it truly makes all matter sing,
your violet flame does all restore,
with you we are becoming more.**

4. Saint Germain, radiate into the collective consciousness the awareness that it is necessary for people to realize that this elite is not made up of lifestreams who are stupid. They are highly intelligent and sophisticated and therefore they will seek to use whatever means are available in a given society.

O Saint Germain, I love you so,
my aura filled with violet glow,
my chakras filled with violet fire,
I am your cosmic amplifier.

**O Saint Germain, what love you bring,
it truly makes all matter sing,
your violet flame does all restore,
with you we are becoming more.**

5. Saint Germain, radiate into the collective consciousness the awareness that there came a point when the power elites of the world accepted that democracy was inevitable so they looked at how to use it. There is no democratic society that does not have people with the elitist mindset who look down on the population and feel that they are entitled to privileges and they are entitled to rule.

O Saint Germain, I am now free,
your violet flame is therapy,
transform all hang-ups in my mind,
as inner peace I surely find.

**O Saint Germain, what love you bring,
it truly makes all matter sing,
your violet flame does all restore,
with you we are becoming more.**

6. Saint Germain, radiate into the collective consciousness the awareness that the larger a country becomes, the more power it has and the more it will attract the lifestreams that want power and will seek to do anything they can to get this power.

O Saint Germain, my body pure,
your violet flame for all is cure,
consume the cause of all disease,
and therefore I am all at ease.

**O Saint Germain, what love you bring,
it truly makes all matter sing,
your violet flame does all restore,
with you we are becoming more.**

7. Saint Germain, radiate into the collective consciousness the awareness that there is no country in the democratic world that has a stronger power elite than the United States. There is hardly a more elitist society than the United States where the members of the elite do not openly control the political process but they control it in hidden ways through the financial system.

25 | *Invoking the exposure of the power elite*

O Saint Germain, I'm karma-free,
the past no longer burdens me,
a brand new opportunity,
I am in Christic unity.

**O Saint Germain, what love you bring,
it truly makes all matter sing,
your violet flame does all restore,
with you we are becoming more.**

8. Saint Germain, radiate into the collective consciousness the awareness that there is hardly any population in the democratic world that is more deceived than Americans for they believe they have the most free nation in the world. Yet there is hardly a nation where a small elite has more control.

O Saint Germain, we are now one,
I am for you a violet sun,
as we transform this planet earth,
your Golden Age is given birth.

**O Saint Germain, what love you bring,
it truly makes all matter sing,
your violet flame does all restore,
with you we are becoming more.**

9. Saint Germain, radiate into the collective consciousness the awareness that you want people to be aware of the elite, but you do not want them to engage in a physical battle against the elite. You do not desire to see violent uprisings and demonstrations against sitting governments.

O Saint Germain, the earth is free,
from burden of duality,
in oneness we bring what is best,
your Golden Age is manifest.

**O Saint Germain, what love you bring,
it truly makes all matter sing,
your violet flame does all restore,
with you we are becoming more.**

Part 2

1. Saint Germain, radiate into the collective consciousness the awareness that we will not further the descent of the Golden Age through force and violence. We will not help you bring the Golden Age by fighting the power elite.

O Jesus, blessed brother mine,
I walk the path that you outline,
a great example to us all,
I follow now your inner call.

**O Jesus, let the Fire of Joy,
consume the devil's subtle ploy,
transfigured is our planet earth,
the Golden Age is given birth.**

2. Saint Germain, radiate into the collective consciousness the awareness that we will help you bring the Golden Age by helping to expose the power elite, by awakening the people to the existence of the power elite and then awakening the people to the mindset that is beyond the epic mindset, beyond the dualistic mindset.

> O Jesus, open inner sight,
> the ego wants to prove it's right,
> but this I will no longer do,
> I want to be all one with you.
>
> **O Jesus, let the Fire of Joy,**
> **consume the devil's subtle ploy,**
> **transfigured is our planet earth,**
> **the Golden Age is given birth.**

3. Saint Germain, radiate into the collective consciousness the awareness that we will not manifest the Golden Age as long as the elite rules society, yet we will not overcome the elite through violence and force. We will not overcome the elite by destroying the elite but by transcending the elitist mindset.

> O Jesus, I now clearly see,
> the Key of Knowledge given me,
> my Christ self I hereby embrace,
> as you fill up my inner space.
>
> **O Jesus, let the Fire of Joy,**
> **consume the devil's subtle ploy,**
> **transfigured is our planet earth,**
> **the Golden Age is given birth.**

4. Saint Germain, radiate into the collective consciousness the awareness that a small power elite can rule a nation as large as the United States by taking advantage of the mindset of the majority of the people, namely black-and-white thinking, the dualistic mindset and the epic struggle.

> O Jesus, show me serpent's lie,
> expose the beam in my own eye,
> as Christ discernment you me give,
> in oneness I forever live.

> **O Jesus, let the Fire of Joy,**
> **consume the devil's subtle ploy,**
> **transfigured is our planet earth,**
> **the Golden Age is given birth.**

5. Saint Germain, radiate into the collective consciousness the awareness that there are still so many people who are trapped in this mindset that the elite can rule America because the people cannot even ask the questions—they are so blinded by this mindset.

> O Jesus, I am truly meek,
> and thus I turn the other cheek,
> when the accuser attacks me,
> I go within and merge with thee.

> **O Jesus, let the Fire of Joy,**
> **consume the devil's subtle ploy,**
> **transfigured is our planet earth,**
> **the Golden Age is given birth.**

6. Saint Germain, radiate into the collective consciousness the awareness that the spiritual people need to ask these questions and transcend the epic mindset that portrays the world as a struggle between good and evil.

O Jesus, ego I let die,
surrender ev'ry earthly tie,
the dead can bury what is dead,
I choose to walk with you instead.

**O Jesus, let the Fire of Joy,
consume the devil's subtle ploy,
transfigured is our planet earth,
the Golden Age is given birth.**

7. Saint Germain, radiate into the collective consciousness the awareness that the epic struggle between good and evil is a struggle between the two dualistic polarities of the fallen consciousness. It has nothing to do with the ascended master consciousness.

O Jesus, help me rise above,
the devil's test through higher love,
show me separate self unreal,
my formless self you do reveal.

**O Jesus, let the Fire of Joy,
consume the devil's subtle ploy,
transfigured is our planet earth,
the Golden Age is given birth.**

8. Saint Germain, radiate into the collective consciousness the awareness that the ultimate goal of the spiritual path is to transcend the fallen mindset. We can demonstrate by example that it is possible and necessary to transcend it for the birth of the Golden Age to become a reality.

> O Jesus, what is that to me,
> I just let go and follow thee,
> with this I do pass ev'ry test,
> to find with you eternal rest.

> **O Jesus, let the Fire of Joy,**
> **consume the devil's subtle ploy,**
> **transfigured is our planet earth,**
> **the Golden Age is given birth.**

9. Saint Germain, radiate into the collective consciousness the awareness that the goal of an awakened society is to extend equal opportunity to all people and to respect the humanity and the spirituality of each human being, therefore helping people to raise their consciousness on an individual basis.

> O Jesus, fiery master mine,
> my heart now melting into thine,
> I love with heart and mind and soul,
> the God who is my highest goal.

> **O Jesus, let the Fire of Joy,**
> **consume the devil's subtle ploy,**
> **transfigured is our planet earth,**
> **the Golden Age is given birth.**

Part 3

1. Saint Germain, radiate into the collective consciousness the awareness that life on earth is not the way it is meant to be because life on earth is not geared towards giving people equal opportunity, equal rights, equal worth.

> O Saint Germain, you do inspire,
> my vision raised forever higher,
> with you I form a figure-eight,
> your Golden Age I co-create.

> **O Saint Germain, what love you bring,**
> **it truly makes all matter sing,**
> **your violet flame does all restore,**
> **with you we are becoming more.**

2. Saint Germain, radiate into the collective consciousness the awareness that there is an elite whose members are always seeking to set themselves up to have privileges and power over the population. They do not have the mindset that all people have equal worth for they believe they are worth more than ordinary people.

> O Saint Germain, what Freedom Flame,
> released when we recite your name,
> acceleration is your gift,
> our planet it will surely lift.

**O Saint Germain, what love you bring,
it truly makes all matter sing,
your violet flame does all restore,
with you we are becoming more.**

3. Saint Germain, radiate into the collective consciousness the awareness that the members of the elite do not want people to have this awareness because they do not want to be exposed, they do not want to be seen for what they are.

O Saint Germain, in love we claim,
our right to bring your violet flame,
from you Above, to us below,
it is an all-transforming flow.

**O Saint Germain, what love you bring,
it truly makes all matter sing,
your violet flame does all restore,
with you we are becoming more.**

4. Saint Germain, radiate into the collective consciousness the awareness that members of the elite know that if people see the elite and see that they are like the Emperor who has noting on, then they will not be willing to submit to them.

O Saint Germain, I love you so,
my aura filled with violet glow,
my chakras filled with violet fire,
I am your cosmic amplifier.

25 | Invoking the exposure of the power elite

**O Saint Germain, what love you bring,
it truly makes all matter sing,
your violet flame does all restore,
with you we are becoming more.**

5. Saint Germain, radiate into the collective consciousness the awareness that we will see that the elite has no power when we recognize that we are more than human beings. We are spiritual beings, and therefore we do not have to submit to any power on earth.

O Saint Germain, I am now free,
your violet flame is therapy,
transform all hang-ups in my mind,
as inner peace I surely find.

**O Saint Germain, what love you bring,
it truly makes all matter sing,
your violet flame does all restore,
with you we are becoming more.**

6. Saint Germain, radiate into the collective consciousness the awareness that as the Buddha and Jesus demonstrated, we can all attain a state of consciousness where we can walk the earth in a physical body, but we will not be subject to any power on earth.

O Saint Germain, my body pure,
your violet flame for all is cure,
consume the cause of all disease,
and therefore I am all at ease.

> **O Saint Germain, what love you bring,**
> **it truly makes all matter sing,**
> **your violet flame does all restore,**
> **with you we are becoming more.**

7. Saint Germain, radiate into the collective consciousness the awareness that we can all be the open door for the power of God, and the power of God cannot be controlled by the power elite.

> O Saint Germain, I'm karma-free,
> the past no longer burdens me,
> a brand new opportunity,
> I am in Christic unity.

> **O Saint Germain, what love you bring,**
> **it truly makes all matter sing,**
> **your violet flame does all restore,**
> **with you we are becoming more.**

8. Saint Germain, radiate into the collective consciousness the awareness that the elite cannot maintain their power over the people when sufficient numbers among us begin to see ourselves as spiritual beings with the potential to be the open door for the power of God.

> O Saint Germain, we are now one,
> I am for you a violet sun,
> as we transform this planet earth,
> your Golden Age is given birth.

> O Saint Germain, what love you bring,
> it truly makes all matter sing,
> your violet flame does all restore,
> with you we are becoming more.

9. Saint Germain, radiate into the collective consciousness the awareness that the last thing the power elite wants on earth is for people to follow Jesus' example so there are suddenly 10,000 people with full Christhood in embodiment and millions with a smaller degree of Christhood.

> O Saint Germain, the earth is free,
> from burden of duality,
> in oneness we bring what is best,
> your Golden Age is manifest.

> O Saint Germain, what love you bring,
> it truly makes all matter sing,
> your violet flame does all restore,
> with you we are becoming more.

Part 4

1. Saint Germain, radiate into the collective consciousness the awareness that when there are people who have attained a degree of Christhood, they will not be subject to the consciousness of the elite, who see themselves as separate beings, separated from God and other people.

Maitreya, I am truly meek,
your counsel wise I humbly seek,
your vision I so want to see,
with you in Eden I will be.

**Maitreya, kindness is the cure,
in fires of kindness I am pure.
Maitreya, now release the fire,
that raises me forever higher.**

2. Saint Germain, radiate into the collective consciousness the awareness that the consciousness of separation leads to the consciousness of inequality.

Maitreya, help me to return,
to learn from you, I truly yearn,
as oneness is all I desire
I feel initiation's fire.

**Maitreya, kindness is the cure,
in fires of kindness I am pure.
Maitreya, now release the fire,
that raises me forever higher.**

3. Saint Germain, radiate into the collective consciousness the awareness that the consciousness of elitism is based on a fundamental inequality so that all people are not created equal, they are not all endowed with inalienable rights that no power on earth can take away from them.

25 | *Invoking the exposure of the power elite*

Maitreya, I hereby decide,
from you I will no longer hide,
expose to me the very lie
that caused edenic self to die.

**Maitreya, kindness is the cure,
in fires of kindness I am pure.
Maitreya, now release the fire,
that raises me forever higher.**

4. Saint Germain, radiate into the collective consciousness the awareness that the elite can have power, they can have a privileged position, only if they are not equal to a majority of the population. They must define a philosophy that puts people down and divides them into distinct categories.

Maitreya, blessed Guru mine,
my heart of hearts forever thine,
I vow that I will listen well,
so we can break the serpent's spell.

**Maitreya, kindness is the cure,
in fires of kindness I am pure.
Maitreya, now release the fire,
that raises me forever higher.**

5. Saint Germain, radiate into the collective consciousness the awareness that even the Christian religion was used to create, sustain and support an elitist society where the king, the noble class and the church hierarchy formed a privileged class and the majority of the population were their slaves.

Maitreya, help me see the lie
whereby the serpent broke the tie,
the serpent now has naught in me,
in oneness I am truly free.

**Maitreya, kindness is the cure,
in fires of kindness I am pure.
Maitreya, now release the fire,
that raises me forever higher.**

6. Saint Germain, radiate into the collective consciousness the awareness that the elite can rule only because the majority of the population are also blinded by this illusion of separation. This is what makes it possible that we can see such incredible inequality between rich and poor nations.

Maitreya, truth does set me free
from falsehoods of duality,
the fruit of knowledge I let go,
so your true spirit I do know.

**Maitreya, kindness is the cure,
in fires of kindness I am pure.
Maitreya, now release the fire,
that raises me forever higher.**

7. Saint Germain, radiate into the collective consciousness the awareness that when we begin to attain a degree of Christ discernment, we see that all human beings originated as spiritual beings.

Maitreya, I submit to you,
intentions pure, my heart is true,
from ego I am truly free,
as I am now all one with thee.

**Maitreya, kindness is the cure,
in fires of kindness I am pure.
Maitreya, now release the fire,
that raises me forever higher.**

8. Saint Germain, radiate into the collective consciousness the awareness that Christhood is characterized by oneness instead of separation. There is the vertical oneness with Spirit and horizontal oneness with other people.

Maitreya, kindness is the key,
all shades of kindness teach to me,
for I am now the open door,
the Art of Kindness to restore.

**Maitreya, kindness is the cure,
in fires of kindness I am pure.
Maitreya, now release the fire,
that raises me forever higher.**

9. Saint Germain, radiate into the collective consciousness the awareness that to the Christ consciousness, it is not acceptable that some nations have such a high degree of material welfare while there are two billion people living under the poverty level and millions of people starving.

Maitreya, oh sweet mystery,
immersed in your reality,
the myst'ry school will now return,
for this, my heart does truly burn.

**Maitreya, kindness is the cure,
in fires of kindness I am pure.
Maitreya, now release the fire,
that raises me forever higher.**

Part 5

1. Saint Germain, radiate into the collective consciousness the awareness that only the consciousness of separation can explain that many among the richest nations are completely absorbed in their affluent lifestyle, only focused on getting more money and material possessions.

O Saint Germain, you do inspire,
my vision raised forever higher,
with you I form a figure-eight,
your Golden Age I co-create.

**O Saint Germain, what love you bring,
it truly makes all matter sing,
your violet flame does all restore,
with you we are becoming more.**

2. Saint Germain, radiate into the collective consciousness the awareness that only people trapped in separation can fail to have compassion for the fact that not everyone has a lifestyle that is worthy of spiritual beings.

> O Saint Germain, what Freedom Flame,
> released when we recite your name,
> acceleration is your gift,
> our planet it will surely lift.

> **O Saint Germain, what love you bring,**
> **it truly makes all matter sing,**
> **your violet flame does all restore,**
> **with you we are becoming more.**

3. Saint Germain, radiate into the collective consciousness the awareness that what will bring the Golden Age into manifestation is that millions of people attain a degree of Christ discernment where they naturally begin to ask these questions and ask them publicly.

> O Saint Germain, in love we claim,
> our right to bring your violet flame,
> from you Above, to us below,
> it is an all-transforming flow.

> **O Saint Germain, what love you bring,**
> **it truly makes all matter sing,**
> **your violet flame does all restore,**
> **with you we are becoming more.**

4. Saint Germain, radiate into the collective consciousness the awareness that will awaken those who have it in their Divine plans to speak out in every area of society and fundamentally shift the public debate from separation to oneness.

> O Saint Germain, I love you so,
> my aura filled with violet glow,
> my chakras filled with violet fire,
> I am your cosmic amplifier.

> **O Saint Germain, what love you bring,**
> **it truly makes all matter sing,**
> **your violet flame does all restore,**
> **with you we are becoming more.**

5. Saint Germain, radiate into the collective consciousness the awareness that it is possible to create a worldwide umbrella organization that has as its goal to raise awareness of the spiritual side of life through all means possible.

> O Saint Germain, I am now free,
> your violet flame is therapy,
> transform all hang-ups in my mind,
> as inner peace I surely find.

> **O Saint Germain, what love you bring,**
> **it truly makes all matter sing,**
> **your violet flame does all restore,**
> **with you we are becoming more.**

6. Saint Germain, radiate into the collective consciousness the awareness that civilization cannot fulfill its potential if we do not acknowledge that life has a spiritual side. Only when we achieve Christ discernment, will be able to step back and ask the questions that we cannot even ask from the consciousness of separation.

> O Saint Germain, my body pure,
> your violet flame for all is cure,
> consume the cause of all disease,
> and therefore I am all at ease.
>
> **O Saint Germain, what love you bring,
> it truly makes all matter sing,
> your violet flame does all restore,
> with you we are becoming more.**

7. Saint Germain, radiate into the collective consciousness the awareness that to the Christ consciousness, it is not acceptable that democratic nations continue to build up their armies, continuing to create more and more sophisticated weapons even though there truly is no enemy for which they need these weapons.

> O Saint Germain, I'm karma-free,
> the past no longer burdens me,
> a brand new opportunity,
> I am in Christic unity.
>
> **O Saint Germain, what love you bring,
> it truly makes all matter sing,
> your violet flame does all restore,
> with you we are becoming more.**

8. Saint Germain, radiate into the collective consciousness the awareness that to the Christ consciousness, it is not acceptable that the United States maintains an armed force that can strike anywhere around the globe at any time and overturn governments or start wars anywhere the elite desires.

> O Saint Germain, we are now one,
> I am for you a violet sun,
> as we transform this planet earth,
> your Golden Age is given birth.

> **O Saint Germain, what love you bring,**
> **it truly makes all matter sing,**
> **your violet flame does all restore,**
> **with you we are becoming more.**

9. Saint Germain, radiate into the collective consciousness the awareness that to the Christ consciousness, it is obvious that the money put into arms and the research into more arms could be freed up to solve real problems.

> O Saint Germain, the earth is free,
> from burden of duality,
> in oneness we bring what is best,
> your Golden Age is manifest.

> **O Saint Germain, what love you bring,**
> **it truly makes all matter sing,**
> **your violet flame does all restore,**
> **with you we are becoming more.**

Sealing

In the name of the Divine Mother, I call to all ascended masters for the sealing of myself and all people in my circle of influence in the creative flow of the Divine Mother, the River of Life. I call for the multiplication of my calls by all ascended masters so that we form the perfect figure-eight flow of "As Above, so below." Thus, I accept that this is fully manifest, because the mouth of the Lord, the Divine Mother that I AM, has spoken it. Amen.

26 | INVOKING A NEW AWARENESS OF HISTORY

In the name I AM THAT I AM, Jesus Christ, I call to all ascended masters working on manifesting the Golden Age, especially Gautama Buddha, Sanat Kumara and Saint Germain to radiate into the collective consciousness a vision of how the power elite has influenced history. Help people see that we can build a new future by working with the ascended masters and letting go of the old way of looking at life, including…

[Make personal calls.]

Part 1

1. Saint Germain, radiate into the collective consciousness the awareness that to the Christ consciousness, it is obvious that the minds of the scientists who are right now focusing on weapons research could be freed up to do other things, such as alternative forms of energy, eradicating disease, eradicating poverty and hunger.

> O Saint Germain, you do inspire,
> my vision raised forever higher,
> with you I form a figure-eight,
> your Golden Age I co-create.
>
> **O Saint Germain, what love you bring,**
> **it truly makes all matter sing,**
> **your violet flame does all restore,**
> **with you we are becoming more.**

2. Saint Germain, radiate into the collective consciousness the awareness that the members of the elite do not want this shift to happen. They want to maintain their power and their privileges.

> O Saint Germain, what Freedom Flame,
> released when we recite your name,
> acceleration is your gift,
> our planet it will surely lift.

> **O Saint Germain, what love you bring,
> it truly makes all matter sing,
> your violet flame does all restore,
> with you we are becoming more.**

3. Saint Germain, radiate into the collective consciousness the awareness that the members of the elite want to maintain the sense that they are special, that they belong to an elite that has more than the people.

> O Saint Germain, in love we claim,
> our right to bring your violet flame,
> from you Above, to us below,
> it is an all-transforming flow.

> **O Saint Germain, what love you bring,
> it truly makes all matter sing,
> your violet flame does all restore,
> with you we are becoming more.**

4. Saint Germain, radiate into the collective consciousness the awareness that the members of the elite do not want equality, they do not want equal opportunity; they want privileged positions that no one can challenge.

> O Saint Germain, I love you so,
> my aura filled with violet glow,
> my chakras filled with violet fire,
> I am your cosmic amplifier.

**O Saint Germain, what love you bring,
it truly makes all matter sing,
your violet flame does all restore,
with you we are becoming more.**

5. Saint Germain, radiate into the collective consciousness the awareness that members of the elite loved the feudal societies of Europe for they were born into a position and stayed in it for a lifetime. They have been trying to recreate this kind of a society under the disguise of democracy and a so-called free-market economy.

O Saint Germain, I am now free,
your violet flame is therapy,
transform all hang-ups in my mind,
as inner peace I surely find.

**O Saint Germain, what love you bring,
it truly makes all matter sing,
your violet flame does all restore,
with you we are becoming more.**

6. Saint Germain, radiate into the collective consciousness the awareness that members of the power elite financed Lenin and the Bolshevik revolution. They continued to extend credit to the Soviet Union so that they could continue to build the arms that necessitated the ongoing arms race between East and West.

O Saint Germain, my body pure,
your violet flame for all is cure,
consume the cause of all disease,
and therefore I am all at ease.

**O Saint Germain, what love you bring,
it truly makes all matter sing,
your violet flame does all restore,
with you we are becoming more.**

7. Saint Germain, radiate into the collective consciousness the awareness that members of the elite believe that if you don't have a real enemy, you have to create one. Then you have the dualistic battle between the two sides, which is the hallmark of the dualistic consciousness.

O Saint Germain, I'm karma-free,
the past no longer burdens me,
a brand new opportunity,
I am in Christic unity.

**O Saint Germain, what love you bring,
it truly makes all matter sing,
your violet flame does all restore,
with you we are becoming more.**

8. Saint Germain, radiate into the collective consciousness the awareness that no society can afford to allow its government and the media to shut down the people who dare to speak out.

O Saint Germain, we are now one,
I am for you a violet sun,
as we transform this planet earth,
your Golden Age is given birth.

> O Saint Germain, what love you bring,
> it truly makes all matter sing,
> your violet flame does all restore,
> with you we are becoming more.

9. Saint Germain, radiate into the collective consciousness the awareness that what truly endangers a nation is when the government does not have transparency.

> O Saint Germain, the earth is free,
> from burden of duality,
> in oneness we bring what is best,
> your Golden Age is manifest.

> O Saint Germain, what love you bring,
> it truly makes all matter sing,
> your violet flame does all restore,
> with you we are becoming more.

Part 2

1. Saint Germain, radiate into the collective consciousness the awareness that it is always the members of the power elite that do not want transparency because they know they can rule only by remaining hidden from the people.

> Gautama, show my mental state
> that does give rise to love and hate,
> your exposé I do endure,
> so my perception will be pure.

**Gautama, Flame of Cosmic Peace,
unruly thoughts do hereby cease,
we radiate from you and me
the peace to still Samsara's Sea.**

2. Saint Germain, radiate into the collective consciousness the awareness that members of the power elite were very concerned about the emergence of democracies. The essence of a democracy is that each person has one vote and that all votes count the same.

Gautama, in your Flame of Peace,
the struggling self I now release,
the Buddha Nature I now see,
it is the core of you and me.

**Gautama, Flame of Cosmic Peace,
unruly thoughts do hereby cease,
we radiate from you and me
the peace to still Samsara's Sea.**

3. Saint Germain, radiate into the collective consciousness the awareness that in a democracy each person must cast his or her vote based on what they know. A democracy can function at its highest potential only when there is complete transparency in the government, businesses and in all aspects of society.

Gautama, I am one with thee,
Mara's demons do now flee,
your Presence like a soothing balm,
my mind and senses ever calm.

> Gautama, Flame of Cosmic Peace,
> unruly thoughts do hereby cease,
> we radiate from you and me
> the peace to still Samsara's Sea.

4. Saint Germain, radiate into the collective consciousness the awareness that the members of the power elite saw that democracies would have to become more and more transparent and therefore the power elite could not stay hidden.

> Gautama, I now take the vow,
> to live in the eternal now,
> with you I do transcend all time,
> to live in present so sublime.

> Gautama, Flame of Cosmic Peace,
> unruly thoughts do hereby cease,
> we radiate from you and me
> the peace to still Samsara's Sea.

5. Saint Germain, radiate into the collective consciousness the awareness that the members of the power elite decided that they needed to stop this, and they did so by creating an enemy of democracy, namely the Soviet Union.

> Gautama, I have no desire,
> to nothing earthly I aspire,
> in non-attachment I now rest,
> passing Mara's subtle test.

> Gautama, Flame of Cosmic Peace,
> unruly thoughts do hereby cease,
> we radiate from you and me
> the peace to still Samsara's Sea.

6. Saint Germain, radiate into the collective consciousness the awareness that with the creation of the Soviet Union, the power elite had the justification for limiting transparency in democratic nations.

> Gautama, I melt into you,
> my mind is one, no longer two,
> immersed in your resplendent glow,
> Nirvana is all that I know.

> Gautama, Flame of Cosmic Peace,
> unruly thoughts do hereby cease,
> we radiate from you and me
> the peace to still Samsara's Sea.

7. Saint Germain, radiate into the collective consciousness the awareness that the need to keep things secret for the Soviet Union was just an excuse. The real issue was that the power elite wanted to keep things secret from the people in democratic nations.

> Gautama, in your timeless space,
> I am immersed in Cosmic Grace,
> I know the God beyond all form,
> to world I will no more conform.

**Gautama, Flame of Cosmic Peace,
unruly thoughts do hereby cease,
we radiate from you and me
the peace to still Samsara's Sea.**

8. Saint Germain, radiate into the collective consciousness the awareness that the members of the power elite in embodiment are tools for the darker forces that are out of embodiment and who see even more of a negative potential than people in embodiment.

Gautama, I am now awake,
I clearly see what is at stake,
and thus I claim my sacred right
to be on earth the Buddhic Light.

**Gautama, Flame of Cosmic Peace,
unruly thoughts do hereby cease,
we radiate from you and me
the peace to still Samsara's Sea.**

9. Saint Germain, radiate into the collective consciousness the awareness that there is only one force that can counteract this and it is that more people become the open doors for the ascended masters. The masters are the only force that can counteract the dark forces and the embodied power elite that seek to take the earth down into a self-destructive spiral.

Gautama, with your thunderbolt,
we give the earth a mighty jolt,
I know that some will understand,
and join the Buddha's timeless band.

> **Gautama, Flame of Cosmic Peace,**
> **unruly thoughts do hereby cease,**
> **we radiate from you and me**
> **the peace to still Samsara's Sea.**

Part 3

1. Saint Germain, radiate into the collective consciousness the awareness that the earth is in an upward spiral only because some people have dared to be open doors for the spiritual light and higher ideas.

> O Saint Germain, you do inspire,
> my vision raised forever higher,
> with you I form a figure-eight,
> your Golden Age I co-create.
>
> **O Saint Germain, what love you bring,**
> **it truly makes all matter sing,**
> **your violet flame does all restore,**
> **with you we are becoming more.**

2. Saint Germain, radiate into the collective consciousness the awareness that society needs to educate children in how to deal with their own personal psychology, overcome their limitations, so that they can have happier and more fulfilled lives.

> O Saint Germain, what Freedom Flame,
> released when we recite your name,
> acceleration is your gift,
> our planet it will surely lift.

> **O Saint Germain, what love you bring,
> it truly makes all matter sing,
> your violet flame does all restore,
> with you we are becoming more.**

3. Saint Germain, radiate into the collective consciousness the awareness that the reason this has not already happened is that the power elite does not want people to overcome their wounds because it is through the wounds that both the embodied power elite and the dark forces behind them can control people.

> O Saint Germain, in love we claim,
> our right to bring your violet flame,
> from you Above, to us below,
> it is an all-transforming flow.

> **O Saint Germain, what love you bring,
> it truly makes all matter sing,
> your violet flame does all restore,
> with you we are becoming more.**

4. Saint Germain, radiate into the collective consciousness the awareness that billions of people are leading lives of intense suffering because of their internal psychological wounds. The rich nations need to provide psycho-spiritual welfare instead of only material welfare.

> O Saint Germain, I love you so,
> my aura filled with violet glow,
> my chakras filled with violet fire,
> I am your cosmic amplifier.

*O Saint Germain, what love you bring,
it truly makes all matter sing,
your violet flame does all restore,
with you we are becoming more.*

5. Saint Germain, radiate into the collective consciousness the awareness that Jesus sought to start a movement that could help people attain healing through the power of the Holy Spirit and Christ awareness. People could then express their discernment in society without being psychologically destroyed by the dark forces.

O Saint Germain, I am now free,
your violet flame is therapy,
transform all hang-ups in my mind,
as inner peace I surely find.

*O Saint Germain, what love you bring,
it truly makes all matter sing,
your violet flame does all restore,
with you we are becoming more.*

6. Saint Germain, radiate into the collective consciousness the awareness that many of the people in history who have attempted to change things, had their own internal psychological issues and did not fulfill their missions.

O Saint Germain, my body pure,
your violet flame for all is cure,
consume the cause of all disease,
and therefore I am all at ease.

**O Saint Germain, what love you bring,
it truly makes all matter sing,
your violet flame does all restore,
with you we are becoming more.**

7. Saint Germain, radiate into the collective consciousness the awareness that there is an incredible potential for any nation that would make a determined policy to teach children from an early age how to heal their psychology and find inner peace and resolution.

O Saint Germain, I'm karma-free,
the past no longer burdens me,
a brand new opportunity,
I am in Christic unity.

**O Saint Germain, what love you bring,
it truly makes all matter sing,
your violet flame does all restore,
with you we are becoming more.**

8. Saint Germain, radiate into the collective consciousness the awareness that the power elite wants to abort Christhood before it can manifest. Many things in society are specifically designed to magnify people's psychological limitations.

O Saint Germain, we are now one,
I am for you a violet sun,
as we transform this planet earth,
your Golden Age is given birth.

> O Saint Germain, what love you bring,
> it truly makes all matter sing,
> your violet flame does all restore,
> with you we are becoming more.

9. Saint Germain, radiate into the collective consciousness the awareness that the power elite took over the Christian religion and used it to control the population.

> O Saint Germain, the earth is free,
> from burden of duality,
> in oneness we bring what is best,
> your Golden Age is manifest.

> O Saint Germain, what love you bring,
> it truly makes all matter sing,
> your violet flame does all restore,
> with you we are becoming more.

Part 4

1. Saint Germain, radiate into the collective consciousness the awareness that when the elite became aware that the Christian religion could no longer dominate the intellectual life of Western societies, they started to create the opposite, namely scientific materialism.

> Sanat Kumara, Ruby Fire,
> I seek my place in love's own choir,
> with open hearts we sing your praise,
> together we the earth do raise.

**Sanat Kumara, Ruby Ray,
bring to earth a higher way,
light this planet with your fire,
clothe her in a new attire.**

2. Saint Germain, radiate into the collective consciousness the awareness that the power elite has managed to create a society that is divided. Democratic nations have an inconsistency for they cannot decide what kind of people they are ministering to from their governments.

Sanat Kumara, Ruby Fire,
initiations I desire,
I am for you an electrode,
Shamballa is my true abode.

**Sanat Kumara, Ruby Ray,
bring to earth a higher way,
light this planet with your fire,
clothe her in a new attire.**

3. Saint Germain, radiate into the collective consciousness the awareness that if we have a democratic nation that recognizes that people have rights, yet at the same time this nation will not recognize that people are spiritual beings, then we have an inconsistency.

Sanat Kumara, Ruby Fire,
I follow path that you require,
initiate me with your love,
the open door for Holy Dove.

> Sanat Kumara, Ruby Ray,
> bring to earth a higher way,
> light this planet with your fire,
> clothe her in a new attire.

4. Saint Germain, radiate into the collective consciousness the awareness that societies cannot recognize that people are spiritual beings because of the opposition from scientific materialism.

> Sanat Kumara, Ruby Fire,
> your great example all inspire,
> with non-attachment and great mirth,
> we give the earth a true rebirth.

> Sanat Kumara, Ruby Ray,
> bring to earth a higher way,
> light this planet with your fire,
> clothe her in a new attire.

5. Saint Germain, radiate into the collective consciousness the awareness that there is also the opposite polarity, defined by the power elite, which makes people think that if they do recognize that people are spiritual beings, then we go back to the old days of being dominated by Christianity.

> Sanat Kumara, Ruby Fire,
> you are this planet's purifier,
> consume on earth all spirits dark,
> reveal the inner Spirit Spark.

> Sanat Kumara, Ruby Ray,
> bring to earth a higher way,
> light this planet with your fire,
> clothe her in a new attire.

6. Saint Germain, radiate into the collective consciousness the awareness that there is an alternative to traditional Christianity and to scientific materialism. It is a universal form of spirituality.

> Sanat Kumara, Ruby Fire,
> you are a cosmic amplifier,
> the lower forces can't withstand,
> vibrations from Venusian band.

> Sanat Kumara, Ruby Ray,
> bring to earth a higher way,
> light this planet with your fire,
> clothe her in a new attire.

7. Saint Germain, radiate into the collective consciousness the awareness that when societies begin to recognize this, they can create an educational system that teaches children that they are psycho-spiritual beings with the potential to overcome the limitations in their psychology.

> Sanat Kumara, Ruby Fire,
> I am on earth your magnifier,
> the flow of love I do restore,
> my chakras are your open door.

**Sanat Kumara, Ruby Ray,
bring to earth a higher way,
light this planet with your fire,
clothe her in a new attire.**

8. Saint Germain, radiate into the collective consciousness the awareness that we can then give children tools to rise above their psychology. Within a generation we will have children who were brought up with an understanding of their own psychology and the potential to master their psychology.

Sanat Kumara, Ruby Fire,
Venusian song the multiplier,
as we your love reverberate,
the densest minds we penetrate.

**Sanat Kumara, Ruby Ray,
bring to earth a higher way,
light this planet with your fire,
clothe her in a new attire.**

9. Saint Germain, radiate into the collective consciousness the awareness that children will then have a sense of purpose and know that one of the purposes of life is to attain self-mastery.

Sanat Kumara, Ruby Fire,
you are for all the sanctifier,
the earth is now a holy place,
purified by cosmic grace.

> **Sanat Kumara, Ruby Ray,
> bring to earth a higher way,
> light this planet with your fire,
> clothe her in a new attire.**

Part 5

1. Saint Germain, radiate into the collective consciousness the awareness that today, most parents export their own unresolved psychology onto their children, which is why we see so many dysfunctional families.

> O Saint Germain, you do inspire,
> my vision raised forever higher,
> with you I form a figure-eight,
> your Golden Age I co-create.

> **O Saint Germain, what love you bring,
> it truly makes all matter sing,
> your violet flame does all restore,
> with you we are becoming more.**

2. Saint Germain, radiate into the collective consciousness the awareness that the most affluent nations have more and more psychological, family and social problems, more and more dysfunctional families, more and more divorces, more and more shipwrecked children.

> O Saint Germain, what Freedom Flame,
> released when we recite your name,
> acceleration is your gift,
> our planet it will surely lift.

> **O Saint Germain, what love you bring,**
> **it truly makes all matter sing,**
> **your violet flame does all restore,**
> **with you we are becoming more.**

3. Saint Germain, radiate into the collective consciousness the awareness that when we have reached a certain level of material affluence, it is necessary for society to step up and look at the psycho-spiritual welfare of its members. Unless this becomes the goal of society, it will become subject to the second law of thermodynamics and start to disintegrate.

> O Saint Germain, in love we claim,
> our right to bring your violet flame,
> from you Above, to us below,
> it is an all-transforming flow.

> **O Saint Germain, what love you bring,**
> **it truly makes all matter sing,**
> **your violet flame does all restore,**
> **with you we are becoming more.**

4. Saint Germain, radiate into the collective consciousness the awareness that there is hardly any child that was not negatively affected by the unresolved psychology of the parents. Psychological wounds are inherited from generation to generation.

O Saint Germain, I love you so,
my aura filled with violet glow,
my chakras filled with violet fire,
I am your cosmic amplifier.

**O Saint Germain, what love you bring,
it truly makes all matter sing,
your violet flame does all restore,
with you we are becoming more.**

5. Saint Germain, radiate into the collective consciousness the awareness that when we are willing to raise our awareness, we can reverse the trend so that we can pass on better opportunities to our children.

O Saint Germain, I am now free,
your violet flame is therapy,
transform all hang-ups in my mind,
as inner peace I surely find.

**O Saint Germain, what love you bring,
it truly makes all matter sing,
your violet flame does all restore,
with you we are becoming more.**

6. Saint Germain, radiate into the collective consciousness the awareness that the highest potential for the modern affluent democracies is the potential to serve other nations, to seek to raise up the whole of the family of nations.

O Saint Germain, my body pure,
your violet flame for all is cure,
consume the cause of all disease,
and therefore I am all at ease.

**O Saint Germain, what love you bring,
it truly makes all matter sing,
your violet flame does all restore,
with you we are becoming more.**

7. Saint Germain, radiate into the collective consciousness the awareness that until these nations acquire enough Christ-perspective that they can begin to serve others, even to serve the whole of humanity, they will go into various downward spirals.

O Saint Germain, I'm karma-free,
the past no longer burdens me,
a brand new opportunity,
I am in Christic unity.

**O Saint Germain, what love you bring,
it truly makes all matter sing,
your violet flame does all restore,
with you we are becoming more.**

8. Saint Germain, radiate into the collective consciousness the awareness that it often seems as if there is no way *out,* but there is a way *up*. There is no way out for we cannot solve these problems horizontally. We can transcend them by going up and by looking at how we can serve others.

O Saint Germain, we are now one,
I am for you a violet sun,
as we transform this planet earth,
your Golden Age is given birth.

**O Saint Germain, what love you bring,
it truly makes all matter sing,
your violet flame does all restore,
with you we are becoming more.**

9. Saint Germain, radiate into the collective consciousness the awareness that when we begin to serve others, we do become the open doors for the ascended masters who are here only to serve humanity and who have the solutions to all of the problems we face.

O Saint Germain, the earth is free,
from burden of duality,
in oneness we bring what is best,
your Golden Age is manifest.

**O Saint Germain, what love you bring,
it truly makes all matter sing,
your violet flame does all restore,
with you we are becoming more.**

Sealing

In the name of the Divine Mother, I call to all ascended masters for the sealing of myself and all people in my circle of influence in the creative flow of the Divine Mother, the River of Life. I call for the multiplication of my calls by all ascended masters so that we form the perfect figure-eight flow of "As Above, so below." Thus, I accept that this is fully manifest, because the mouth of the Lord, the Divine Mother that I AM, has spoken it. Amen.

www.ingramcontent.com/pod-product-compliance
Lightning Source LLC
Chambersburg PA
CBHW030514230426
43665CB00010B/614